WITHDRAWN
UTSA LIBRARIES

Industrial Policy in Europe, Japan and the USA

Also by Khalid Sekkat

LES RELATIONS VERTICALES INTER-ENTREPRISES: Objectifs Et Instruments

TRADE AND JOBS IN EUROPE: Much ado about Nothing (*co-edited with M. Dewatripont and A. Sapir*)

EUROPEAN INTEGRATION AND THE FUNCTIONING OF PRODUCT MARKETS (*co-edited with A. Dierx and F. Ilzkovitz*)

VERTICAL RELATIONSHIPS AND THE FIRM IN THE GLOBAL ECONOMY

L' ÉCONOMIE MACROCAINE EN QUESTIONS (*co-edited with L. Achy*)

COMPETITION AND EFFICIENCY IN THE ARAB WORLD (*co-edited volume*)

Also by Pierre-André Buigues

THE ECONOMICS OF ANTITRUST AND REGULATION IN TELECOMMUNICATION: Perspectives for the New European Regulatory Framework (*co-edited with Patrick Rey*)

COMPETITIVENESS AND THE VALUE OF INTANGIBLE ASSETS (*co-edited with A. Jacquemin*)

EUROPEAN POLICIES OF COMPETITION, TRADE AND INDUSTRY: Conflicts and Complementaries (*co-edited with Jacquemin and A. Sapir*)

MARKET SERVICES AND EUROPEAN INTEGRATION: The Challenges for the 90's (*co-edited with A. Sapir and J. Gual*)

Industrial Policy in Europe, Japan and the USA

Amounts, Mechanisms and Effectiveness

Pierre-André Buigues

and

Khalid Sekkat

© Pierre-André Buigues and Khalid Sekkat 2009

All rights reserved. No reproduction, copy or transmission of this publication may be made without written permission.

No portion of this publication may be reproduced, copied or transmitted save with written permission or in accordance with the provisions of the Copyright, Designs and Patents Act 1988, or under the terms of any licence permitting limited copying issued by the Copyright Licensing Agency, Saffron House, 6-10 Kirby Street, London EC1N 8TS.

Any person who does any unauthorized act in relation to this publication may be liable to criminal prosecution and civil claims for damages.

The authors have asserted their rights to be identified as the authors of this work in accordance with the Copyright, Designs and Patents Act 1988.

First published 2009 by
PALGRAVE MACMILLAN

Palgrave Macmillan in the UK is an imprint of Macmillan Publishers Limited, registered in England, company number 785998, of Houndmills, Basingstoke, Hampshire RG21 6XS.

Palgrave Macmillan in the US is a division of St Martin's Press LLC,
175 Fifth Avenue, New York, NY 10010.

Palgrave Macmillan is the global academic imprint of the above companies and has companies and representatives throughout the world.

Palgrave® and Macmillan® are registered trademarks in the United States, the United Kingdom, Europe and other countries.

ISBN: 978–0–230–57988–0 hardback

This book is printed on paper suitable for recycling and made from fully managed and sustained forest sources. Logging, pulping and manufacturing processes are expected to conform to the environmental regulations of the country of origin.

A catalogue record for this book is available from the British Library.

A catalog record for this book is available from the Library of Congress.

10 9 8 7 6 5 4 3 2 1
18 17 16 15 14 13 12 11 10 09

Printed and bound in Great Britain by
CPI Antony Rowe, Chippenham and Eastbourne

To **Chantal**
Pierre-André Buigues

To **Claude and William**
Khalid Sekkat

Contents

List of Tables   x
List of Figures   xii
List of Acronyms   xiii
Acknowledgements   xvi
Introduction   xvii

Part I Theory and Empirical Evidence

1. **Public Support to Business: An Overview**   3
   1.1 Motivations   3
   1.2 Types of public support to business   5
   1.3 Instruments of public support to business   6
   1.4 Conclusion   9

2. **Cases for Public Support: Market Failures**   10
   2.1 Information   10
   2.2 Externalities   11
   2.3 Imperfect competition   16
   2.4 Conclusion   18

3. **Argument Against Public Support: Government Failures**   20
   3.1 Information   20
   3.2 Conflicts with other policies   22
   3.3 Political economy   25
   3.4 Conclusion   27

4. **Instruments of Support: Subsidies and Public Procurement**   29
   4.1 Subsidies   29
   4.2 Public procurement   43
   4.3 Conclusion   54

5. **Effectiveness of Public Support**   55
   5.1 Assessment issues   55
   5.2 Empirical evidence on the arguments in favour of public support   57

		5.3 Empirical evidence on the arguments against public support	73
		5.4 Conclusion	81

Part II   Quantitative Assessment

6	**Subsidies and State Aid**	85
	6.1 Public support policies in the OECD countries (1998)	89
	6.2 Quantitative analysis of state aid in the EU	91
	6.3 Public support policies in the EU, the USA, and Japan	94
	6.4 Conclusion	98
7	**Public Procurement**	101
	7.1 Divergences in assessments	101
	7.2 Aggregate assessment using the EU definition	102
	7.3 Public procurement by functions (the EU definition)	105
	7.4 Conclusion	111

Part III   Country Studies

8	**Public Support in Germany**	115
	8.1 Objectives of public support	116
	8.2 Actors	121
	8.3 Instruments	125
	8.4 Industry sector and structure	127
	8.5 Public sector structure and public procurement	128
	8.6 Evaluation and efficiency of instruments	132
	8.7 Conclusion	137
9	**Public Support in France**	140
	9.1 Objectives of public support	142
	9.2 Actors	145
	9.3 Industry sector and structure	150
	9.4 Public sector structure and public procurement	152
	9.5 Evaluation and efficiency of public support policy	155
	9.6 Conclusion	157
10	**Public Support in the United Kingdom**	160
	10.1 Objectives of public support	160
	10.2 Actors	161
	10.3 Instruments	162
	10.4 Outcomes of public support in the United Kingdom	167
	10.5 Conclusion	169

11	**Public Support in the United States**	**170**
	11.1 Objectives of public support	171
	11.2 Actors	172
	11.3 Instruments	173
	11.4 Outcomes of public support in the United States	179
	11.5 Conclusion	182
12	**Public Support in Japan**	**184**
	12.1 Objectives of public support	187
	12.2 Actors	189
	12.3 Instruments	191
	12.4 Industry sector and structure	194
	12.5 Public sector and public procurement	196
	12.6 Evaluation and efficiency of public support policy	198
	12.7 Conclusion	201

Conclusions	**203**
Notes	206
Bibliography	213
Index	225

Tables

4.1	Classification of state aid by objective	33
4.2	Different approaches of subsidies	35
4.3	The use of countervailing mearsures by reporting members from 1995 to 2006	39
4.4	The sectoral distribution of measures by reporting members from 1995 to 2006	40
6.1	Differences between data sources on subsidies	87
6.2	Sectoral allocation of subsidies notified by WTO members: Yearly average 1999/2002 (percentage)	88
6.3	EU Member States: Rankings for average subsidy	88
6.4	Reported expenditures (on manufacturing) by policy objective in OCED	91
6.5	Sectoral distribution of aid by Member State (2006)	92
6.6	State aid for horizontal and sectoral aid in 2006	93
6.7	International trends in government subsidies (as percentage of GDP)	95
6.8	Trends in government subsidies (as percentage of GDP)	95
6.9	Classification of subsidies by functions (2004)	97
7.1	Public procurement	102
7.2	Public procurement (own definition)	103
8.1	Total aids of the Federation in 2006	119
8.2	Industry support of the Federation in 2006	119
8.3	SME support in 2006	121
8.4	The financial equalization system between the Länder	122
8.5	Total aids by instrument and source	126
8.6	Aid mechanisms, ranked in descending order of budgetary cost (Federation)	127
8.7	Total aids of the Federation in 2006	128
8.8	Public procurement in Germany in 2005	131
8.9	Federation public procurement in 2005	131
9.1	Breakdown of aid by objective	144
9.2	Breakdown of competitiveness clusters by sector and type	148
9.3	R&D project funding: Clusters with a global dimension	148
9.4	Public support by instrument	149

9.5	Aid mechanisms, ranked in descending order of budgetary cost	149
9.6	Sectoral aid by sector	151
9.7	Public procurement in France (2006)	154
10.1	Selected government expenses	163
11.1	Selected Federal expenses	174
12.1	Expenditure by policy objectives in Japan	185
12.2	Distribution of public funding in R&D in Japan	189
12.3	SME financing in Japan (September 2006)	193
12.4	SME favourable tax system	193
12.5	Entities with large procurement in 2005	197
12.6	Total value and number of government procurement contacts in Japan	197

Figures

3.1	Competition, industrial and trade policies	23
7.1	The share of public procurement in GDP	104
7.2	Components of public procurements as a percentage of GDP	105
7.3	Public procurement by function	106
8.1	Economic growth in the Länder	123
8.2	Unemployment rate in the Länder in 2006	124
8.3	Debt interest burden and investment ratio of the Länder in 2006	124
8.4	The German public procurement system	130
8.5	Total private 'private equity' in Germany	134
8.6	Seed and start-up financing provided by private 'private equity' firms	134
8.7	Seed and start-up financing vs all remaining private 'private equity'	135
9.1	Presents the main actors of public support for R&D and SMEs in France	145
9.2	Organization of procurement at the national level	153
12.1	Trends in new business launches and closures by number of enterprises	188
12.2	Distribution of public funding in R&D in Japan	190
12.3	Framework for SME policy	191

Acronyms

ACI	American Competitiveness Initiative (The United States)
AII	Agence de l'Innovation Industrielle (France)
ANR	Agence Nationale de la Recherche (France)
APEC	Asia-Pacific Economic Cooperation
ARD	Annual Respondents Database
ATP	Advanced Technology Program (The United States)
BEEPS	Business Environment and Enterprise Performance Survey
BMBF	Federal Ministry for Education and Research
BMWi	Federal Ministry for Economics and Technology
CVD	Countervailing Duty
CIADT	Regional Planning and Development Committee (France)
CMPE	Commission des Marchés Publics de l'Etat (France)
CNRS	Centre Nationale de la Recherche Scientifique
COFOG	Classification of the Functions of the Government
DBERR	Department for Business, Enterprise & Regulatory Reform (The United Kingdom)
DC	Developed Countries
DG-ECFIN	Directorate General Economic and Finance (European Commission)
DIUS	Department for Innovation, Universities and Skills (The United Kingdom)
DTI	Department of Trade and Industry (The United Kingdom)
EBRD	European Bank for Reconstruction and Development
EC	European Communities
EDA	Economic Development Administration (The United States)
EDF	Electricté de France (France)
EPL	Employment Protection Legislation
ERP	European Recovery Plan
EU	European Union
E&S	Equipment and Software
FAR	Federal Acquisition Regulation (The United States)

FCE	Fonds de compétitivité des entreprises (France)
FDI	Foreign Direct Investment
GDP	Gross Domestic Product
GEM	Global Entrepreneurship Monitor
GNP	Gross National Product
GPA	Government Procurement Agreement
IMF	International Monetary Fund
INSEE	Institut National de Statistique et d'Etudes Economiques (France)
KfW	Kreditanstalt für Wiederaufbau (the former bank for the rebuilding of Germany)
LDC	Less Developed Countries
MEP	Manufacturing Extension Partnership (The United States)
METI	Ministry of Economy Trade and Industry (Japan)
MITI	Ministry of International Trade and Industry (Japan)
NAICS	North American Industry Classification System
NAO	National Audit Office
NAS	National Account Statistics
NCG	Net Cost to Government
NEG	new economic geography
NERA	National Economic Research Associates
NIST	National Institute of Standards and Technology (The United States)
NPISH	Non-Profit Institutions Serving Households
OECD	Organisation of Economic Cooperation and Development
OFPP	Office of Federal Procurement Policy (The United States)
OFT	Office of Fair Trade (The United Kingdom)
OGC	Office of Government Commerce (The United Kingdom)
OMB	Office of Management and Budget (The United States)
PAT	Prime d'Aménagement du Territoire
PMR	Product market regulation
R&D	Research and Development
RDA	Regional Development Agencies (The United Kingdom)
RIETI	Research Institute of Economy, Trade and Industry (Japan)
RSA	Regional Selective Assistance (The United Kingdom)
S&T	Sciences and Technology
SAMIS	Selective Assistance Management Information System
SAP	Structural Adjustment Programs
SBA	Small Business Administration
SBIR	Small Business Innovation Research (The United States)
SBS	Small Business Service (The United Kingdom)

SEC	scale efficiency change
SCM	Subsidies and Countervailing measures
SGEI	Services of General Economic Interest
SMART/SPUR	Small Firm Merit Awards for Research and Technology (The United Kingdom)
SME	Small and Medium Enterprise
SNA	System of National Accounts
SNCF	Société Nationale des Chemins de fer Français
STEP	Science, Technology, and Economic Policy
STT	strategic trade theory
STTR	Small Business Technology Transfer program (The United States)
TAA	Trade Agreements Act (The United States)
TC	technical change
TEC	technical efficiency change
TFP	Total Factor Productivity
VAT	value-added tax
VC	Venture Capital
VCRs	video-cassette recorders
VW	Volkswagen
WCR	World Competitiveness Report
WTO	World Trade Organisation

Acknowledgements

The authors are grateful to Fabienne Ilzkovitz, Paul Seabright, Damien Neven, David Encaoua, Dominique Guellec, Elie Cohen, Patrick Messerlain, and Jean Pisani for very helpful discussions. Japanese government officials and economists also helped us to better understand the specificities of the Japanese model to support the industry: Akira Kawamoto, Akira Goto, Sumita, Hirose, Motohashi. The book has benefited from valuable inputs provided by Christian Lechner and Eugenie Kulozhenko. Needless to say, the opinions expressed in the book do not reflect the policy lines of the institutions to which the authors are affiliated.

Introduction

Over the past half century the mainstream view of public support to business, also called industrial policy, has varied markedly. From the early 1950s to the early 1970s industrial policy was seen as the panacea to growth and development problems. The apparent success of some East Asian economies has for a long time supported the conviction of those who were in favour of such policy. However, since the end of 1970s and until recently such conviction has been challenged. Evidence was provided to show that industrial policy may lead to misallocation of resources, not improve long-run growth, and give rise to rent-seeking. Therefore, the widespread consensus among economists limited the role of the state mainly to the protection of property rights and contract enforcement, maintenance of macroeconomic stability and the creation of a good general-purpose business environment, in addition to public goods provision and social protection. As a result, a number of industrialized countries initiated a dramatic reversal of their discourses toward supporting business and, under their persuasion, the IMF and the World Bank incited developing countries to reduce or stop support to business under the framework of the Structural Adjustment Programs (SAP).

At present, convictions seem to be softening. The Berlin Wall has been broken. New economic theories have been developed (new growth, geography, trade, etc.) and tested. As a result, few people still seriously think that state planning and intervention can act as the main driving force of economic development. At the same time, it is increasingly recognized that public action can, in some circumstances, combine with private initiative to foster restructuring, diversification, and technological dynamism beyond what market forces on their own would generate. As a result, public support to business can take an intermediate attitude between the two extremes. While market forces and private initiative remain the driving force, governments could set strategies for the productive sphere beyond simply ensuring property rights, enforcing contracts, and stabilizing the economy.

As Wade (2003) points out, there is no clear-cut evidence that the creation of efficient, rent-free markets coupled with transparent public sectors is even close to being a necessary or sufficient for a dynamic economic development. Moreover, it is increasingly recognized (Rodrik, 2004) that appropriate incorporation of private initiative into a framework of public action allows mitigation of idiosyncratic risks and can become a driving force for economic development and growth. Theses arguments, along with traditional reasons for public interventions, provide another insight to public support policies and their role in dynamic economic development and welfare growth.

The mainstream rationale for public interventions principally lies in the necessity to offset some pre-existing market failures (efficiency objective) and correct for social inequalities (equity objective). These failures can take the form of imperfect competition, technological, information, coordination, and other externalities. Public intervention is therefore justified provided that the government is able to improve upon market outcomes.

However, this approach is often confronted with a sceptical posture towards government involvement in the economy. In particular, as noted by Rodrik (2006), there are two fundamental arguments that cast doubts on bureaucrats' capacity to correct market failures: information and incentive issues. The first refers to the fact that governments may not be able to substitute for the decentralized information processing that markets, in general, can achieve. Secondly, even if it were possible, the incentives that rule public interest are not always clear. Thus, the fear of market failures must be balanced with the risks of government failures. For instance, studies by Leahy and Neary (2001) and Bond and Samuelson (1986) provide good illustrations of the difficulty for a government to identify instruments that can achieve a given target with the least possible distortion to the economy. Others document the risk (Dewatripont and Seabright, 2006) of wasteful public spending by governments seeking to signal their diligence in order to incite voters to re-elect them.

The potential net benefit or loss from government support to business is, therefore, the result of the relative importance of the two types of 'failures'. In practice, the literature reports both cases of successful and failing government intervention. The main message from empirical analyses is that the outcome depends on the failure government seeks to address, the policy instrument used, and the way this is implemented.

In contrast with the free market orientation of many structural reforms, governments have often followed some sort of 'public support policies'. They use various instruments (e.g. Credit conditions, taxes cut, subsidized energy prices, targeted public procurements, and research and development subsidies) to foster the development of favoured sectors. It is well documented, for instance, that the superiority of the US information technology industry owes much to military procurements (Montani, 2005). The post-war Japanese economic performance was achieved through policies that directly provide resources to industries and, even, policies that reduce competition between firms (Tilton, 1996). Korean economic development relied on government measures promoting the development of large firms that could compete on international markets while at the same time encouraging fierce competition between these firms. In exchange for government subsidies and trade protection the Korean government also set stringent performance standards. Firms were penalized when they performed poorly (Rodrik, 1995).

Observation of reality also shows that governments' intervention may lead to distorted policy decisions such as expensive prestige projects like Concorde or support to struggling firms such as Crédit Lyonnais, Alsthom, and MG Rover (Dewatripont and Seabright, 2006). Active industrial policy may open doors to corruption as in South Korea in 1993, where investigations convicted 39 generals of getting bribes for arranging contracts in defence procurements (Ades and Di Tella, 1997). There are also circumstances where firms in transition economies have been able to shape the rules of the game to their own advantage (i.e. state capture) at considerable social cost (Hellman et al., 2000).

In the light of the above discussion, an up-to-date analysis of the debate and evidence on the opportunity of pursuing industrial policy is timely. This is not only useful for academics or students who need to keep on track of advanced economic analysis but also for policymakers (often lost in debate among experts) who need to understand successful (or unsuccessful) policies, why they succeeded and how. To our best knowledge, this is the first book (at least for a long time) to offer a structured and up-to-date analysis linking theoretical arguments, implementation approaches, and effectiveness of industrial policy.

To help clarify the debate about the opportunity for a more direct intervention of public authorities to foster growth and welfare, the book draws on recent developments in the theoretical and empirical literature and on the experience of five industrialized countries (Germany, the United Kingdom, France, the United States and Japan). The comparison between public supports to business across the five countries includes the objectives, mechanisms, amounts, and outcomes. For clarity and efficacy, the analysis is limited in two respects. First, it concerns only the three biggest European countries (France, Germany and the United Kingdom) and the two most important non-European countries (the United States and Japan). Second, the focus is on two main instruments: subsidies and public procurements. These are two widely used instruments but with markedly different importance and purpose across the five countries.

With the recent financial crisis and its consequences on the global economy, public support to business is publicly debated between governments, central bankers, and economists. The global economy is confronted by a major economic crisis with a deepening global slowdown of the stock markets, pessimistic growth prospects, and a trembling consumer confidence. The industry is asking for major public support: the European automotive industry demanded a 40 billion euro loan to support their sector. Public support to industry considered by governments includes the recapitalization of banks, government guarantees on loans, targeted state support for big business facing the challenge of the renewing expiring credit lines, and major state aid for R&D in clean technology, as in the car industry. This book, which presents the economic theory behind and critical views on the implementation of public support policies, is an essential element of the debate that opened with the current financial crisis.

The book is structured in three main parts. The first part presents the main theoretical arguments for and against public support to business, the instruments of support, and the empirical evidence concerning their effectiveness. The second part compares the quantitative importance of the two instruments across countries, drawing on various statistical sources (the WTO, the OECD, and the European Commission). The third part compares the objectives, actors, instruments, and efficacy of public support to business in the five countries.

Part I
Theory and Empirical Evidence

1
Public Support to Business: An Overview

It is difficult to find a precise and unambiguous definition to public support to business (see Aiginger, 2007 for a discussion). Economists often use the term 'industrial policy' instead of 'public support'. In this book we use interchangeably the terms industrial policy and public support policy. In general, any economic policy which influences industry can be referred to as public support to business. In the broad sense, such a support encompasses public sector intervention aimed at changing the distribution of resources between economic sectors and activities (Caves, 1987). However, the concept of public support to business agreed upon by economists since the early eighties also includes issues linked to innovation, economic growth, technological progress, and entrepreneurship. Public support policy is, therefore, a sort of complement to market forces that reinforce or counteract the allocation that market forces would otherwise produce.

1.1 Motivations

One of the first justifications of public interventions is the infant industry argument, which can be traced back to the last centuries, when the protection of an emerging manufacturing sector was seen as having a key role in the development of an economy's potential comparative advantage. The justification incurred further elaboration and formalization by, among others, Bardhan (1971), Young (1991), and Greenwald and Stiglitz (2006).

In particular, Bardhan (1971) has put forward a simple dynamic model of 'learning by doing' and used it to characterize the time-path of the optimum rate of subsidy to an infant industry. The nature of the learning process is defined as overcoming a historical handicap, a matter of catching up with a foreign country's efficiency level. In fact, Bardhan argues that if the initial stock of experience is small, the optimum rate of subsidy should decrease steadily over time, approaching asymptotically a positive stationary rate. The decreasing subsidy should remain positive due to its property to enhance productivity and generate positive spillovers for other firms.

Young (1991), using an endogenous growth model, investigated the dynamic effects of international trade. In particular, his paper examined the interaction between a developing (LDC) and a developed (DC) country. The latter disposes of a higher initial level of knowledge and there is a 'learning by doing' effect that generates spillovers across goods. A salient finding of this model, contrasting with traditional static ones, is that under free trade the LDC experiences rates of technical progress and Gross Domestic Product (GDP) growth less or equal to those enjoyed under autarky. The situation is different, however, in the case of the DC, which should experience greater or equal growth rates under free trade compared with the situation of autarky. This suggests that public interventions through trade protection may appear justified in the LDC since they may foster technical and GDP growth.

Greenwald and Stiglitz (2006) emphasized that the dynamic benefits of trade restrictions may outweigh their static costs. This is especially true for developing countries for which the possibilities of catching-up in the knowledge gap with advanced industrial economies offers large growth potential. Since the development of a country is determined by a multitude of factors (local conditions, structural changes, etc.), Greenwald and Stiglitz argue that reducing domestic distortions while maintaining external barriers may provide the conditions for dynamic gains. They suggest that a tariff, balancing the long-term benefits of fostering industrial growth against the short-term costs of inefficient acquisition of industrial products, should be applied. However, to be efficient, the tariffs should be broad and uniform, meaning that there should be no attempt to 'pick up winners'. Similarly to Bardhan (1971), Greenwald and Stiglitz pose a second condition for efficiency. This is 'self-limiting', implying that free-trade conditions are to be restored when successful local industries are able to sustain competition in international market.

While the above discussion pertains mainly to LDC, public support to business may be well founded in the case of DC too. The literature summarizes the argument for and against public support in both groups of countries as a trade-off between 'markets failures' and 'government failures', that is, in cases where the market (government) can do better than the government (market) in achieving a given objective.

Provided that all markets are perfectly competitive, information is complete, and there is no externality, the market mechanism will be the first-best solution for an optimal resources allocation while the function of the government will be limited in its traditional role. However, there are a number of cases when market forces fail to fulfil their 'responsibility' of the optimal allocation of resources.

Market failures are related to imperfect information, externalities, and market power.[1] Imperfect information may be an obstacle to firm's innovation if fund's providers, for instance, are sceptical about profitability because of their limited knowledge. Externalities may be related to information, network, or geography. If such externalities are not taken into account, the agent's decision may be sub-optimal. Market power allows producers to capture excess rents and may motivate government intervention to achieve a better outcome for its population.

While these factors suggest that in some cases the market may fail to achieve the first best, public intervention is justified only if 'government failures' do not induce a worse outcome than market mechanisms. The risk of government failures is related to the fact that public intervention should target a clearly defined market shortcoming and should be designed in a way to correct for it with the least possible distortion to the economy. Moreover, governments may be confronted with conflicts with other policies (e.g. competition and trade policies). Finally, other sources of government failures are related to self-interest seeking (e.g. elections or corruption) and the risk of capture.

1.2 Types of public support to business

Following the economic literature (Caves 1987; Gual 1995a; Valila, 2006), we distinguish two types of public support to industry, namely horizontal and vertical support.[2]

Horizontal support refers to the measures that target economic activities that are common to a large number of sectors and firms that suffer market failures. For instance, it can provide support to innovation, addressing in this fashion a wide range of knowledge externalities. Broadly speaking, in the context of public interventions it implies the absence of selectivity in terms of the sectors or individual firms supported.

In contrast to the non-selectivity of horizontal policy, the chief aim of vertical policy consists in supporting a specific sector or an individual firm. There are several potential economic justifications for such selectivity, including economies of scale or spatial externalities, incomplete markets or abuse of market power. Strategic trade and merger policy are examples of 'vertical' public intervention. Both horizontal and vertical industrial policies imply an allocation of resources different from a free-market outcome.

1.3 Instruments of public support to business

At the beginning of this chapter we referred to public support as any public sector intervention aimed at changing the distribution of resources between economic sectors and activities (Caves, 1987). It follows that the instruments of public support are numerous and include such measures as grant, trade protection, or protection of intellectual property. For the purpose of this study, we will split such instruments into two broad categories, namely structural and monetary instruments. The former concerns every measure that does not involve transfer of funds from the government to firms. It encompasses a large spectrum of measures such as tariff and non-tariff barriers to trade, merger policy, the protection of intellectual property, regulation (targeting products or producers), as well as the provision of skills, infrastructure, and other public goods and services. The latter, which concerns measures that involve transfer of funds from the government to firms, will be the focus of the rest of the study. To keep coherence with the literature, we distinguish inside this category between subsidies and public procurement.

1.3.1 Subsidies[3]

Subsidies are one of the most important tools of public support but they are also redistributive political tools (Aydin, 2007) and they have been an important public concern across the world. Government expenditure on subsidies is high in many countries and may represent many percentage points of GDP. At the same time, as mentioned in the World Trade Organisation (WTO) World Report on Subsidies (2006), even if a large number of governments maintain extensive subsidy programmes with a multiplicity of objectives to justify these programmes, the amount and the impact of subsidies remain under-researched. For Schwartz and Clements (1999) from the International Monetary Fund (IMF), 'In the most general terms, a subsidy can be defined as any government assistance that (1) allows consumers to purchase goods and services at prices lower than those offered by a perfectly competitive private sector, or (2) raise producers incomes beyond those that would be earned without intervention'.

Therefore, some economists argue that a natural benchmark for identifying subsidization is hypothetical market equilibrium without the presence of government 'when the government enters to picture through tax and expenditure policies, it will alter equilibrium prices and output. Activities for which the net returns are reduced will be discouraged to some degree, and those activities can be said to be "taxed". Activities for which the net returns are enhanced will be encouraged to a degree and they may be said to be "subsidized"' (Sykes, 2003: 24).

However, the difficulty with this concept of subsidy is that it is exceedingly difficult to apply as a practical matter. The observation of the hypothetical market equilibrium without government intervention is not possible in practice, and the quantitative evaluation of the deviation from any benchmark equilibrium that result from government intervention is quite complex.

The Organisation of Economic Cooperation and Development (OECD) has defined public support to business as any form of direct or indirect selective financial support, such as grants, low interest loans and tax breaks (OECD, 1998). Subsidies are defined as any form of state support to industry that is granted selectively to certain firms or sectors.

More precisely subsidies can be grouped in the following seven categories (see Schwartz and Clements, 1999):

- Cash subsidy: direct government payments to consumers or producers
- Credit subsidies: government guarantees, interest subsidies, and soft loans (credit subsidies)
- Tax subsidies: reduction of specific taxes
- Equity subsidies: government equity participation
- Subsidies in kind: government provision of goods or services at below market prices
- Procurement subsidies: government purchases of goods and services at above-market prices
- Regulation subsidies: government regulatory actions that change market price.

However, even this classification presents shortcomings. For example, grants given to a project which are only repayable if the project is successful may be considered as a cash grant if the project is unsuccessful and a credit subsidy if the project is successful (interest rate below the normal market rate). Overvalued exchange rates also contain to a certain extent a subsidy element for those who purchase imported goods and entail cost for the exporters. However, the evaluation of the subsidy components of overvalued exchange rate will be extremely difficult to measure.

1.3.2 Public procurement

Government support to business directly through subsidies or indirectly through the provision of adequate skills or infrastructure is generally classified by economists among *'push factors'*. Public procurements belong to another category called *'pull factors'*. *Pull factors* create an early-stage customers and a market demand that enables business to innovate. By securing a certain level of demand to the firms, they may help them support the cost of sometimes risky research and innovation. As such they may prove a powerful instrument of public support to business (McCrudden, 2004; Henten, 2005; Evenett and Hoekman, 2005).

Public procurement is the term used to describe the purchasing of works, supplies, and services by national, regional, and local public bodies, including central government, local authorities, fire and police authorities, defence, health services, joint consortia of public bodies, and public and private utilities.

Public procurement possess a significant 'arsenal' in order to create a favourable climate for encouraging demand for innovative solutions inciting thereafter the supply side of the market to adapt accordingly. In the meantime, another important difference between public procurement and public interventions by the means of subsidies is in the fact that the former acts within a system of a liberal market. While subsidies are set at the government discretion or in the framework of some institutional rules, public procurements are, in principle, awarded though auctions and competitive tendering. The distortions are expected to be relatively less important although the effects on competition considerably depend on particular procurement settings and market characteristics.

Public procurement policies may be a powerful instrument of public intervention which is important from a development perspective. Efficient public procurement enables government to get the most out of the limited funds available for state purchases of goods, services, and infrastructure. In addition, as pointed out by Hunja (2003), successful procurement practices also contribute towards the sound management of public expenditure more generally, because procurement planning helps the government in identification of major investment expenditure, which in turn facilitates budgetary decision-making. Besides, there is a growing appreciation of the linkage between specific national objectives and public procurement practices. In fact, by virtue of procurement contracts government is able to provide support to Small and Medium Enterprises (SMEs), assist development of lagging regions, or pursue equity objectives. The manner in which a state implements its public procurement policies has implications for achievement of such objectives, and for the cost of doing so. Therefore knowing what the various objectives are and how effective and efficient procurement policies are in attaining them should be an important dimension for government's performance assessment.

1.4 Conclusion

Public support to business has a long history. One of its first justifications is the infant industry argument. The latter can be traced back to the beginning of the last century. Protection of an emerging manufacturing sector was seen as the key factor in the development of an economy's potential comparative advantage. Since then the argument has been elaborated and formalized according to 'learning by doing', the dynamic effects of international trade, and the possibilities of catching-up in knowledge. While these arguments pertain mainly to LDC, public support has been shown be also well founded in the case of DC. The literature sees the necessity of public support as a result of the trade-off between 'markets failures' and 'government failures'.

There are several different approaches to industrial policy such as horizontal, vertical, or support to structural changes approaches, each of them having their own goals, depending on the level of economic development. There are also numerous instruments of public support, including tariff and non-tariff barriers to trade, merger policy, regulation, subsidies, and public procurement. The outcome of public support depends on the failure government seeks to address, the policy instrument used, and the way this is implemented.

2
Cases for Public Support: Market Failures

Market failures refer to situations where market forces fail to fulfil their 'responsibility' of the optimal allocation of resources. They may be due to information imperfection, externalities, or imperfect competition and may justify public intervention. In this chapter we discuss the three kinds of market failures.

2.1 Information

Information issues mainly encompass two aspects: information incompleteness and uncertainty. Either might give rise to departure from the first best. Consider, for instance, investment. To choose the best investment project, the investor attempts to evaluate the expected outcomes of various projects. Information incompleteness and/or uncertainty may force the investor to resort to close substitutes as a basis for its estimations of expected profitability. It entails, therefore, a risk of significant bias in relevant inferences. Moreover, estimations become more problematic for non-traditional activity because the market cannot reveal the profitability of a resource that does not yet exist (Rodrik, 2004). The inadequacy or scarcity of information about the market might, therefore, result in a number of unfavourable outcomes. A number of decisions to launch new activities might not be taken because of underestimated project profitability. In turn, this diminishes the potential level of business activity and investments in the economy.

Imperfect information has been identified as a major obstacle to SMEs development. SMEs have restricted access to information and encounter difficulty assessing innovation and new technologies. They also face the reluctance of capital and credit markets to fund their establishment and development. Imperfect information is also an important characteristic of labour markets where the wide variety of skills induces non negligible 'search cost' for enterprise and workers (Meiklejohn, 1999).

The uncertainty about the profitability of a project may also come from the doubt about the realization of other projects. In many circumstances, the profitability of a project requires simultaneous investment in another project. Once both investments are put in place all of them end up profitable. Yet market force itself may not ensure that this will happen, and hence to give sufficient incentives for incurring such investment expenses at a venture. A typical solution for the public authority in this case is to provide a guarantee to both investors, for example in a form of state aid or public procurement contracts. Alternatively, if only one project works out, government could ensure the elaboration of the other.[1]

2.2 Externalities

An externality is a cost or benefit from an economic activity that the parties 'external' to it receive or support. There are positive and negative externalities. The positive ones occurs when economic agents enjoy the benefit generated by the activity of others without rewarding the latter and bearing no costs in the created advantage (i.e. R&D spillovers). Conversely, a negative externality is observed when an external cost is imposed upon others (i.e. pollution). As a result, positive externalities are frequently associated with a free-riding behaviour with the consequence of a less-than-optimal level of the activity producing the externality. Meanwhile, the negative one tends to induce 'over-production' since the individual cost is lower than the public one. Whatever the externality, it generates sub-optimal market outcomes and calls for public intervention.

There are a number of ways to improve overall social utility when externalities are involved. The most efficient one is 'internalization'. In particular, Ronald Coase argued that provided that three requirements are accomplished, externalities can be internalized by private agents and therefore do not result in an inefficient allocation of resources. The requirements are that property rights are well defined, people act rationally, and transaction costs are insignificant. However, there are cases when Coase's statement is difficult to apply and government intervention is justified.

Externalities, either positive or negative, are very important in three main fields: knowledge generation, network effects, and space. In what follows we examine each field in turn.

2.2.1 Knowledge

One of the most common examples of externalities concerns knowledge externalities. As was demonstrated by Arrow (1962), the cost of obtaining knowledge or scientific information can be prohibitive, but once it has been acquired, its dissemination cost drops significantly. These intrinsic characteristics make knowledge a public good since it can be shared among an unlimited number of consumers and generates positive externalities. The latter means that the level of spending by private agents on knowledge generation may be sub-optimal because of the difficulties in appropriating the total benefit of the created knowledge. In other words, the market fails in providing appropriate incentives to knowledge creation. Specifically, the benefits that a firm can generate from investment in R&D can be the same for other firms. However, the level of investments in R&D of private companies left on their own could be chosen in order to maximize their private profits without taking into account social benefits of knowledge spillovers.

A variant of such externality has been recently proposed by Hausmann and Rodrik (2003). This concerns self-discovery leading to diversification of the productive structure. Entrepreneurs try new product lines and adapt them to local conditions. This activity has important social value while being poorly remunerated. Should the entrepreneur discover that the activity is profitable, other producers may follow his example and flock into the new activity. If the venture fails, the first-movers bear the whole cost.

Due to knowledge externalities the private returns from engaging in activities such as R&D or self-discovery are lower than the social benefits and the market incentives are inefficiently low. Economically justified public intervention would provide a subsidy in order to bring the private returns in line with the social ones. However, such first-best policy response to the knowledge externalities might be hard to implement because of the difficulty in monitoring the use of the subsidy. Among the possible solutions, Hausmann and Rodrik (2003) suggested a carrot-and-stick strategy implementation. Under such settlement, support may take a form of a subsidy of any kind, trade protection, or the provision of venture capital or soft loans, but, on the other side, the rents that investors receive should be subject to either performance requirements (for example, export requirements) or close monitoring. Following Wade (2003), East Asian industrial policy has used both elements, while Latin American policy has used too much of the 'carrot', and too little of the 'stick', which explains the fact that Latin America has ended up with a considerable degree of inefficiency.

Closely related to knowledge externality is labour training, which is another source of spillovers (Rodrik, 2006). Specifically, a training provided by a company to its labour can be beneficial to other companies as well. As with other externalities, this dampens the incentive to provide the optimal level of training for fear of losing the investment. While labour mobility is an efficiency enhancing factor, since it diminishes the labour-market rigidity, it may dissuade companies from training expenses. Public support for training programmes can be a solution for the problem.

However, it is much easier for the government to meet the needs of already established activities and provide the necessary training in order to improve upon sub-optimal market solution than to support the development of new activities. As emphasized earlier, such activities require highly specified knowledge training. The imperfection of government's mechanisms to elicit the information about the needed training is due to the self-discovery property of a new activity. An alternative solution would be to support a wide range of research activities and training, leaving the market to choose the necessary ones. In addition, new activities with their learning-by-doing can adapt and improve the factors and capabilities that an economy has already developed for other purposes.

2.2.2 Network

In markets where network externalities are present, the economic value of a particular good is composed of two parts: the 'intrinsic' value of the good itself and the value of its 'network'. The network effect exists because the utility of consuming the good depends positively on the total number of consumers who purchase compatible products. Katz and Shapiro (1985) distinguished between direct and indirect network effects. A direct effect arises when there is 'a direct physical effect of the number of purchasers on the quality of the product'. This is, for instance, the case of communication technologies such as telephone networks and facsimile standards where the value of joining a network depends on the number of other consumers who join by adopting the same, or a compatible, technology. The indirect effect exists when the consumption benefits do not depend directly on the size of the network (the total number of consumers who purchase compatible products) per se but on the size of the market of complementary products. Users of Macintosh computers are better off the greater the number of consumers who purchase Macs. This is because the larger the number of Mac users the greater the demand for compatible software. If matched by an appropriate supply, such demand will lead to lower prices and/or a greater variety of software, which benefits all Mac. This effect applies to many markets, including most consumer electronic technologies, including video-cassette recorders, televisions, and audio technologies as well as non-electronic goods such as cars, credit cards, and natural gas filling stations.

With network externalities a central question concerns the compatibility of goods. This can be achieved through the adoption of a standard by all producers, which may bring positive welfare effects, reducing inefficiencies linked to inertia, by which potential users wait to adopt the new technology so as to minimize the risk of choosing the less diffused or less performing one. Standards also reduce consumers' search and coordination costs. On the supply side, by ensuring interoperability and compatibility in a large market, standards provide stronger incentives to invest in commercially viable innovations.

However, an important issue concerns the choice of a standard. There may be many possible standards, all with different degrees of efficiency. Leaving market forces themselves to select a standard may result in the choice of a non-efficient standard. Moreover, the choice of a rigid standard may prevent the emergence of innovative products or alternative technological paths. In individual cases, there may also be a trade-off between the positive network externalities and the costs linked to limited diversity and competition.

The discussion implies that the cost of a mistake in the standard selection process is likely to be very high. Public intervention may help in picking up the right standard. Whenever there are network externalities, there is a potential for welfare-improving public intervention. The latter can take various forms: mandating a standard of a technology, subsidizing investments in a particular standard, or relying on public procurement. However, this presupposes that government is able to identify the most efficient standard, which may not the case in reality.

2.2.3 Space

Brander (1986), Krugman (1993), and Baldwin et al. (2003) have shown that a sector or an industry characterized by high fixed costs, and therefore exhibiting economies of scale, or the one where some of the inputs are non-tradable (e.g. because they are immobile) tend to concentrate production geographically in order to benefit from external economies (e.g. diffusion of tacit knowledge, common infrastructure, availability of skilled workers, etc). This may lead to a higher concentration of economic activities in some regions than in others.

From the perspective of economic efficiency, agglomeration is desirable in sectors where positive spatial externalities are important. For instance, companies that are technologically and organizationally close have an interest in moving closer together geographically in order to benefit from economies of scale, to take advantage of public infrastructure, support in research and education, and to build up flexible competences (Cohen, 2006). Moreover, agglomeration may lead to a pool of labour with appropriate skills and informal exchanges of information/know-how. However, agglomeration can give rise to negative externalities, such as congestion or regional disequilibrium. In such cases, public intervention may prove necessary in order, for instance, to prevent an unbalanced development of the country where some regions are becoming richer and others poorer.

A relevant question is, why particular industries tend to be heavily concentrated in certain geographic locations and why do these concentrations generally persist over long periods? The new economic geography (NEG) literature, while not denying the relevance of comparative advantage, argues that non-economic factors, path dependence, chance, and cumulative process frequently account for the origins and concentration of manufacturing and many other economic activities in particular areas.

According to NEG, the initial location and concentration of economic activities in a particular region is frequently a matter of chance or historical accident. However, once an industry or economic activity is established, cumulative forces and feedback mechanisms can lead to continued concentration of economic activities in that region for an extended period of time. Production of motor vehicles in Detroit and the computer industry in Silicon Valley can serve as examples of economic activities that cluster in a particular region due to an arbitrary event and the effects of path dependence.

Another non-negligible facet of agglomeration is its potential to reinforce cooperation based on geographical proximity and to enhance industrial competitive advantages. Advocates of this viewpoint see the forces of cooperation and spatial proximity as key conditions for the capacity to adapt more rapidly to technological and organizational change. In particular, Lorenz (1992) argues that successful industrial agglomerations are characterized by a particular balance between cooperation and competition among the companies.

However, the incentives for cooperation as well as the benefits from spatial externalities are conditional on a particular industry's characteristics, specifically on its inherent pace of technological change. When technological change is quite slow the incentives for cooperation in a view of technological development are quite weak. By the same token, there is no strong stimulus for clustering in order to take advantage of knowledge spillovers. The situation is different when technological change is rapid and incremental. Under such circumstances, the incentives for cooperation and clustering are particularly strong.

2.3 Imperfect competition

Imperfectly competitive markets, high fixed costs, and starting capital, presence of scale economies, and market power create situations when a first mover captures excess rents to the detriment of potential entrants and consumers. In cases involving only domestic companies, competition policy is a good instrument to cope with such inconveniences. For cases involving domestic and foreign companies, intervention may be pursued through strategic trade policy or domestic merger policy.

In the early 1980s, the strategic trade theory (STT) was developed by James Brander, Barbara Spencer, Avinash Dixit, Gene Grossman, and Paul Krugman. It incorporates models of imperfect competition and game theory into traditional trade theory. The theory of strategic trade provides a rationale to use protectionist measures or other forms of public support in order to provide national companies with a tangible advantage in both domestic and international markets. The idea is that owing to protection measures taken by the government, 'favoured' companies can take advantage of increasing returns, positive feedbacks associated with path dependence, and so forth. They could, therefore, augment their competitiveness in the international markets.

The significance of strategic trade measures can be appreciated through consideration of the fundamental differences between perfect and imperfect competition. In the sectors/industries where there is perfect competition, the behaviour of one firm cannot change the rules of game. Hence, the firm cannot gain advantage through strategic behaviour. However, in industries where there is imperfect competition the market can eventually be dominated by only a few firms, that is, lead to an oligopolistic market. This means that their behaviour can make a difference and alter the decisions of other firms. Under oligopolistic market settings, abnormally high profits are captured by a few or even a single company. The central idea of the strategic trade policy is that, under such circumstances, firms and governments can behave strategically to improve a country's trade balance and overall national welfare. Specifically, the government can support a domestic firm to increase its productive capabilities or to cope with sharp price competition from foreign firms. By granting a direct subsidy to a firm or by giving outright protection to a domestic industry, the government may deter foreign firms from entering in a particular industrial sector. Oligopolistic competition is most likely to occur in certain high-tech industries characterized by economies of scale and learning-by-doing. These include the aerospace, advanced materials, computer and semiconductors, and biochemical industries. Most of these industries possess an important property of dual technologies. They are of particular importance to economic competitiveness since their good performance can spill over into other industries and boost their performance. They are also of particular importance to the military industry, as empirical analyses of the case of the United States show. Often, this gives an additional 'security' reason for public intervention.

Another motivation for strategic trade policy is proposed by Zysman et al. (1990). This concerns the effects of imperfect competition on industrial sectors characterized by rapid technological change. Considering such issues, an important question is whether it is justified to subsidize some sectors or companies that cannot, or fail to be, financed by the private sector, but that are essential for the nation's competitiveness. However, this notion is ambiguous and refers, more or less, to the control by a country of the production of a good that is 'essential'. This notion influenced the trade policy of the United States under the Clinton administration (Tyson, L. A., 1992). Krugman (1991a) severely criticized such a strategy. He argued that while competitiveness is a seductive idea, it promises easy answers to complex problems and results in misallocation of resources, trade frictions, and distorted economic policies domestic economic policies.

Another rational for strategic trade is illustrated by the case of South Korea. Because the country was dependent on imports of raw materials, such as oil, a major government objective was to significantly increase the level of exports in order to finance necessary imports. The government combined a policy of import substitution with the export-led approach. Policy planners selected a group of strategic industries to back, including electronics, shipbuilding, and the automotive industry. New industries were nurtured by making the import of such goods difficult. When the new industry was on its feet, the government worked to create good conditions for exporting. Incentives for exports included a reduction of corporate and private income taxes for exporters, tariff exemptions for raw materials imported for export production, business tax exemptions, and accelerated depreciation allowances.

Strategic trade theory implies that governments assist national firms in order to shift profits from foreign firms to domestic ones and to the national economy. But there is an important difference between conventional and strategic trade theory exists on this point. Trade theory puts forward the possibility for a nation with sufficient power to impose an optimum tariff and thereby shift the terms of trade in its favour.[2] By restricting imports and decreasing the demand for a product, a large economy may be able to cause the price of the imported good to fall. Strategic trade policy, however, is able to go beyond the optimum tariff theory through its recognition of a nation's ability to intervene effectively in trade matters and thus to gain disproportionately.

2.4 Conclusion

Provided that all markets are perfectly competitive, information is complete, and there is no externality, the market mechanism should be the first-best solution for an optimal resource allocation. However, there are a number of instances of market failures that justify public intervention. These failures are related to imperfect information, externalities, and market power.

Information issues encompass two aspects; information incompleteness and uncertainty. Incomplete information has been identified as an obstacle to the development of SMEs. The latter have difficulty assessing the benefit of innovation and new technologies and face the reluctance of capital markets. Moreover, for non-traditional (e.g. innovative) activities and long-term projects, there is uncertainty about future profitability. If the investment returns ate hazy, market forces may be unlikely to ensure the implementation of such projects.

Externalities are a separate case of market failure and they generate sub-optimal market solutions. Knowledge externalities are one of the most common examples of externalities. The most efficient means of correcting for externalities is to 'internalize' the costs and benefits. However, internalization is not always possible and public intervention for supporting innovation activity can contribute to total welfare by enabling productivity growth and restructuring.

Another case of market failure arises due to the presence of spatial externalities. An industry characterized by high fixed costs and economies of scale tends to concentrate production geographically in order to benefit from external economies. Public intervention is able to foster the creation of clusters and cooperation between firms that generate agglomeration externalities, overcoming the coordination failure and resulting in higher allocative efficiency. However, the risks are that governments may not dispose of all the necessary information to determine the industries with agglomeration effects and the strategy for the best knowledge dissemination.

Imperfectly competitive markets allow situations where a first mover captures excess rents to the detriment of potential entrants and consumers. Strategic trade theory provides an economic rationale for government to support particular industries with imperfect competition and to provide national companies with a tangible advantage in international markets. Oligopolistic (or monopolistic) competition is most likely to occur in certain high-tech industries. However, strategic trade policy remains a highly controversial subject among economists. It is difficult to assess the welfare effect of public support in oligopolistic markets.

3
Argument Against Public Support: Government Failures

Government failures refer to situations where government intervention prevents the economy from achieving 'the first best'. As for the market, government failures may occur because of information imperfection. They may also occur because of conflict with other public policies or self-interest seeking by government officials. While the first two arguments are inherent in many public policies (including public support to business) the third is more likely with public support to business. Since government officials have the power to grant concrete benefits to specific actors in the economy, they may be prone to corruption.

3.1 Information

This is one of the most powerful arguments against government intervention. The issue is whether the government has enough adequate information to substitute for the decentralized information processing that markets, in general, can achieve. The problem for the government is twofold: identifying instruments that can achieve a given target and choosing the one that entails the least possible distortion of the economy.

3.1.1 Identifying instruments

Broadly speaking, one can distinguish two categories of instruments, namely structural and monetary. The former concerns all measures that do not involve transfer of funds from the government to firms (e.g. tariff and non-tariff barriers to trade, merger policy, protection of intellectual property and regulation). The latter concerns measures that involve transfer of funds from the government to firms (e.g. grants, tax breaks, or public procurement).

Depending on the nature of market failure or externality to alleviate, different types of industrial policy resort to various policy tools better adapted to attaining the policy targets. To tackle knowledge externalities and support innovation activities, governments therefore use fiscal instruments, such as subsidies for R&D and innovation, loan guarantees, and soft loans, or tax breaks and deferrals aimed at encouraging private expenditure on R&D activity (OECD, 2001). A number of other instruments are now available to governments; these may enhance innovation activities. They may include public research centres (e.g. university-based research centres), business support agencies, public procurement and so forth (Toivanen, 2006).

Spatial externalities and agglomeration support may be addressed though both fiscal and structural policy tools. Relocating firms may enjoy tax breaks, soft loans, or loan guarantees, or even direct budgetary subsidies. However, this may conflict with anti-trust regulations. Moreover, regional policy instruments can also promote agglomeration. Better infrastructure, education, and health care can enhance agglomeration incentives.

Strategic trade and merger policies rely on fiscal, structural, and trade policy instruments. Domestic producers can be granted different kind of subsidies (export, investment, production, etc.) or be protected by import tariffs or quotas. There may also be preferential procurement or financing agreements in favour of national producers. Strategic merger policy involves competition policy instruments, such as merger control and fiscal instruments such as tax breaks, or different kind of budgetary subsidies.

3.1.2 Optimality of instruments

While the wide range of instruments available to governments for addressing a market failure leaves room for manoeuvre, it does not make the choice any easier. A number of restrictions or obstacles (lack or difficultly of obtaining information, high costs, or contradiction with other economic policies) may still impair the efficiency of an otherwise perfect instrument.

For instance, a subsidy may allow direct targeting of a given market failure but raises the issue of the optimal size of a subsidy that is difficult to calibrate given the limited knowledge of the government (market and costs structures, etc.). Tax breaks (holidays or deferrals) designed to stimulate private incentive for innovations and R&D activities seem to be more 'market-oriented' measures that preserve the entrepreneur's incentives and competition, but the fact that they address the failure rather indirectly makes them potentially less effective.

Some economists have tried to map instruments against the various types of market failures. For instance, Caves (1987) and Gual (1995a, 1995b) argued that when the objective is to shift excessive rent from a foreign company present in a imperfectly competitive national market, the best possible intervention instrument is the import tariff. In contrast, a subsidy is better for promoting national producers on the international market. Eaton and Grossman (1985) showed that, when two national companies compete in prices with a foreign company (Bertrand behaviour) the best possible instrument may be an export tariff, which is supposed to reduce the pre-tax price for the domestic producer, allowing the undercutting of the foreign company and the increase of their market share. Other studies deal with different instruments (see Leahy and Neary [2001] on investment subsidy, Bond and Samuelson [1986] and Doyle and van Weinberger [1996] on tax holidays) but do not provide clearly defined recommendations.

3.2 Conflicts with other policies

There are two main policies that interplay with public support to business: competition and trade policies. The two policies are closely related because their areas of application overlap, inducing the risk of conflicts. Figure 3.1 illustrates such a risk using a very simple configuration. If one sees competition policy as the fight against any kind of monopolization, collusion and other restrictive practices (labelled 'strong') and trade policy as the steady progress towards free trade (labelled 'low'), there may be little room for public support to business, and so conflicts are likely.

The best policy mix is not very realistic in practice. First, the services or the people in charge of one of these policies may not be aware of what is done by the services in charge of the other policies. Second, the implementation of each of these policies is the result of forces different from the simple objective described above. For example, several competition laws aim more towards the protection of Small and Medium Enterprises (SMEs) against big business instead of promoting efficiency only. The general result is that each country has found some form of unstable equilibrium between industrial, competition, and trade policies, creating confusion within each of these policies as well as amongst them. The presence of conflicts entails the opportunity costs of undertaking public intervention.

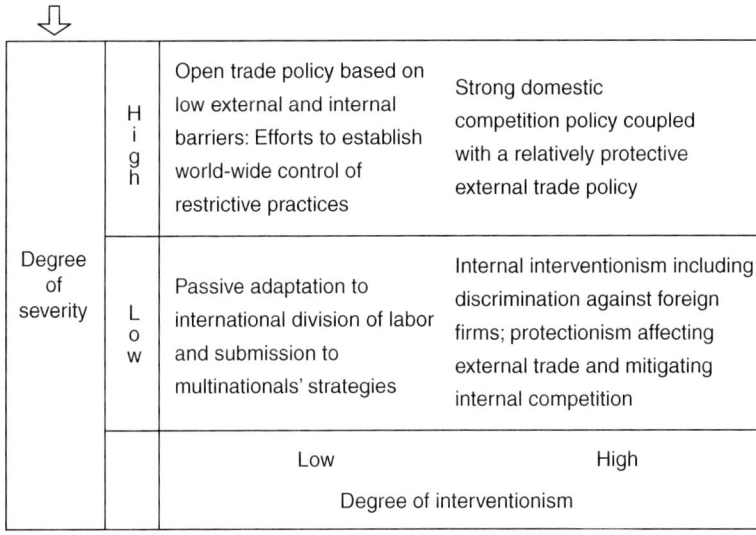

Figure 3.1 Competition, industrial and trade policies
Source: Buigues et al. (1995).

Less evident at the outset, more difficult to qualify, and less amenable to precise estimates are the indirect (or opportunity) costs involved in the execution of industrial policy. In fact, a public intervention that is economically quite sensible in isolation may counteract other policies. The issue to consider, therefore, is the trade-off between industrial and other policies. The importance of the point lies in an event when the outcome for the entire economic system would be better should industrial targets be disregarded. To put it differently, the losses that public interventions may bring about in terms of potential mishaps to other policies may appear more important than the potential improvements they may create.

3.2.1 Competition policy

The goal of competition policy, as defined by the European Commission is to 'promote and protect competition'.[1] Imperfect competition is associated with lower allocative efficiency and a reduction of consumer welfare. An improvement in market competitiveness therefore increases economic welfare. In practice, this goal is targeted though antitrust control and regulations, liberalization of potentially competitive markets, merger control, and state aid screening and control, and so on.

Although competition is the first-best solution for the maximization of welfare, there are several exceptions. Temporary market power may prove welfare-enhancing in cases where it is generated by innovation. (i.e. patent protection, temporary monopoly induced by innovation, etc.). This situation was discussed above in association with market failure due to knowledge externalities. Under these settings, therefore, the goals of industrial and competition policies may be compatible in the long run, but may contradict in the short run.

Another hindrance to perfect competition aimed at welfare maximization is the case of markets with economies of scale, when marginal costs are likely to decrease along with an increase in market size. The situation was also examined in detail earlier in the text in relation to market failure arising because of spatial externality. In this case, the second-best solution seems is to limit entry to the point when increase in efficiency from the larger scale of production exceeds the loss in allocative efficiency from reduced competition. However, while encouraging agglomeration may, under certain conditions, be the goal for both policies, it also makes collusion and cartels between firms easier, running against competition principles.

By the same token, strategic trade policy yields contradictory results when assessed from the perspective of competition policy. As far as domestic competition is concerned, subsidies to a national producer make no difference if the national producer is a 'natural' monopolist. If, however, other producers are present in the market, such subsidies to a selected firm will skew the market and come into conflict with competition policy. With respect to strategic merger as a tool of industrial policy (rent shifting from foreign producers to the national economy), the earlier discussion makes clear that there is an evident conflict between the policies if the production technology is characterized by constant returns to scale. By supporting such a merger, industrial policy helps a national producer to withstand the challenge of a foreign producer but, on the domestic market, it results in lower domestic competition with no gains in productive efficiency.

Finally, the compatibility of national industrial policy and EU competition policy is not evident if we are not concerned with domestic welfare. In the context of European Union (EU) competition policy, a national industrial policy in support of a specific sector is always discriminatory and therefore will distort competition.

3.2.2 Trade policy

As for other policies, the outcome of trade policy interventions might be an allocation of resources different from that implied by a non-restricted international trade pattern. Similarly, it may be accompanied with loss of economic efficiency and the potential benefits that free trade ensures at the global level. There are some exceptions, however. In particular, a country can be better off (provided it is able to affect prices on the international market) by imposing an import tariff, which leads to lower import prices. The necessary condition, however, is that the gain for the economy should exceed the cost of the tariff in terms of distorting production and consumption (Valila, 2006).

Moreover, the outcomes in the static and dynamic settings might differ significantly. Krugman and Obstfeld (1994), and Gual (1995a, 1995b) stressed failures in domestic markets for inputs. Specifically, during structural change, a tariff protection might appear a second-best response to labour and capital market rigidities (the first-best solution would clearly be flexibility; however, it is often non-feasible, at least, in the short run). Nonetheless, this argument remains very controversial, because of difficulties in defining the market failure and doubts that a tariff is the best possible instrument for remedying the situation.

3.3 Political economy

The use of industrial policy raises certain political economy issues which induce some non negligible costs and may outweigh the benefit of the policy. We examine three of these issues below: elections, lobbying, and the possibility of capture and corruption (or favouritism).

3.3.1 Elections

There is a vast literature in the field of political economy devoted to elections, referred to as political cycles. The central assumption in this literature is that governments choose policy instruments, and thereby affect policy outcomes, in line with political considerations, such as the desire to win elections or to promote ideologies.

The theory of political cycles has two strands. One postulates that politicians are 'opportunistic', choosing policies in order to further their chances of re-election. The other assumes, instead, that politicians behave in a 'partisan' manner, acting in accordance with their ideology. The two strands developed in parallel in two phases. During the 1970s, the two schools relied on the traditional assumption that governments have a great deal of influence on policy outcomes. By contrast, in the

1980s and 1990s, researchers of both schools adopted rational expectations models, which imply limited ability of policymakers to influence economic outcomes. At present, therefore, the theory contains four types of models: traditional and rational opportunistic models, and traditional and rational partisan models.

Each of these four types of models produces different implications, in terms of policy instruments and policy outcomes. For instance, opportunistic models imply policy instrument manipulations and impacts on policy outcomes before elections, whereas partisan models generate policy effects after elections. These implications have been extensively tested by Alesina and several co-authors on data for the United States and most other Organisation of Economic Cooperation and Development (OECD) countries. They found that partisan models perform much better than opportunistic models both for the United States and other OECD countries.

While the above discussion naturally implies the need for better accountability on the part of the government, Dewatripont and Seabright (2006) suggest that accountability, in itself, may generate wasteful public spending. Their paper develops a model in which politicians fund wasteful projects as a way of advertising their diligence, and voters rationally reward them for this. In fact, they argue that wasteful spending by politicians can sometimes arise as a by-product of political accountability. Hence, simply strengthening these mechanisms would not necessarily improve – and might even worsen – the quality of spending decisions. Politicians may sometimes engage in wasteful spending not because of negligence or lack of information but because of their desire to improve their chances of re-election by showcasing their commitment to the supply of public goods.

3.3.2 Lobbying and capture

Another political economy argument against industrial policies stems from the role of lobbying and the risk of capture of public authorities when supporting specific industrial sectors. The specific public authorities in question and the industries being supported may become so interdependent that there will be a distortion of the economic decision processes.

This argument has been formally examined by Laffont (1996), but goes back to Montesquieu and Marx who argued that governments may favour special interest groups. Taking a more disaggregated view of government, which distinguishes regulatory agencies from political executives and recognizes the multi-principal nature of governments, these authors have emphasized the distorting role that can be played by various intermediaries that are needed in the implementation of industrial policies.

More recently, various authors, assuming that politicians control the various agencies in charge of implementing policies, have investigated how various interest groups influence the democratic process or the elected politicians to favour their own interests (Pelzman, 1976; Becker, 1985).

The dead-weight losses generated by such activities must be added to the original dead-weight loss associated with the original distortions, for example due to monopoly pricing, in order to obtain a complete assessment of social cost. This implies that industrial policy should also be designed at the constitutional level to deal with the capture problems with firms, interest groups or politicians. It also necessitates that governments or agencies be structured to mitigate the costs of capture.

3.3.3 Corruption

Theoretical contributions by, among others, Laffont and Tirole (1991) and Compte et al (2005), have shown that favouritism and corruption may emerge as an equilibrium outcome in procurement auctions. They highlight that the scope for favouritism and corruption in a procurement auction depends much on what is being procured and how the procurement is organized. The risk of corruption is particularly high when the object of bidding is very complex; there are potentially major quality differences in the bids that these qualities of bids are initially the bidders' private information, and delegation is inevitable.

There is some evidence of the negative impact of corruption on economic performance. Rose-Ackerman (1997) showed that a firm may be able to pay high bribes simply because it will compromise on the quality of the goods that it will produce if it gets a license. Tanzi and Davoodi (1997) found that higher corruption is associated with higher public investments which are not directed towards the most efficient awards of contract. Finally, Mauro (1998), observed a significant negative relationship between corruption and private investment that extended to growth. These findings were confirmed by Brunetti and Weder (1998) and Mo (2001).

3.4 Conclusion

Market failures imply that in some cases public authorities should intervene to achieve the first best. However, such intervention is well founded only if 'government failures' do not induce an outcome worse than market mechanisms. As for the market, government failures may occur because of information imperfection. They may also occur because of conflict with other public policies or self-interest seeking by government officials.

The issue of information is one of the most powerful arguments against government intervention. The question is whether the government may have better information than private agents inside the markets. Moreover, the government should choose the policy instrument that can achieve a given target and entails the least possible distortion in the economy.

Industrial policy interplays with other government policies; in particular competition and trade policies. The areas of application of the two policies may overlap, inducing the risk of conflicts. If one sees competition policy as the fight against any kind of monopolization, collusion, and other restrictive practices and trade policy as the steady progress towards free trade, there may be little room for public support to business and conflicts are likely.

The use of industrial policy also raises political economy issues. These are related to elections, lobbying (and capture), and corruption (and favouritism). A part of the literature in the field of political economy shows that governments may choose policies on the basis of purely political considerations, such as the desire to win elections or to promote ideologies. Furthermore lobbying groups may become so influential that there will be a distortion of the economic decision processes. Finally, the representative of an authority granting support to business may be inclined to ask (or accept) a 'reward' from the beneficiary.

4
Instruments of Support: Subsidies and Public Procurement

4.1 Subsidies

In practice, there is no commonly accepted definition of subsidy and state aid, and existing definitions differ in the scope of policy which they consider (OECD, 2001). Schwartz and Clements (1999) define a subsidy as any government assistance that allows consumers to purchase goods and services at prices lower than those offered by a perfectly competitive private sector or that raise producers' incomes beyond those that would be earned without intervention. The authors proposed a list of government assistance that can be considered as subsidies.

Besides the definition issues, subsidies also pose measurement problems. There are almost as many measures as the number of (national or international) institutions in charge of assessing subsidies. This section discusses the differences in definition and measurement of subsidies.

4.1.1 Definition of subsidies in the WTO

The issue of state aid and subsidies in an international context is a permanent source of conflict because of their alleged distortive effects on trade (Messerlin, 1999). The Agreement on Subsidies and Countervailing Measures ('SCM Agreement') addresses the issue of multilateral disciplines regulating the provision of subsidies to goods. Part 1 of the Agreement defines the term of 'subsidy' and the concept of 'specificity'. Only specific subsidies, as opposed to general measures, are subject to ASCM disciplines. The defining characteristics of subsidies are listed in SCM Article 1: 'definition of a subsidy'.

The definition contains three basic elements: (1) financial contribution (2) the contribution comes from a government or any public body within the territory of a Member (3) the contribution confers a benefit to the recipient of the contribution. All three of these elements must be satisfied in order for a subsidy to exist. That implies that the agreement covers a financial contribution such as grants, loans, equity subsidies, fiscal incentives, the provision of goods and services, or the purchase of goods. The financial contribution must be made by or on behalf of a government or any public body and the financial contribution is not a subsidy unless it confers a 'benefit'. The existence of a 'benefit' is not always very clear, in particular in the case of loan, or purchase by governments.[1]

Only 'specific' subsidies are subject to the SCM Agreement disciplines (e.g. enterprise-specificity, industry-specificity).

The SCM Agreement requires that World Trade Organisation (WTO) members notify all specific subsidies, at all levels of government covering all goods sectors to the SCM Committee. That implies that subsidies to the services sector are not covered by WTO notification requirements. New and full notifications are due every two years. However, 29 of the current WTO members, particularly Less Developed Countries (LDCs), have so far not submitted any notification. Other WTO members do not provide quantitative or complete information systematically.

In the notification submitted to the Committee, the country may indicate certain measures that may not constitute 'subsidies' under the WTO definition and certain subsidies which may not be 'specific'. Some of the horizontal subsidies are also notified to achieve the maximum transparency by certain countries. Therefore, there are important differences between countries' notifications. Over the period 1995 to 2002, a total of 54 countries notified quantitative information on industrial and/or horizontal subsidies to the WTO under the SCM notifications requirement.

For example, the notification of Japan on Subsidies to the Committee on Subsidies and Countervailing measures of the WTO (G/SCM/123/JPN, 7 July 2005) presented 92 measures, one fiche for each different programme. Each fiche presents the title of the subsidy programme, the period covered by the notification, the policy objective, the background and authority for the subsidy, the legislation under which it was granted, the form of the subsidy, to whom the subsidy was granted, subsidy per unit, and the duration of the subsidy. However, even if the SCM Agreement requires members to provide quantitative information on the annual amount budgeted for the subsidy, members, in particular those from less developed countries, frequently indicate in their notification that no quantitative information is available.

4.1.2 Definition of subsidies in National Accounts statistics

National account statistics published by government are the most complete standardized information on subsidies. In National Accounts, OECD defines subsidies as 'current unrequited payments that government units, make to enterprises on the basis of their production activities or the quantities or value of the goods or services which they produce, sell or import'. Other subsidies on production consist of 'subsidies, except subsidies on products, which resident enterprises may receive as a consequence of engaging in production (e.g. subsidies on payroll, or workforce or subsidies to reduce pollution)'.[2]

Therefore, National Accounts statistics reveal only direct payment to enterprises. In the national account statistics approach, subsidies involve money directly flowing from government to domestic enterprises but subsidies may take less obvious form. In government fiscal accounts, other types of subsidies than cash subsidies are not classified in the budget category 'subsidies', such as credit, tax, equity, in-kind, procurement and regulatory subsidies. Tax subsidies are reduced tax revenue and therefore not included in the budget category 'subsidies'. Loans to state enterprises are often not classified as subsidies, even if these loans are used to cover deficits. This is often the case with utility companies which may be obliged by government to sell their products or services at low prices (railway, energy, etc.).

The definition is also restricted to the producers as recipients. Direct transfers to households are not considered as subsidies but as social benefits. Moreover, the definition of subsidies in national account statistics refers only to payments linked to their production activities and not to payments 'not linked' to their production activities, as pure income revenue such as. Information on subsidies in the National Accounts approach covers the following categories: defence, education, public order and safety, social protection, general public services, economic affairs, environment protection, housing, recreation, culture and religion, health.[3] However, on the basis of the data on subsidies in National Accounts, it is not possible to get information on the nature of public support policies and on the priorities adopted by government R&D, environment, Small and Medium Enterprises (SMEs), region, declining sector, or high-tech industries.

4.1.3 Definition of subsidies in the EU

In the EU, Articles 87–9 of the European Communities (EC) Treaty relate to state aid, which overlaps to some extent with the concepts of subsidy described above. State aid is defined in Article 87(1) EC Treaty as a state intervention through transfer of state resources that effectively confers advantages by favouring certain economic activities or certain undertakings and that distorts competition and trade within the common market. To determine whether a government measure can be defined as state aid, a distinction is drawn between general measures, which are equally applicable to all undertakings throughout the Member States, and measures which are selective, that is, directed at certain undertakings, sectors, or economic activities.

To qualify as state aid, a measure needs to satisfy all the criteria listed under Article 87(1):

- *Transfer of state resources:* this includes national, regional, or local authorities, not necessarily granted by the state itself but also by public companies, or intermediate bodies appointed by the state. Moreover, the transfer of state resources can take can different forms: grant, interest rate rebates, loan guarantees, accelerated depreciation allowances, capital injections, etc.
- *Economic advantage:* this applies to the economic advantage that an undertaking could not have received in the normal course of business, for example, if a company buys land from the state at less than market price, or obtains risk capital under conditions more favourable than those that would have applied had it purchased from a private investor.
- *Selectivity:* this is what differentiates state aid from general economic measures which apply without distinction to all firms in a Member State. General measures, such as nationwide fiscal measures which apply to all firms, are not considered as state aid. *The distinction between state aid measures and general economic measures is not always clear-cut.* Certain general economic measures open to all sectors and undertakings may be selective to a certain extent if there is an element of discretion by the Member States authorities. The interpretation of this concept of selectivity has evolved following Court rulings and Commission decisions.
- *Effect on competition and trade:* such aid must have a potential effect on competition and trade between the Member States. It is sufficient to prove that the beneficiary operates in a market in which there is trade between Member States. In the present set of rules, aids below €200,000 (per beneficiary over three years) are considered de facto to have no impact on trade and competition and do not need to be notified.

Table 4.1 Classification of state aid by objective

Horizontal objectives	Research and development
	Environment and energy saving
	Small and medium-sized enterprises
	Commerce
	Employment aid
	Training aid
	Regional aid not elsewhere classified
	Other objectives
Particular sectors	Manufacturing
	Services
	Coal
	Other non-manufacturing
	Transport (airlines, inland waterways, maritime, road and combined)

Source: State Aid Scoreboard, conceptual and methodological remarks.

State aid reports classify the different forms of state aid by objectives Table 4.1).

However, as mentioned in the scoreboard report, the classification of state aid by objective is not so clear and easy. The classification of aids to the manufacturing sector is related to the principal objective for which aid is given. For example, generally, aid classified under the objective of R&D is managed through specific R&D programmes. But this is not always the case for aid classified under the objective of regional aid. In fact, regional aid may be paid primarily to SMEs, or for employment purposes. This implies that the differences in objectives between Member States are not always very clear and conclusions have to be drawn cautiously.

4.1.4 Differences between the definitions

We have presented definition of subsidies in WTO, in national account statistics and in the EU. Many differences exist between the different definitions and approaches. The WTO notification database has a much wider coverage of different forms of subsidies than the national account finance statistics, in particular tax subsidies. However, the WTO notification database has a much narrower sectoral coverage than the national account finance statistics, as *services industries* are not included in the WTO notifications. Moreover, many horizontal subsidies are not included in the WTO notification database, as they are not 'specific subsidies' and the information collected in the notification is not always completed and sufficiently precise.

Table 4.2 presents the different definitions used in the reports and empirical studies on subsidies and state aid.

An agreed definition of subsidies is important if subsidies are to be measured and compared between countries. In practice, the cross-country comparison of the amount of subsidies is particularly complex and very often the empirical work relies on pragmatic subsidy definitions that allow quantification. Moreover, what can be measured may only be a fraction of what is spent in the real economic world by governments. The United Nation's system of National Accounts, which defines subsidies relatively narrowly, is the only standardized information in subsidies covering the EU Member States, the United States, and Japan.

4.1.5 Impact of subsidies on competition

While subsidies can help correcting for market failures, they will also distort competition. In particular, subsidy targeted on particular firms or sectors will inevitably lead to distortions of competitions.

The objective of a study prepared for the Office of Fair Trading (2004) was precisely to provide an understanding of the competition effects that can arise from public subsidies, and to identify the factors which affect the magnitude of the distortions of competition.

The report underlines that subsidies can affect decisions of the firms in many ways: entry and exit, pricing and output, and R&D investment decisions. The identification of the characteristics of the market where the subsidy is operating, is important to understand whether the impact of subsidy is likely to materialize.[4] The Office of Fair Trade (OFT) report (2004) identifies the following market characteristics, to determine the effect of the subsidy:

- *Market concentration:* subsidies affecting pricing decisions are most likely to raise competition concerns where concentration is high and the number of firms small. Less product differentiation increases the distortions of competition. The effects on pricing are likely to be large and more likely to result in exit. Where the number of firms is small but product differentiation is strong, the effects on pricing are likely to be smaller. If the subsidy results in an additional firm in a market already concentrated with moderate product differentiation, this entry is likely to give rise to competition concerns.

If the concentration is high, with large firms facing a fringe of several smaller competitors, the impact on competition is more ambiguous. Subsidy to the large firms will potentially further reduce the competition.

Table 4.2 Different approaches of subsidies

Sources	Transactions covered	Sectoral coverage	Measurement basis[a]	Country coverage	Comments
NAS	Cash subsidies	All	Gross cost to government	UN Member states	
EU (State aid scoreboard)	Cash subsidies soft loans guarantees equity subsidies tax subsidies + sale of inputs below market price + purchase above market prices (but no transfers from Community budget)	All	Grant equivalent	EU Member states	Covers only EU Member States
OECD (public support to industry project)	Cash subsidies soft loans guarantees equity subsidies tax subsidies	Manufacturing	Net cost to government	OECD Member countries	Ad hoc project, covering the period 1989–1993
WTO (WTO notification based on SCM agreement)	Financial contribution by a public body which confers a 'benefit'. For the EU it includes transfers from the Community budget	Services are not covered	Net cost to government	WTO Member countries	Lack of clarity and consistency in the quantitative information

[a] The differences between the 'gross cost to government' and the 'net cost government' are the following. Under the 'gross concept', the full amount of government payment is a subsidy whereas under the net concept, subsidies take into account the possible recovery operations. For example, for equity subsidies under the net concept, equity subsidy are calculated as the difference between the cost of the government borrowing and the dividends received (value of shares).

Sources: WTO report (2006), Schwartz and Clements (1999), EU State Aid Scoreboard.

A subsidy to smaller or fringe firms which allow them to compete more effectively with the large firm is likely to increase competition. However, if the subsidy increases competition between the small firms, this may lead to the exit of small firms and may have a negative effect on competition.

- *Barriers to entry and exit:* the importance of entry and exit barriers gives incumbent firms an advantage since they can raise prices without the threat of potential entering. An incumbent facing a subsidized competitor will be less likely to exit in the face of short-run losses, as barriers to exit tend to be high. The competition effects may be in that case reduced but if this exit occurs, the competition effect may be high, since high barriers to entry make it difficult to return in the market.

R&D investment decision: subsidies can affect R&D competition by increasing the quantity or the focus of investment decisions. However, there is no clear rule on how subsidies may change the future incentives to innovate. That will depend on whether the subsidy is for the technology leader or for its competitors and the intensity of product market competition. The Office of Fair Trading (2007) has recently published guidance on how to assess the competition effects of subsidies. The objective is to enable subsidy providers assessing whether a proposed subsidy is likely to affect competition. This guidance report concludes that a subsidy undermines the mechanisms for ensuring efficiency in the market when (1) competitors are forced to exit the market; (2) the recipient is under less financial pressure to be competitive; (3) an inefficient recipient is able to remain in the market and; (4) firms spend significant sums of money seeking subsidies.

The problem of assessing the effects on competition of state aid is particularly complex when the beneficiaries and even the affected markets are not known. This is often the case when the European Commission examines proposed aid schemes rather than aid to individual firms (Fingleton et al., 1999). Buelens et al. (2007) suggests 'a series of indicators that can contribute to identifying conditions (e.g. aid, firm, or market characteristics) which would give rise to or exacerbate the negative effects of aids'. However, as underlined by these authors, work remain to be done as regards the quantification of some of these indicators, in particular the determination of thresholds.

As discussed in Section 4.1 above, the principal justifications for state aid are the existence of market failures. However, in the case of existing market failure, one of the main problems for economists is the quantification issue. This is particularly the case for R&D and SME state aid. The European Commission guidelines give convincing economic arguments for the favourable treatment of state intervention for R&D, in particular positive externalities. These guidelines also introduce different thresholds. For example, the treatment of R&D is based on the differences between fundamental and applied research. However, the form and the degree of government intervention must be suited to the importance and nature of the problems. The core question for economists is to design state aid so as to correct a clearly defined market failure.

From an empirical viewpoint, one of the main difficulties for the European Commission is to quantify the degree of market failures. For economists, the evaluation of market failures poses very practical problems. For example, existing studies on externalities and the financial disadvantages faced by SMEs do not provide adequate guidelines for the clear quantification of state aid, which would correctly compensate for market failures (Buigues, 2001). Externalities are generally not the subject of market transactions and are therefore not easily measured. It is clear, as underlined by Rey (2001), that 'it is usually a better idea to correct the sources of the market failure, rather than to try to correct the undesirable consequences of the market failure'.

At an aggregate economic level, Gual (1999) has tried to define optimal aid levels when aid pursues efficiency objectives, that is, correct market failures. Since the externality cannot be observed, the methodology was based on allowing deviations from a common rate of aid when justified by divergences in the factors determining the magnitude of externality. The main conclusion of the study is, however, disappointing: 'the evidence shows that even when program pursues an efficiency objective, the actual disbursement of aid across countries bears no relationship to reasonable proxies of the magnitude of the market failures being targeted' (Gual, 1999).

Therefore, economic analysis of subsidies (impact on competition and evaluation of market failures) has still to be developed. As stated recently, 'Most of the analysis in the practice of European state aid control is not firmly rooted in economic principles' (Friederiszich et al., 2008). This situation is explained by a number of reasons such as the existence of multiple objectives of subsidies and the existence of several theories of the competitive impact of subsidies (e.g. dynamic theories and political economy). For the authors, further economic analysis of state aid control is needed to get a better picture of the impact of state aid on competition (Friederiszick et al., 2008). This implies a clear assessment of market failures on the one hand and of the distortions of competition on the other.

4.1.6 Rules for subsidies: WTO disciplines and EU state aid control

Government subsidies can be useful instruments in correcting market failures but can also distort competition and trade. As some types of public support are clearly controversial and can be damaging, it is important to understand the relevance of WTO disciplines on subsidies and the interface with EU state aid control.

WTO disciplines

Having defined subsidies based on three basic elements (financial contribution by a government or a public body conferring a benefit) the SCM Agreement creates two basic categories of subsidies, prohibited subsidies and actionable subsidies:

- *Prohibited subsidies*: there are two types of prohibited subsidies. The first type consists of subsidies contingent on export performance ('export subsidies'). The annex to the SCM Agreement presents a list of export subsidies. The second type of prohibited subsidies consists of subsidies contingent upon the use of domestic over imported goods ('local content subsidies'). As mentioned by WTO, 'these two categories of subsidies are prohibited because they are designed to directly affect trade and thus are most likely to have adverse effects on the interest of other members' (Subsidies and Countervailing measures overview, WTO). In practice the scope of these prohibitions is relatively narrow.
- *Actionable subsidies*: most subsidies fall into this category. They are not prohibited but are subject to challenge, through multilateral dispute settlement or unilateral imposition of countervailing duties. To be challenged, they have to cause adverse effects to the interest of other member of the WTO. Three types of adverse effects mentioned are:
  - *Injury to a domestic industry* of a complaining member caused by subsidized imports; this is the only basis for countervailing action;
  - *Serious prejudice*, which usually arises as a result of adverse effects such as export displacement. It can serve as a basis for complaint related to a member's export interest;
  - *Nullification or impairment* of benefits which arise typically where the improved market access following tariff reduction is undercut by subsidization.

When it is clearly demonstrated that there are subsidized imports, injury to a domestic industry, and a clear causal link between the subsidized import and the injury, the WTO member may impose a countervailing duty (CVD). However, the need in many cases to demonstrate the economically adverse effects arising from subsidies is a real difficulty. To allow WTO members to challenge actionable subsidies causing adverse effects, a system of multilateral dispute settlement was created.

- *Countervailing measures*: the SCM Agreement sets out detailed procedural requirements regarding the countervailing investigation that must be fulfilled in order to impose a countervailing duty. When we look at how WTO rules have imposed discipline on subsidies, it is clear that the imposition of countervailing duties enforced unilaterally is the preferred instrument (Ehlermann and Goyette, 2006). The reason explaining the success of CVDs is that it is faster than going through the WTO dispute settlement process. Generally, CVDs are sufficient to meet the industry concern and national interest (WTO, 2006) when injury occurs in the domestic market. Taking the CVD route is also easier since it places the onus on the exporting country to challenge the CVD measure. The burden of proof falls upon the countries whose export have been affected by the CVD, and will play in favour of the member imposing the CVDs.

Table 4.3 presents the use of CVD measures by reporting members. The EU has in the period from 1995 to end of 2006 taken 23 CVD measures compared with 47 measures by the United States, and only one by Japan. The sector 'Base metals and articles of base metal' alone represents nearly 50% of the measures by reporting members from 1995 to 2006 (Table 4.4).

Table 4.3 The use of countervailing measures by reporting members from 1995 to 2006

	01/01/95 to end 2000	End 2000 to end 2006	Total
European Community	15	8	23
Japan	0	1	1
United States	21	26	47
Total reporting member	66	49	115

Source: Statistics on subsidies and countervailing measures WTO.

Table 4.4 The sectoral distribution of measures by reporting members from 1995 to 2006 (top 4 sectors representing 74% of total)

1. Base metals and articles of base metal	57	49.6%
2. Prepared foodstuffs: beverages, spirits and vinegar, tobacco and manufactured tobacco substitute	12	10.4%
3. Vegetable products	8	7.0%
4. Plastics and articles thereof: rubber and articles thereof	7	6.1%
Total	115	100.0%

Source: Statistics on subsidies and countervailing measures WTO.

However, CVDs will not suffice where the national industry is not so much concerned about the effects of the subsidies on its home market but on third country markets. This would also be true of anti-dumping measures in cases where they are preferred to CVD. In such case, the WTO dispute settlement is the only way.

- *Dispute Settlement:* only a limited number of cases have addressed complaints against actionable subsidies and most of the WTO subsidy dispute settlement cases have concerned export subsidies.[5] The dispute settlement system is based on clearly defined rules with timetables for completing a case. As reported by WTO, the objective is not to pass judgment but to settle disputes, through consultation process. By July 2005, only about 130 of the nearly 332 dispute settlement cases had reached the full panel process.

EU State aid control

The point of departure of the EU approach to subsidy is laid down in Article 87(1) of the EC Treaty. This article states that state aid is, in principle, incompatible with the common market: 'any aid granted by a Member State or through state resources in any form whatsoever which distorts or threatens to distort competition by favouring certain undertakings or the production of certain goods shall, in so far as it affects trade between Member States, be incompatible with the common market'. Article 88 requires Member States to notify the Commission in advance the intention to grant state aid. The standstill obligation implies that state aid cannot be granted before it has been authorized by the Commission on the basis of the exceptions to the principle of incompatibility which are set out in Articles 87(2) and (3). The Commission has been charged with the exclusive competence to control state aid, subject to judicial review by the European Courts. The control of state aids is an almost unique feature of competition policy applied in the European Union. Even federal states lack such mechanism of control of subsidies granted by their constituent parts.[6]

The principle of the incompatibility of state aid with the Treaty is not, however, absolute. Thus, Article 87(2) states a number of exemptions from this general prohibition. It includes aid of a social character, or related to natural disasters, and aid granted to the economy in certain areas of Western Germany affected by the division of Germany (after the German reunification, exemptions were only applied in two cases: in 1992 for Potsdamer Platz – Berlin (West) and in 1994 for Tettauer Winkel (Bavaria). They are not applicable to Eastern Germany COM ((90) 400). Besides, Article 87(3) foresees some discretionary exceptions, such as aid for the development of certain (underdeveloped) regions or economic activities, aid to support projects of common European interest, aid to dealing with serious economic disturbances, and for culture and heritage conservation.

The European Commission and the Council have adopted regulations and guidelines in order to specify administrative procedures for implementing control over state aid.

WTO discipline on subsidies and EU state aid control

The question of the consistency between the WTO discipline and EU state aid control is the subject of many papers (Tietje, 2004; Weiss, 2005; Ehlermann and Goyette, 2006). What is important to notice is that for certain academics, 'WTO law has a much broader scope of application with regard to subsidies' (Tietje C., 2004: 9).

Claus-Dieter Ehlermann and Martin Goyette (2006) have analysed the interface between EU state aid control and the WTO disciplines on subsidies. For these authors, the approaches retained in the WTO and in the EC present certain different characteristics:

- *Cost to government:* for the EU Court of justice, 'only advantages granted directly or indirectly through State resources are to be considered aid' (Case C-379/98-PreussenElektra AG, paragraph 58). The Court rejected a Commission argument that the state aid concept ought to be interpreted in such a way as to include support measures which are decided upon by the state but financed by private undertakings (ibid., paragraph 65). Under WTO law, government measures that do not impose a transfer of state resources may be regarded as subsidy. For Ehlermann and Goyette, 'In principle, the requirement in EC law that a measure correspond to a charge on the

public account signifies that EC state aid law is more lenient than the WTO's disciplines on subsidies' (ibid., p. 699). This is a somewhat counter-intuitive result.
- *Benefit:* the WTO and EC contain similar requirements on a measure which will constitute a subsidy or state aid from the viewpoint of the benefit. In EC law, in order for state aid to exist, it must confer an economic advantage to the recipient. This is similar to the WTO law for the determination of the benefit. The WTO test is whether this benefit would have been obtained under normal market conditions.
- *Specificity:* the concepts of 'specificity' under EC law and WTO law are to a certain extent similar but differ in their treatment of regional specificity (some measures that would be selective under the EC rules would not be specific under the WTO rules) and general measures (where the EC law would consider as selective, for example, SME aid which may fall outside the concept of specificity in the WTO).

Compatibility: the EU Commission has to assess state aid by weighing the benefits and the potential negative impact on competition before authorizing the aid. But the Commission does not assess the international trade effects of a measure before authorizing it, although it never authorizes subsidies in the WTO's 'prohibited' category. In principle, all state aid authorized by the Commission is 'actionable' under the WTO rules if the necessary requirements are met, as discussed earlier (e.g. material injury, causal link, etc.).Ehlermann et al. (2006), mention particular concerns of a risk of conflicts on the following aids:

- ad hoc regional aid to large investment projects. Providing the undertakings are exporting to the world markets, they are likely to cause adverse trade effects;
- aid to promote important projects of European interest such as alleged aid for Airbus;
- rescue and restructuring aid, has the potential of causing adverse effects.

The authors conclude, however, that 'the most significant difference between the two systems relates not to the definition of state aid and subsidy, but what happens once a measure meets to such definition'. Potentially problematic subsidies in the WTO are subject to only poorly enforced notification requirements and to inconsistent challenge by governments. This implies that the consequences of WTO discipline are relatively unpredictable. By contrast, EC state aid control provides for an *ex ante* assessment and state aids are subject to extensive scrutiny prior to implementation. Moreover, where unlawful and incompatible aid has been paid, it will be recovered with interest. Under the WTO, remedies imply removal of a subsidy or of its effects, or a countervailing duty. However, at the same time, the EU state aid control provides for flexibility, since the Commission has the power to authorize state aid measures.

4.2 Public procurement

Public procurement is the term used to describe the purchasing of works, supplies, and services by national, regional, and local public bodies, including central government, local authorities, fire and police authorities, defence, health services, joint consortia of public bodies, and public and private utilities.

Government support to business directly through subsidies or indirectly through the provision of adequate skills or infrastructure is generally classified by economists among the 'push factors'. When public procurements are used to support business they play the role of 'pull factors'. They may create an early-stage customer and a market demand that enables business to innovate. By securing a certain level of demand to the firms, they may help them supporting the cost of (sometimes risky) research and innovation. As such they may prove a powerful instrument of public support to business (McCrudden, 2004; Henten, 2005; Evenett and Hoekman, 2005).

4.2.1 Public procurement and international trade

Public procurements are attracting much attention in international negotiations (Evenett and Hoekman, 2005) because these contracts may condition access to foreign markets. In the frame of international trade negotiations the government defines terms and conditions for foreign firms' eligibility for taking part in competition in the domestic market of public procurement. WTO supervises these procedures, even if its disciplines on procurement are made currently on voluntary basis, in that they apply only to signatories of a so-called plurilateral agreement, the Agreement on Government Procurement (GPA) that came into force in 1996. This agreement has extended its coverage to include works and services contracts as well as supplies. The new GPA is no longer limited to procurement at central government but comprises contracts awarded by public authorities at regional and local level and also a number of utilities sectors.

Within the EU, public procurement is subject to Community and international rules (GPA, as mentioned above), although not all public procurement is subject to these obligations. Under these rules public sector procurement, which is considered a fundamental part of the single market, must follow transparent open procedures ensuring fair conditions of competition for suppliers. The principle of public procurement is to open up the choice of potential suppliers to the public sector and utilities, which is expected to result in cost reduction, while at the same time opening up potential markets for companies. In particular, the rules aim to ensure the free movement of goods and services within the EU and that public sector purchasing decisions are based on value-for-money achieved through competition. These principles are applied by virtue of the advertising of contracts across the Union, and are supposed to treat all enquiries equally to avoid discrimination, such as on the grounds of nationality or the origins of goods and services.

Some purchases (e.g. military equipment for the defence sector) are, however, excluded, and purchases below thresholds must respect the principles of the Treaty. In particular, related legislative package of public procurement directives was approved in 2004 by the European Parliament and the Council of Ministers. The opening up of public procurement within the internal market is supposed to increase cross-border competition and make the prices paid by public authorities more competitive.

Since (a least a part of) public procurement represents potentially profitable opportunities for companies, there is a risk of corruption. The first order problem is the allocation of scarce resources, in other words, prioritizing. The needs are enormous and ever growing and the problem is how to allocate scarce resources. That is why the concepts of public administration transparency and accountability are important in the field of public procurements.

These considerations give a political dimension to the public procurement process. A procurement decision reflects a political preference and priority. But the decision itself is not always motivated by rational arguments. The issues of government's failures have been discussed above, in particular the fact that politicians or regulators, even if there is no question of power abuse or corruption, are subject to their own incentive systems that may not lead to socially desirable outcomes. Political economy proposes a wide range of frameworks that investigate governments' incentives to give preferences to one or another policy. For instance, in the so-called 'representative democratic model' politicians strive to get re-elected and choose their policies accordingly. The choice might not be always effective in the sense of improving social welfare, however. The optimality condition would require accountability and transparency.

In the same context, Schapper et al. (2006) point out that is it impossible to develop a comprehensive framework for the analysis or management of public procurement independent of its political context. Moreover, besides transparency and accountability requirements, public procurement needs highly qualified public officials capable of effective management in order to deliver good value for money while limiting risks (NPR, 1993). And similarly to industrial policy, it necessitates the demand for coherence with other public policies and between the actions of relevant authorities, due to its importance for business environment and the economy as a whole (Harland et al., 2000).

Many jurisdictions worldwide, implicitly or explicitly, follow similar objectives for public procurement. Yet, while the policies pursued are often alike, there are important variances in methodologies and operational practice (Thai, 2001; Jones, 2002). For instance, the Government Procurement Experts Group within the forum for Asia-Pacific Economic Cooperation countries (APEC) has elaborated a set of non-binding principles that include transparency, value for money, fair dealing, open and effective competition, accountability and due process (APEC, 1999). In general, outlined principles serve a foundation for majority of public procurement policies, the differences consist only in the importance that is assigned to a particular one. In fact, a country taking into account the peculiar characteristics of the economy and the cost and benefits of adopting specific measures privileges certain of them giving the role of second fiddle to others.

Three basic objectives of public procurement policy may be sketched out (Schapper, et al., 2006):

Public confidence – an essential requirement for transparency, equity, and fair dealing in respect with procurement process;
Efficiency and effectiveness – the utilization of public resources so as to achieve optimal balance between risk and value for money;
Policy compliance and consistency – the process of public procurement and its outcomes should be compatible with the objectives of other economic policies, such as environmental issues, support of SMEs, training, regional impacts, international obligations.

If drafted in this way, the objectives of public procurement policy are entirely consistent with the common understanding of public management. They stress its principal pillars of transparency, efficiency, and efficacy, and are in line with other targets of governmental economic and social policies. Meanwhile, despite outer simplicity, delivering these objectives into operational reality involves issues and policies that are frequently in conflict if not mutually incompatible. Generally, three main approaches, each focusing on particular facet of procurement process (i.e. regulation, management, and centralization), are used to ensure adequate public procurement policy. However, there are a number of combinations that are better suited to the particular economic or cultural traditions of a country.

4.2.2 Public procurement and competition

The nature of the competition effects of public procurement varies considerably across different procurement settings. It reflects that fact that

- public procurement covers a wide range of different goods and services;
- conditions in a particular market;
- differences in procurement practices stipulated by the nature of the goods and services bought.

In fact, competition takes place in many dimensions, for example in price, quality, innovation, and so on. The intensity of rivalry between firms to sell their products or services to consumers/customers or the public sector depends on a number of factors. For a case of public procurement, the principal factor can be the ease with which customers can switch between suppliers, the facility with which a supplier of a particular product can switch to a different one, whether a new firm can enter the market without much difficulty, and so forth. There is no rule of thumb that would allow assessing whether competition becomes more or less intense as a result of particular change in market conditions. Yet some indicators – such as the number of suppliers in a market, whether they are similar or different, or the level of entry barriers – can give some insight about the level of competition in a market.

As mentioned above, competition effects from procurement can be both positive and negative. The public sector, by virtue of its overall demand in certain markets, may be in a position to protect and promote competition, for example by maintaining a competitive market structure through deliberately sourcing its requirements from a range of suppliers, by providing incentives to suppliers to invest and innovate, or by helping firms to overcome barriers to entry. By the same token, a government may, however, restrict and distort competition by adopting procurement practices that have the effect of restricting participation in public tenders and that might even discriminate against particular types of firms.

However, because of the complexity of the competition effects of public procurement, it is difficult to determine any clear rules that suggest where procurement might entail competition concerns. This means that procurement practices have to be assessed on a case-by-case basis where the background of the market within which procurement takes place should also be taken into account. Hence, a conceptual analysis of the basic mechanism through which public procurement can affect competition might be helpful for a number of reasons. First, it provides a framework for the detailed review of specific procurement practices in particular markets and equips the public sector with a measure of guidance for its decisions as to how to design procurement processes. Second, conceptual analysis allows identification of the markets where competition concerns are most likely to arise, and where further investigation might be appropriate.

It is evident that for public procurement to be in a measure to affect competition in a market, the public sector needs to possess buyer power. Although there are numerous ways of endowing buyer power, all are encompassed in one of two principal categories: either due to the fact that the size of demand of the public sector is relatively much more significant in comparison to the total demand in a particular market, or because a buyer (public sector) is a strategically important customer for its suppliers. The two categories are closely related, though, because the strategic importance of a buyer tends to be associated with its size. Therefore, a powerful buyer can be defined as a buyer who is large in relation to the total demand within a particular market.

The public sector of any country consists of many independent agents. This point should be kept in mind, because the fact that public sector demand is large does not mean that the public sector enjoys buyer power. For example, if the demand of the public sector is fragmented, and/or if different public authorities act in an uncoordinated fashion, there may not be any significant public sector buyer power. On the other hand, it does not mean that the attempts to attain buyer power though consolidation of demand and/or coordinated action where the public sector accounts for a large share of demand in a market will not be taken.

Concerning the buyer power of the public sector, two important differences in relation to private sector's buying power should be stressed. First, there is a legal and regulatory framework for public sector procurement that does not apply to the private sector. As we have seen, the GPA and EU directives on public procurement define rules that have to be followed by contracting authorities. This makes it much more difficult for the public sector to exercise buyer power. Moreover, transparency and non-discrimination obligations, together with formal requirements with which public procurement contracts have to comply, limit the possibilities for buyer power abuse. Second, there is a significant difference in the way buyer decisions are taken and in the reasons that lead to these decisions. For example, among first priorities of the public sector is to avoid failures while pursuing efficiency and effectiveness of their decisions. Any failure of procurement that jeopardizes the ability of the public sector to deliver services to the public is highly visible. As a result, the public sector is normally much more risk-adverse than private agents and reluctant to experiment with novel ways of organizing its procurement, or to choose new or alternative suppliers. Another important point about public procurement decisions is that, while trying to get the best value for money they are not driven by pure profit-maximizing considerations. This means that the public sector is not likely to engage in the exercise of buyer power with the purpose of obtaining unfair advantages over other buyers of similar goods and services. Nonetheless, the public sector may be vulnerable to corruption issues and exposed to other kind of government failures, as was discussed earlier and confirmed by empirical studies.

Meanwhile, the public sector may pursue other policy objectives through its procurement decision. Such objectives could potentially lead to or in particular cases even require a restriction of distortion of competition among suppliers. In other words, although some policy objectives may be in line with the broad objective of improving competition, for instance minimizing barriers for SMEs to participate in public tenders, others may have an adverse impact on competition.

4.2.3 Impact of public procurement on competition

The complexity of the competition effects of procurement makes it difficult to apply hard and fast rules that prevent competition concerns.

Public procurement can affect competition in a number of ways. The economic literature distinguishes between the short-term effects, long-term effects, and knock-on effects on competition (OFT, 2004). The short-term effect is mainly related to the risk of collusion while the long-term effect concerns changes in market structure and technology (e.g. investment and innovation). The knock-on effect is the potential impact on other buyers (i.e. non-public sector buyers).

Short-term effect

The main short-term effect of public procurement on competition concerns the risk of collusion, which depends principally on the number and similarity of potential suppliers.

As simple economic reasoning predicts, more bidders implies more intense competition, resulting in lower prices and higher quality. However if additional bidders are weak, the incremental benefits from having more participants in a tender may become smaller as the number of bidders increases.. Nonetheless, any feature of procurement processes that limits participation has a detrimental impact on competition in the short-term.

On the other hand, there are a number of reasons that would justify certain limits on participation. The requirement for procurement to deliver higher performance in terms of improved *value-for-money* and *fit-for-purpose* outcomes has led to the development of more complex supply chains (e.g. through outsourcing and partnering arrangements) to deliver comprehensive service solutions, requiring more sophisticated relationships with suppliers. These more complex supply chains represent a move away from simple competitive markets and require a deeper understanding of industry structures and capabilities (Martin, 2002). This makes evaluating bids ever-more costly, in particular where buyer's (public sector) needs are complex and requirements cannot be specified in a simple way. Hence, the trade-off between the higher costs of assessing a larger number of bids and the likelihood to decrease a final purchase cost (resulting from more intense competition) may level out. The evidence suggests that applying certain criteria to limit the number of bidders, such as bidders' *reputation* or a proven ability to meet the particular requirements and probably to opt for short contracts with possibility to re-auction, may appear efficient measures in cases where the characteristics of the goods or services are difficult to define contractually (OFT, 2004). The other features of these reputational commitments are a risk of collusion and higher barriers for new entrants. As Calzolari and Spagnolo (2006) have shown, there is a general trade-off between reputation for quality and collusion. Reduced competition due to small number of eligible suppliers facilitates non-contactable quality provision, but also collusive agreements among suppliers. However, when non-contractible quality and variability in suppliers' efficiency are both important, short contract duration and a collusive agreement between a few eligible sellers may be notwithstanding desirable for the buyer and also welfare-maximizing.

The supposition that more intense competition results in lower prices and better quality, may appear misleading in public procurement. There are conditions in which increasing the number of bidders can lead to higher prices because everyone would bid more cautiously if a buyer does not define its reserve price strategically, or if its value is large compared with the seller's costs. This is the case where bidders are concerned about the risk of bidding too low and make a loss as a result of having won the tender[7] and also can make collusion sustainable (Thomas, 2001).

Among further reasons for limiting the number of participants is the consideration that competition is generally more intense the more similar the bidders are. However, this means that increasing the number of bidders may not necessarily increase competition, if the qualifications of participants are very different. More generally, designing procurement processes in a way that ensures that participants are more alike would increase competition, whereas processes that lead to participants to be very dissimilar are likely to have the opposite effect, for example, to reduce competition. The remedy might be *prequalification criteria* for restricted tenders. This would determine the characteristics of bidders and thus their similarity.

As is evident from the previous discussion, one of the most important concerns of public procurement process is the likelihood of collusion (Bajari and Summers, 2002; Lambert and Sonin, 2005). Generally, it is more difficult to sustain collusion as the number of bidders increases, and as bidders become more dissimilar, even though it may counteract the positive impact on competition as a result of more similarity across bidders. There are a number of other factors, as we have seen, which, while being tangible for an efficient procurement process, may have an impact on the likelihood of collusion.

In particular, collusion is more easily sustained if bidders can observe when other firms are trying to change prices below the collusive level or when a competitor's costs are easily estimated (Brosig et al., 2006). In other words, increased *transparency*, such as information about the terms and conditions offered by winning and losing bidders in a competitive tender, may increase the risk of collusion.[8]

Other circumstances that might favour collusion are likely to arise when bidders interact repeatedly, either in the same market over time or in different markets. Such repeated interaction can increase efficiency (e.g. learning-by-doing, etc.) but, on the other hand, allows for more effective 'punishment' of firms trying changing prices below the collusive level. Thus, the same reasons may simultaneously favour efficient and corruptive behaviour. This means that splitting up a requirement across multiple tenders that would necessitate repeated interaction between agents can increase the risk of collusion. (Lambert and Sonin, 2005).

One more factor that is likely to play a non-negligible role is *stability of demand*. Stable and predictable demand from the public sector creates the situation where collusion is more easily sustained. Should demand be volatile, attempts by firms to grab a larger share of the market by charging lower prices are more difficult to detect; by the same token, the incentives to under-bid competitors are larger when demand is large at present but is expected to fall in the future. However, when demand is predictable and stable, the incentives of collusion are the strongest.

Long-term effect

Short-term restrictions and distortions to competition, applied for one or another reason, may lead to long-term effects. They arise when the changes in market structure and market positions caused by short-term effects cannot be easily reversed, which means that the threat of potential competition form new entrants is not effective. When the entry barriers are significant and/or when winning a contract is crucial for the viability of firms, public intervention is practically indispensable (OFT, 2004). Such intervention is able to affect market structure by awarding contracts of a larger or smaller number of firms or by helping firms to overcome entry barriers.

Even without changing the number of suppliers in the market, public procurement may have long-term effects on competitiveness. For example, it can increase the gap between market leaders and other suppliers or create incumbency advantage[9] for public contractors in future tenders (i.e. *reputation* or a proven ability to fulfil the requirements, pre-qualification criteria). Apart from the fact that a firm enjoying incumbent advantages might have better chances, this may discourage other firms with low chances of winning from participation, which is likely to weaken competition overall.

The repeated selection of the same firm would further increase incumbency advantages (e.g. though learning-by-doing, investment, etc.) Under such circumstances, a buyer (public sector) awarding a contract to the cheapest supplier risks finding itself in the long run with a rather short list of potential suppliers (Calzalari and Spagnolo, 2006).

To the extent that some bidders might anticipate such an outcome, they have an incentive to reduce the price when a tender is put out in the expectation of higher profits in the future. In other words, when public sector attempts to privilege *value for money* in the short run, it can entail a risk that competition is reduced over time, that is, in the long run. This situation may have repercussions for the economy as a whole, since through procurement contracts government can increase the gap between market leader and smaller firms. Such systematic discrimination may lead to less vigorous competition in the market as a whole.

In order to prevent reduction in competition as described above, the government in its procurement process should attempt to award multiple contracts and select different bidders for each of the contracts, even if bidders do not offer the best price, meaning that the principle of cost saving will not be realized in the short term (OFT, 2004). However, competitiveness of the market and a number of other advantages (investments, learning-by-doing, technological correspondence, etc.) will be stimulated due to public procurement contracts in the long run.

Grouping together different procurements may allow the government affecting the vertical organization of supply. For instance, in providing advantages to a vertically integrated supplier, the government is able to affect decisions of firms to integrate vertically (e.g. in the sectors susceptible to benefit of spatial externalities or economies of scale). Conversely, by increasing unbundled purchases, the government might remove or weaken incentives for vertical integration (OFT, 2004).

As was mentioned earlier, public procurement may also have a significant effect on investment and innovation, and produce a *'pull-effect'* for an economy due to its ability to create early-stage customers and a market demand that enables business to innovate. An overly strong focus on price in public tenders, for instance, may discourage innovation because bidders may not be able to benefit fully from their investments. At the same time, significant public sector demand can be used to provide incentives for investment and innovation, not least in order to ensure that capacity in the long run is sufficient to meet the public sector's needs and attain social objectives, beyond which it is also expected to produce spillover effects to other sectors (McCrudden, 2004; Evenett and Hoekmann, 2005).

Where public procurement is used in order to promote investment and innovation, handle a network externality problem, or ensure an optimal standard (as, for example, in the case of public procurement of broadband services, where public demand was initially regarded as one of the main consumers), it may determine the range of products available, and the firms supplying them. In this way, public procurement decisions may be the main factor determining competition in the market at large, having helped to create it in the first place (OFT, 2004).

Knock-on effect
Where the public sector accounts for much, but not all, demand in a market, other buyers will be affected by the impact of procurement decisions in the number of suppliers, the range of products available, and the technologies used (these are the knock-on effects). To the extent that other buyer do not enjoy buyer power, they may be more exposed to a long-term lessening of competition than the strong public sector buyer.

In addition to these side-effects, there may also be cases in which the public sector benefits at the expense of other buyers. For instance, where public contractors gain advantages over those firms not supplying the public sector, and these advantages result in restricted or distorted competition in the supply of other buyers, intense competition for the public sector contract may arise. Expected profits from restricted competition in the supply of other buyers would result in better terms and conditions for the public sector.

It is at least theoretically possible that the public sector could improve the terms and conditions it obtains from bidders in public tenders if it increases the extent to which public contractors are advantaged in the supply of other buyers.

Overall effect
As becomes evident from earlier discussions, these effects can sometimes work in opposite directions. Notably, the strong promotion of short-term competition among suppliers can reduce long-term competitiveness, or may discourage innovation and investment. Where the government, through its procurement, exercises countervailing buyer power, it should keep a check on supplier market power, making suppliers compete more vigorously for public contracts than they would otherwise. The exercise of countervailing buyer power may sustain a competitive market in the long run, or even help new suppliers overcome entry barriers. On the other hand, a strong public sector buyer may also reduce competition, for instance, by increasing the gap, as it was mentioned earlier, between large and small firms within a market, or because failing to prevent collusion or stave off corruption issues.

The discussion of potential competition effect of procurement demonstrates clearly that such effects are complex, depend on the particular details of the procurement settings, and can be both positive and negative. This complexity often requires a trade-off between costs (e.g. the administrative cost of running a tender with more bidders) and benefits (e.g. the expected benefits in price as a result of more intense competition). Where these decisions are made on the basis of distorted incentives, in may be the case that public procurement fails to promote competition as much as it could, or leads to avoidable restrictions or distortions of competition. Therefore, a detailed analysis of procurement practices in a particular market would be necessary in order to establish whether they cause competition concerns.

4.3 Conclusion

While there is no one accepted definition of subsidy, the most common refers to any government assistance that allows consumers to purchase goods and services at prices lower than those offered by a perfectly competitive private sector or that raise producers' incomes beyond those that would be earned without intervention. Public procurement concerns the purchasing of works, supplies, and services by national, regional, and local public bodies, including central government, local authorities, fire and police authorities, defence, health services, joint consortia of public bodies, and public and private utilities. Beside the definition issues, subsidies and public procurement also pose measurement problems. There are almost as many measures as the number of (national or international) institutions in charge of assessing them.

Subsidies and public procurement can be useful instruments in correcting market failures but can also distort competition and trade. The discussion of possible distortions demonstrates clearly that the effects are complex, depend on the particular objective and design of the subsidy or procurement, and can be both positive and negative. This complexity often requires a trade-off between costs and benefits. Where these decisions are made on the basis of distorted incentives, it may be the case that they fail to promote efficiency as much as they could, or lead to avoidable restrictions or distortions of competition.

5
Effectiveness of Public Support

5.1 Assessment issues

In Chapters 1 to 3, the discussion focused mainly on the theoretical arguments in favour of and/or against public support to industry as well as on the instruments of support. The latter includes state aid, public procurements, strategic trade policy, provision of public goods, regulations, policies directed towards factor markets, and so forth. The arguments in favour of public support are related to information issues (imperfect information, uncertainty and information spillovers), externalities (network and spatial externalities), strategic trade and merger (incomplete markets, oligopolistic competition) and the new growth theories (in particular R&D issues). The arguments against public support put forward the conflict with other policies (competition, trade and macroeconomic policies), political economy issues (elections, lobbying and capture, corruption and favouritism) and the difficulties of choice of appropriate instruments.

Accurate evaluation of each of these policies is essential but arduous, not only because it is often hampered by a lack of knowledge of what would have happened without them but also because many are often used simultaneously entailing, consequently, interactions between policies. Indeed, evaluations are always rather *ex post* assessments of the activities of beneficiaries. Such evaluations can be subject to a selection-bias problem. Successful delivery of research results may reflect the influence of factors other than the availability of public financial support. Even a comparison of funded and non-funded firms may fail to fully control for some selection bias should funding decisions be made using an accurate *ex ante* evaluation of project quality. Such projects would be the most likely to succeed even in the absence of public support. Moreover, potential knowledge spillovers should also be separated out. R&D programmes may succeed in producing innovations that are used by other firms outside the programmes, raising the social returns from publicly funded innovative activity. Moreover, there is a problem of measurability. While the existence a market failure is widely admitted, their magnitudes in a particular market is hard to measure. The amount of aid needed to correct for the market failure depends on a large number of factors, such as market structure, production function, cost structure, and so forth. Because of the problem of asymmetric and/or incomplete information, it is almost impossible in practice to determine the exact amount of state aid needed. Finally, the 'effectiveness' of public funding (i.e. the extent to which public funding is able to reach its primary objective and give a positive impulse to the market) should be considered. This is related, but not limited, to the crowding out and crowding in issues. More precisely, crowding in can occur if firms face financial constraints that prevent them from undertaking projects that are expected to yield high returns. Public support has a value added in this case. Crowding out may occur if diminishing marginal returns to R&D lead grant recipients to reduce their own funding for R&D expenditure. It may also occur if rivals' R&D expenditure decreases as a result of the grant.

Attempts to address these issues rely mainly on two types of empirical approaches: case studies and econometric analysis. The former are typically retrospective event studies in which the aim is to investigate how the introduction of a certain mechanism has affected the economic environment. They tend to be focused on a limited number of economic issues providing thus the advantage that, in principle, the investigator controls for other factors. Case studies may, however, suffer from two important drawbacks. First, constructing a good counterfactual, which really controls for other factors, may be very difficult in practice. Second, as researchers are free to pick a case for their studies, the chosen cases may be subject to a selection bias. Researchers may, for some reasons, pick only the positive or negative examples.

Econometric analysis allows for a stochastic relationship between public support and the policy objective. Inclusion of proper control variables enables to isolate the true impact of public support from the impact of other factors (country effects, institutional settings, etc.). For instance, one might construct an equation that predicts the level of R&D investment as a function of past R&D, past output, expected demand, cash flow, and price variables. A dummy variable is included, equal to one when the credit is available and zero otherwise. Alternatively, a time series of, for instance, tax credits can be included. If econometric estimation is rightly conducted (especially controlling for potential endogeneity of explanatory variables), the magnitude of the estimated coefficient of the dummy or the tax credit variable gives an unbiased estimate of the impact of the policy on the amount of R&D. The advantage of this method is that it is better grounded in economic theory and estimates the response of R&D directly.

The next two sections focus on state aid and public procurements and present empirical evidence that support the earlier advanced arguments both for and against public support.

5.2 Empirical evidence on the arguments in favour of public support

5.2.1 Public procurement

While the theoretical arguments in favour of public support cover a wide range of 'market failures', empirical studies regarding public procurements only dealt with a part of them. Available empirical studies are presented in this chapter and concern the ability of government procurement to induce technological progress and alleviate network externalities.

Network externality

Goods or services are affected by network externalities when the economic agent's utility of using them depends on the number of other customers using the same goods or services. With positive network externality the choice of standard allows the use of the same good or service by the maximum number of persons. This, in turn, increases each consumer's utility. Many standards might be available in the market but only one (or few) is optimal. The cost of a mistake in the standard-selection process is likely to be very high. Public intervention may help picking up the right standard. Cabral et al. (2006) cite cases where the market alone fails to select an optimal standard and cases where government fosters its adoption. An example in the first category refers to video-cassette recorders (VCRs). Many industry experts considered that the Betamax system of Sony and Philips was superior to Victory Company of Japan's (JVCs) Video Home System (VHS). Indeed, until the advent of digital recording technology, Betamax remained the first choice for TV professionals. However, the VHS standard took advantage of the situation when, during the 1980s, video rental stores and consumers faced a need to agree on a single standard. Once most video stores were equipped with mostly VHS tapes, even users who would otherwise prefer the Betamax system opted for the JVC standard. An example in the second category concerns computer operating systems. The Brazilian government has recently decided to expand the use of free source software in the public sector. In September 2004, a relevant agreement with IBM led to the establishment of a knowledge and technology promotion centre in charge of development of open source and Linux solutions in Brazil. Other governments (e.g. the United States, France) adopted a similar attitude.

Technical progress: R&D

Some attempts to estimate the impact of public procurement on R&D by virtue of econometric modelling were taken by some researchers (Cozzi and Impulitti, 2004; Becker and Pain, 2003). An important conclusion is that government funding of R&D does have a positive impact and is able to give rise to private R&D expenditures and provide, besides, positive incentives to the economy as a whole. However, there are other factors (e.g. macroeconomic, financial, institutional, etc.) that determine to a non-negligible extent the level of R&D expenditures in the economy.

In particular, Cozzi and Impulitti (2004) focused on the impact of the US government's dramatic shift in procurement choices in favour of high-tech sectors in the 1980s and 1990s. Public investment in equipment and software (E&S), which consisted of 20% of total government investment in 1980, climbs to about 40% in 1990 and to more than 50% in 2001. The private demand also switched towards E&S but more than a decade later. The authors also investigated the impact of the introduction of the Research and Experimentation tax credit in 1981 in stimulating private R&D. Companies that qualified for the credit could deduct or subtract from corporate income taxes an amount that in the period 1981–2004 has been in the range of 20 to 25% of qualified research expenses above a base amount.

The research framework adopted a neo-Schumpeterian growth model (with heterogeneous industries) in government spending where R&D subsidies are explicitly incorporated. In order to allow assessment of quantitative effects that the change in government policy produced on the sectors' composition of the economy, the model was calibrated in a way to choose the parameters that would match the salient long-run features of the US economy.

The results showed that government policy, indeed, played a non-negligible role in a surge of innovations that hit the US economy in the recent decades. It confirms, therefore, the theoretical argument

Effectiveness of Public Support 59

put forward earlier, that public procurement could have a 'pull-off' effect. The latter plays an important role in providing producers of new investment goods with the appropriate market size in an early stage of development.

Becker and Pain (2003) looked into the factors behind the decrease in R&D intensity in the United Kingdom during most of the 1990s. This happens both in the economy as a whole as well as in the business sector. In particular, they estimated an econometric model of R&D expenditure using a panel of United Kingdom manufacturing industries.

The model of R&D expenditures at the industry level was constructed with the following explanatory variables: market size (output in the industry), the proportion of R&D undertaken by business and funded by government (either by the mean of subsidies or through public procurement), the proportion of R&D undertaken by foreign owned firms, import competition (the ratio of imports to total home sales), the number of scientists and engineers in the industry relative to its total employment, financial conditions, profit, macroeconomic policies and industry specific fixed effects. The sample covered 11 manufacturing activities over the period 1993–2000, three of which are relatively R&D intensive – chemicals, electrical machinery, and transport. The authors correct for potential endogeneity of some variables (e.g. profit) but not of all. This may impact on the results.

The results highlighted the importance of industry characteristics such as sales and profitability, product market competition, macroeconomic factors (such as real long-term interest rates and the real effective exchange rate), availability of skilled labour, and the composition of R&D expenditure and funding.

However, government funding also appears to play an important role. For instance a sustained rise of one percentage point in the share of business R&D expenditure funded by the government is estimated to raise the level of R&D expenditure by 1.8%. Another important factor appears to be the R&D undertaken by foreign-owned companies. The results have revealed a significant positive impact of R&D undertaken by foreign-owned firms on the aggregate level of R&D expenditures, although the magnitude of this effect is lower than that of government funding. A sustained rise of one percentage point in the share of business R&D expenditure undertaken by foreign firms is estimated to raise the level of R&D expenditure by 0.9%.

The main explanations for the comparatively low level of R&D observed during the 1990s appear to be weak output growth, the declining level of government funding for private industry and the appreciation in the real effective exchange rate since 1996. Taken together these factors have largely outweighed the stimulus being offered by the decline in long-term interest rates during the 1990s, the growing share of R&D expenditure being undertaken by foreign-owned firms, the rising level of competition in product markets and the increase in skilled labour employed on R&D in the latter half of the decade.

5.2.2 State aid

The question of the influence of public support by means of state aid on industry and overall economic development has attracted a much larger interest among researchers compared with that of the impact of public procurement. The analysis mainly focuses on the capacity of state aid to support and speed up the pace of the technological progress. To this end, the studies may be split into those that treat the problem of R&D and those concerned with productivity. Other research efforts are devoted to the question of firms' location. To our best knowledge only few studies attempt to assess the effectiveness of different forms of state aid or evaluate the rescue and restructuring aid impact on international competitiveness of firms affected by such aid.

Technical progress: R&D

Most of the literature on R&D and state aid focuses on the determinants of total R&D expenditures. Only a few studies investigate the determinants of business-sector R&D intensity. A first notable exception is Bloom et al. (2002), which examines the impact of fiscal incentives on the level of private R&D investment. The econometric model of R&D investment is estimated using a panel of data on tax changes and R&D spending in nine Organisation of Economic Cooperation and Development (OECD) countries over a 19-year period (1979–97). The findings show that tax incentives are effective in increasing private R&D intensity. This is true even after allowing for permanent country-specific characteristics, business cycle, macroeconomic shocks, and other policy influences. The estimates suggest that a sustained 1% decline in the user cost of R&D capital (owing to tax reduction) would eventually raise privately funded R&D in the business sector by just under 1%.

As noted by the authors, however, their results may still suffer from endogeneity bias. In a context of international tax competition, the existence of R&D tax rivalry has the implication that governments may be strategically choosing their R&D policies. This implies that government policy and particularly the existence of R&D tax credits should be endogenized.

Guellec and van Pottelsberghe (2003) study the effect of government funding on business R&D across 17 OECD countries for the period 1981–96. They report that government funding stimulates business R&D expenditure if the government research is contracted to the business sector, but tends to partially crowd out business R&D when performed in government laboratories. There found no impact of university research expenditures on business enterprise R&D expenditures. Finally, tax incentives seem to be more effective in stimulating business R&D than other support schemes (direct subsidy).

Quantifying the average stimulatory effect of direct government funding of private R&D, the authors show that each dollar of direct (non-defence) government financing bring 0.70 dollar additional increase in business funded R&D.

Falk (2004) analyses policy and non-policy factors affecting business-sector R&D intensity using a panel of OECD countries for the period 1980–2002. Policy factors include favourable tax treatment for firms undertaking R&D expenditures and direct subsidies to private R&D projects. Non-policy factors comprise expenditure on R&D performed by the public sector,[1] specialization in high-tech industries, Gross Domestic Product (GDP) per capita, openness, price-cost margin, indicators for human capital and physical investment. Estimates of both a static fixed effects and dynamic panel data models suggest that tax incentives for R&D have a significant and positive impact on business R&D expenditures in OECD countries regardless of specification and estimation techniques. The long-run elasticity implies that a 1% increase in generosity of tax incentives for R&D leads to a 0.9% increase in the amount of private R&D spending in the long run. Furthermore, expenditures on R&D performed by universities are significantly and positively related to business enterprise sector expenditures on R&D indicating that public sector R&D and private R&D are complements. Direct R&D subsidies and the specialization in high-tech industries also contributes significantly to business sector R&D intensity but these effects are not robust.

Additional evidence is provided by Hyytinen and Toivanen (2003), Lach (2002) and Parisi and Sembenelli (2003). The former focused on Small and Medium Enterprises (SMEs) in Finland and found that government funding has a greater impact on the R&D expenditures of firms in industries that are more dependent on external finance, consistent with what might be expected if there are capital market imperfections.

Lach (2002) finds that government subsidies in Israel have a significant positive impact on company financed R&D expenditure for small firms, but a negative, though insignificant, impact on expenditures by large firms. One interpretation of this finding is that grants to small firms enable projects to be undertaken that would not otherwise be financed. For large firms, the subsidy is more likely to be directed towards activities that would have been undertaken in any event. For Italy, Parisi and Sembenelli (2003), analysing a panel of Italian manufacturing firms, suggests that the elasticity of R&D with respect to its price could be markedly large: a 1% change in the user cost changing the total company spending in R&D by between 1.5 and 1.8%.

Surveys by Jaumotte and Pain (2005) and OXERA (2006) of previous studies on the role of public support in stimulating innovation reach similar inferences as others. Jaumotte and Pain conclude that while there is 'substantial evidence' that tax incentives have a positive effect on the amount of private sector R&D expenditure, there is little consensus on the effectiveness of subsidies and research programmes.

To sum up, the majority of the empirical studies suggest a positive relation between the various forms of aid schemes and privately funded R&D expenditures. Furthermore, there is a complementarity between government and private expenditures on R&D. However, this result might be sensitive to the aggregation level of the data and a definition of the control group.[2]

Technical progress: productivity

Harris and Robinson (2004) examined the impact of the UK government industrial support schemes on manufacturing plant level Total Factor Productivity (TFP). Although UK industrial policy has three industrial support schemes (science and technology, small firms, and regional policy), the authors focused on two. These are the Regional Selective Assistance (RSA) and the Small Firm Merit Awards for Research and Technology (SMART) programmes. The former, introduced in 1972, seems to be the most important domestic policy instrument in terms of regional industrial policy (Wren, 2001). Its principal aim is to safeguard and create employment opportunities in designated Assisted Areas, through offering a discretionary subsidy to plants in the form of a capital grant. The latter, introduced in 1986, is aimed at encouraging innovative activity in the SME sector.

The empirical analysis regresses the log of real gross output of plant i and time t on the log of its employment, the log of real intermediate inputs, the log of capital stock and a set of control variables. These include 18 industry dummies and 10 region dummies as well as the logarithm of the age of the plant, whether the plant was owned by a foreign company and a time trend (to allow for business cycle effects). The role of industrial support is captured through the introduction *RSAi* and *SMARTi* dummies that have a value of one if the plant was anytime assisted during the period considered and through *RSAit* and *SMARTit* dummies that take on a value of one from the time that a plant participates in RSA or SMART. The latter terms allow the intercept to shift up or down following assistance).

The data were drawn form the Department of Trade and Industry (DTI's) Selective Assistance Management Information System (SAMIS) database for 1990–2000. It gives records on enterprises that received Regional Selective Assistance and SMART grants.

The results suggest that RSA plants had below-average levels of productivity (overall TFP is 4.7% less than the average), which suggest a selection bias in favour of less performing plants. Following assistance, RSA plants improve their TFP by an average of 2.5%. However, when allowing the assistance effect to differ across regions, only Scottish plants seemed to have benefited in a major way; the average improvement in TFP here being some 4.8%. There is little benefit, however, in other regions for RSA-assisted plants when compared to non-assisted plants. Regarding SMART assisted plants, they were better than the average (nearly 8% more productive), but assistance seems to induce little significant change in TFP.

Skuras et al. (2006) addressed a similar question for the food and beverages sector in Greece. This is one of the most important and dynamic sectors of the manufacturing industry in that country. They focused on capital subsidies in the form of free capital and/or interest rate subsidization for invested capital. Their goal is to investigate the impact of selective capital subsidies on the TFP of subsidized firms. They measure TFP using a stochastic production frontier approach. The estimation of the stochastic production frontier treats capital subsidies as a new input. This avoids the restrictions imposed by traditional approaches which just combine the subsidy and the capital stock into a single variable. The authors decompose TFP into three elements: technical change (TC), scale efficiency change (SEC), and technical efficiency change (TEC). TC stems from bringing the combination of labour and capital closer to the frontier of production. SEC is the result of the expansion of production in the presence of scale economies. Finally, TEC is due to shift of the frontier of production itself, stemming from technical progress.

In Greece, a system of regional development incentives providing for, among others, direct capital subsidization, was formally introduced in 1982. Capital subsidies are discretionary, that is, paid to individual new or existing firms meeting *ex ante* criteria, and selective, that is, targeting certain regions of the country and particular industrial sectors. The prime factor influencing the rate of subsidization is the firm's location because capital subsidies aim, among others, at assisting firms in overcoming location disadvantages associated with higher production and/or transportation costs and favour deprived and lagging areas of the country.

Data on individual firm characteristics are derived from the business database maintained by the private financial and business information service company, called ICAP, in Greece. The annual ICAP directories provide key elements from the published balance sheets of almost all Plc and Ltd firms operating in all sectors of economic activity. From the annual directories of ICAP, a panel database of firms operating in the food and drinks manufacturing sector of the Greek economy for the period 1989-94 was extracted. This database was complemented by information derived from the Greek Ministry of National Economy on firm subsidization from the regional and industrial policy frameworks.

The results show that TFP grows by 2.4% during the first year after the subsidy is granted and rises to 6.4% in the fifth year. This growth, when decomposed, is mainly due to TC. More specifically, the TC index grows by 2.3% during the first year after the subsidy is granted and rises to 6.6% in the fifth year. This indicates that firms are more productive because they bring the combination of labour and capital closer to its optimal level (i.e. the frontier of production). The contribution of TEC is relatively small because it falls slightly in the first year after the subsidy is granted to increase again and reach a growth of only 0.5% in the fifth year after the subsidy was granted. The observed decrease in the first year may be caused either by internal cost of adjustment (organizational changes) or by transaction costs arising from the adoption of the new technology. The relative importance of TC vs. TEC implies that most of the gains come from an improvement in the combination of labour and capital rather than form the adoption of a new technology. Surprisingly, the SEC index, despite a marginal increase in the first and second years after the subsidy is granted, decreases substantially after the third year.

The fact that capital subsidies affect TFP growth, especially through TC, and not through SEC change, is interpreted by the authors as a signal that capital subsidies seem to substitute own capital. One would expect that capital subsidies would enhance scale efficiency if they were used in addition to the productive capital already used. The results indicate that subsidized capital does not really increase the scale of operation, but it substitutes the capital aimed to be invested by the firm under conditions of no subsidization.

Bergström (1998) analyses 72 companies in the manufacturing sector that received state aid in Sweden during 1989–95 and compares them with a random sample of 832 non-aid-receiving firms. He analyses selective regional subsidies, that is, subsidies specifically directed towards firms in support areas and for which firms have to apply. These subsidies include localization subsidies and loans, development support, support to sparsely populated areas, and loans to investment firms. Such subsidies must be used primarily for investments in machinery and buildings. He finds that in the short run, the productivity of subsidized firms increased more than the productivity of non-subsidized firms, but that already after three years productivity was lower in subsidized than in non-subsidized firms. Notwithstanding, the overall effect on economic growth is positive. However, the researcher finds evidence that an omitted variable problem may exist, rendering some doubt on the finding. To state it differently, the problem is that the 'economic black box' between policy instruments and TFP is too large.

London Economics (2004) presents the results of an *ex post* evaluation of the impact of rescue and restructuring state aid on firms' performance (e.g. survival, sales and productivity). This study was commissioned by the European Commission Enterprise Directorate General. It examined the state aid decisions made by the European Commission between 1995 and 2003 and focused on ended cases (i.e. either the rescue aid has been reimbursed or the restructuring plan has come to an end). This gives 71 individual companies from different member countries and different sectors including services. The companies belong both to assisted and non-Assisted Areas.

Companies awarded rescue aid suffered mainly from liquidity problems. Those benefiting form restructuring aid suffered, in general, form a heavy financial burden. The most common uses of the aid were capacity reduction, personnel reduction, refocusing on core business activities and cost-cutting.

Out of 71 companies having received rescue and/or restructuring state aid, about one-third ceased operations, one-third were bought by other companies and the remaining part kept their legal status unchanged. In other words, they considered a company to have survived, even if a new owner had acquired it, so long as the original production lines were still a recognizable physical entity. The mortality rate of aid-receiving companies was particularly high in the case of companies having received solely rescue aid: out of 29 companies having received such aid, 14 folded. In contrast, only 8 companies of the 42 companies having received restructuring aid have folded.

An econometric analysis, relating the probability of survival for an aid-receiving company to a number of company, sector and aid characteristics was conducted. The estimates, first, confirm that companies that have benefited from rescue aid are more likely to exit the industry than those that have received restructuring aid. They also show that if the firm was in difficulty due to market decline and poor management,[3] it has a better chance of surviving. Regarding the impact of aids, the study found that by 2002 about half of the aid-receiving companies had actually increased their levels of employment but the magnitudes of the increases were in general much smaller than those of the decreases. A large majority of aid-receiving companies experienced a rise in turnover but less than half of them performed better than comparable companies. About three-quarters of aid-receiving companies improved their profitability but most of them remained markedly below the industry average profitability. Finally, three-quarters of companies recorded labour productivity above the industry average by the end of the period.

Gual and Jódar (2006) assessed the effectiveness of vertical industrial policies within the European Union (EU). Their definition of such policies exclude measures directed to primary sectors as well as those related to non-tradable industries, such as housing services or retail trade. Policies that affect most firms in a country to a similar extent (for example, investment tax credits or subsidies for the employment of a particular kind of labour) were also excluded. The impact of vertical industrial policies is measured through TFP growth and the TFP level of country i in relation to the frontier country (the one with the highest TFP; see below).

The TFP growth is calculated as the discrete-time analogue of the continuous-time formula derived by Solow to measure the rate of technological progress. The difference comes from the use of a translog production function instead of the more standard Cobb–Douglas production function. However, the assumptions of constant returns to scale and perfect competition in the input markets are maintained.

The estimation of the level of TFP of country i compared to the frontier country involves three steps. First, the level of TFP of each country is evaluated in relation to the geometric mean of all countries. Second, for each year, the country with the highest TFP relative to the geometric mean is defined as the frontier country. Note that for the frontier calculations, non-EU OECD countries (e.g. Canada, Japan, and the United States) are also included in the analysis to identify the world technology leader. Third, the TFP level of country *i* relative to the frontier country is just the difference between the TFP country *i* and that of the frontier country.

TFP is modelled as an auto-regressive distributed lag where the level of TFP is co-integrated with the level of TFP of the frontier country. Moreover, the variation in the level of technology around its long-run trend is a function of a set of exogenous factors. These include R&D intensity, public capital, product market regulation (PMR), and employment protection legislation (EPL), the EU-15 output gap (proxy for the business cycle), country dummies and vertical state aid.

The sample includes 11 EU Member States over the period 1992–2003. The data for output, capital stock, and labour come from the OECD STAN database. Data on R&D intensity are drawn from the OECD ANBERD database. Data on public capital are taken from Kamps (2005). Indicators on product market regulation and employment protection legislation are taken from Boylaud et al. (2000). Data on output gap are drawn from the AMECO database of the European Commission. Finally, data on state aid are taken from the State Aid Scoreboard of the European Commission.

The estimation results show a positive and significant effect of vertical aid on manufacturing productivity: an extra percentage point of vertical state aid generates approximately 0.83 percentage points of TFP growth in the manufacturing sector. However, when the authors add to the model the indicator on employment protection legislation and that of product market regulation, the effect of vertical state aid becomes insignificant even after correcting for the endogeneity of some variables. This suggests that the positive and significant effect of vertical aid on manufacturing productivity is not robust.

Summing up, most of the studies examining the impact of the public support with respect to its capacity to enhance TFP come up with inconclusive results. In fact, there is no strong evidence that state aid is able to induce a significant increase in TFP, especially in the long run. When a positive change is observed in productivity level, it comes more often from technical rather than efficiency change. This means that increase in productivity comes from more investment in physical capital (which may replace some workers) instead of higher productivity of the same workers. Moreover, there are cases when subsidy crowds out private investment in physical capital, that is, the subsidy only replaces private funds that could be otherwise have been invested.

However, while a positive impact of state aid might be observed on the overall economic growth in some model specifications, the effect on TFP remains ambiguous. Furthermore, some studies find significant effects, in particular of vertical aid, but the results appear to be sensitive to the specification of the model.

Firm location

Kokko and Gustavsson (2004) used a descriptive analysis to examine whether the investment incentives allowed in the EU affected foreign direct investment (FDI) flows to Sweden. Recall that within the EU investment incentives are restricted by three kinds of provisions. The first one follows from Article 87(1) of the Treaty, which bans aids that might affect trade between Member States. The second comes from the EU's Code of Conduct on business taxation that bans tax measures that may affect investment location within the Union because they are significantly lower than those generally applied in the economy. The third comes from non-discrimination and national treatment regulations, which essentially guarantee that all firms qualifying for a certain kind of support should be treated equally. There are, however, some important exceptions to the general rule that are also outlined by the Treaty.

The data come from Statistics Sweden, Financial Statistics database, and cover all enterprises with 20 or more employees. The firms are classified as foreign-owned (have foreign majority ownership) or domestic and according to their location in Objective 1 and 2 regions.

Comparing FDI in Swedish regions with and without access to Objective 1 and 2 support, the authors found little impact of the regional subsidies at the macro level. Employment in foreign-owned enterprises in provinces qualifying for regional support grew during the 1990s, at the same time as productivity and education levels increased. However, these increases were significantly lower than those in more central provinces, and not very different from those in provinces that were not qualified for regional support. In other words, although the behaviour of some individual firms may have been influenced by the various subsidies available in supported provinces, the effects were not strong enough to show up at the regional level.

The main exception from this conclusion concerns, nevertheless, R&D. There are signs that regional support may have allowed both foreign-owned and domestic firms in supported regions to reach higher R&D intensities than what would be possible otherwise. To the extent that these research activities result in technology diffusion and other positive externalities, they are likely to push regional growth and development. However, the authors question the positive effect of these programmes on the basis of a costs and benefits approach. In particular, the fiscal consequences of regional support are not taken into account.

Mayer (2004) focused on the case of FDI location in France over the period 1985–95 and evaluates how regional policies in favour of French regions by both national and EU authorities compare to other determinants of the location choice. He used conditional logit and nested logit regressions to measure the impact of the determinants of location choice of foreign investors in France. The determinants include the market potential of a region (its closeness to rich or poor regions), the average annual wage per worker at the region and 4-digit industry level and fixed effects for each region. Moreover, the regression takes into account the impact of the number of (i) firms in the region that are owned by foreign direct investors from the same home country, (ii) firms in the region that are owned by foreign direct investors from different countries and (iii) firms in the region that are owned by French investors.

Regarding industrial policy instruments, the author includes the subsidies given by the national government (mainly the Prime d'Aménagement du Territoire; PAT) and the funds granted by the European Commission for economically less developed regions (structural funds). The amount of PAT received by all companies in a region, in the year the investment took place, is introduced in the estimated equation. French regions being also beneficiaries of the European Commission's Objective 1 and Objective 5 funds, grants by Objective and region are also introduced. All three variables are expected to have a positive impact on location choice.

The data on the PAT comes from annual reports of Délégation à l'aménagement du territoire et à l'action régionale, the official body in charge of regional policy in France. Data on grants by Objective and region are published by the European Commission. Data on the location choice of foreign-owned affiliates in all French regions, the nationality of shareholders of the affiliate, date of investment, and type of industry comes from the Direction du Trésor (a division of the French Ministry of Finance) and covers 92 regions.

The results on the impact of regional policies show a low value and weak significance of the regional policy variables. Although PAT is statistically significant, its coefficient is considerably lower than the coefficients of non-policy related variables. The coefficient on PAT indicates that it requires a doubling of the support for a region to increase by 3%

the probability of being chosen. For comparison, the same increase in the probability would result from a 10% rise in the number of foreign firms. These results cast considerable doubt on the scope for regional policy to actually change the location patterns of FDI.

To be complete, the author decomposes the probability of choosing a given location into the contribution of each explanatory variable. The results clearly show that the most important determinant of location choice of foreign firms in France is the location of existing French firms. Market potential is also an important motivation for choosing a region, as well as distance to the home country. The location of competitors from the same home country has a relatively small influence. When wages and regional policies are significant, they have only a marginal impact on the choice of location. These results remain qualitatively robust to alternative specifications and tests.

Devereux et al. (2007) examined whether discretionary government grants influence the location of domestic and multinational firms' new plants, and how the presence of agglomeration externalities interacts with these policy instruments. They use plant-level data for Great Britain, along with individual grant offers under the Regional Selective Assistance (RSA) scheme. RSA grants are offered to firms in designated low income per capita Assisted Areas, which are typically located in regions with low growth rates. The choice of location is modelled in a discrete choice framework as a function of characteristics of each region, plant and industrial sector.

The data come from the Office for National Statistics Annual Respondents Database (ARD) for Great Britain over the period 1986–92. For this period the ARD contains basic information on the population of manufacturing plants and also information on a wider range of characteristics for a random stratified sample at the establishment level. The data are used to identify greenfield entrants and to construct measures of agglomeration. The ARD are complemented by the list of all grant offers of £75,000 or more that is published by the Department of Trade and Industry. This allows considering firms' location choices at the level of the 64 counties and Scottish regions within Great Britain, 38 of which include at least some areas that are classified as Assisted Areas. The measures of industry-county localization are: (1) the number of plants in each industry in each county-year; and (2) the number of foreign-owned plants in each industry in each county-year.

The authors, first, estimate the determinants of the grant offer, and then use this to investigate the effect of expected grants on the location choices. They find evidence that firms are more likely to locate greenfield plants near larger markets and that plants within the same industry tend to co-locate. More importantly, they find that on average greenfield entrants are less likely to locate in Assisted (compared to non-Assisted) Areas and that grant offers have a greater effect on location incentives in areas where there is more existing economic activity in the entrants' industry. Put another way, the results imply that higher grant offers are needed to attract greenfield entrants to locations where industry agglomeration or natural resource benefits are weaker.

Various robustness checks are conducted and confirm that the marginal effects associated with the expected grant remain economically small, and that the expected grant has a greater impact on the probability of location in areas where there are numerous existing activities in the entrant's own industry.

Wren (2005) is critical about the above conclusion. Following the author, the weak effect found for the grants in the econometric studies could arise because they are carried out for individual nations, examining plant location between regions of a country. The survey evidence on 'additionality' is that the grants determine location at the international level, and indeed RSA is not offered for relocations within the United Kingdom. Since such econometric evidence mix entrants that are already located there and those which are entering that country, it does not necessarily contradict the survey evidence, which is that the grants are effective in changing plant location, but at the national rather than regional level.

Moreover, Wren (2005) argued that since the aim of RSA is job creation in the Assisted Areas, the evaluations should focus on this. Although the exact effect on employment is still controversial among UK institutions (ranging form 84,000 to 6,000 jobs created over the four-and-a-half-year period 1991–5), the author proposes an estimate of 12,000 net jobs created per year. The difference among estimates arise because of the difference in the way adjustments are made for the displacement of jobs elsewhere in the Assisted Areas, due to multiplier and linkage effects in supplier firms and because of permanent net job equivalent.

The author also tackled the issue of the cost of such job creation. Recent reports by the Committee of Public Accounts find that the net employment effect of policy is 'disappointingly small'. The National Audit Office (NAO) gives a cost of regional policy of £21,000 per job, while National Economic Research Associates (NERA) put it at around £50,000 per job. Both studies measure the cost in net present-value terms by deducting the future flow-backs to the Treasury from higher corporate tax revenues, so that the difference reflects the measurement of the employment effect. However, the NAO and NERA 'costs per job' both express the jobs as permanent net job equivalents. When the jobs are given as net jobs created, the 'cost per job' is smaller and in the range £8,150 to £25,000. The author retains an average cost per job of around £12,700.

To judge whether these costs are too high or not, Wren (2005) uses two approaches. One is based on the cost of other job creation schemes and the other on benefit payments paid to the unemployed. Regarding the first approach, calculations by Layard (2001) show that the short-run average cost of a person in employment from the New Deal is £7,000 in gross spending terms.[4] However, this estimate makes a deduction from the costs for both benefit and tax savings, whereas the RSA figure makes a deduction for corporate tax savings only. If deductions are not made for these, the 'cost per job' for the New Deal is £14,000, and this is in the same ballpark as that for RSA.

The second comparison can be made with the annual jobseeker's allowance paid to an unemployed person aged 25. This is around £3,000, but it is a recurrent payment, so comparison should be made with the 'cost per present-value net job year' which gives per year £1,600. This seems to confirm that that RSA is at least as cost-effective as measures designed either to reduce or to alleviate unemployment.

Midelfart and Overman (2002) studied the impact of state aids and the European Structural Funds expenditure on location across European countries and regions. The empirical model explains the share of a country (or a region) in an industry in terms of the size of the country (region), the country (region) characteristics, the industry characteristics, total aid from the EU, and total state aid. National level analysis is based on data for 14 EU Member States (the EU-15 excluding Luxembourg) using the OECD STAN database. This provides production data (gross value of output) for 13 EU countries and 36 industries, from 1970 to 1997. The regional analysis is based on gross value-added data for ten EU countries. Regional disaggregated industry data are NUTS 2 level data, for the period 1980–95 from Eurostat which splits the manufacturing sector into nine industries. Aid data are from the European Commission. State aid refers to total state aid to manufacturing, while EU aid refers to the sum of regional fund, social fund and cohesion fund expenditures. The results show that, for both regions and countries, EU expenditure has a particularly large positive impact on the location of R&D-intensive activities but state aid targeted to specific sectors or to specific types of activity, does not attract that sector or activity. Robustness checks confirm both results.

To sum up the discussion on the ability of state aid to influence firms' location several points are worth pointing out. First of all, the different schemes of state support to lagging regions do have positive an influence. However, its capacity to influence firms' location is quite weak. Meanwhile, market's incentives (market size, infrastructure, natural resources, etc.) for agglomeration appear to be stronger comparatively to the government's ones. However, some studies have shown that should the efficacy of state aid be examined with the respect to the employment objective, some positive results can be achieved. Meanwhile, estimation of the cost of employment creation remains highly controversial and sensitive to methods of estimation employed.

Röller et al. (2003) treated somewhat different aspects of state aid: the impact of the level and the interaction among aid schemes on effectiveness. They assessed the effectiveness of different forms of state aid – defined in line with Articles 87–9 European Communities (EC) – with regard to various properly defined policy objectives. They focused on four areas of policy making (R&D, SME, regional policy, and railways) and used three types of methodologies: indices, correlations, and econometric methods. They found that the econometric approach is best suited to uncover the likely factors that impact on state aid effectiveness.

Their analysis identified a number of robust results. First, returns to state aid are significant and positive but there is considerable evidence in the data that the effectiveness of state aid is subject to diminishing returns, that is, more aid lowers its effectiveness. Second, there is overwhelming empirical support for country heterogeneity in all state aid areas. Third, the effectiveness of state aid is affected by state aid granted for other policy area and the type of instrument used (subsidy, tax relief, equity). Fourth, the study finds quite strong evidence that aid for R&D has a positive effect on R&D spending and that there is a complementarity between R&D aid and SME aid – possibly because many SME aid schemes focus on innovation.

5.3 Empirical evidence on the arguments against public support

Empirical analysis that tests systematically and rigorously the theoretical argument against public support to the industry are quite scarce. Among the arguments presented in the theoretical analysis (conflict with other policies, political economy issues and choice of appropriate instruments) we found studies only on political economy issues. These include distorted appreciation by policy makers of the gain from government spending, electoral concerns and corruption.

5.3.1 Some facts

Dewatripont and Seabright (2006) cite various example of distorted appreciation by policy makers including expensive prestige projects such as Concorde or the state support to struggling firms such as Crédit Lyonnais, Alsthom, and MG Rover. They also present a recent case approved by the European Commission. The Portuguese government approved aid of 41.5 million euros to the semiconductor firm Infineon in order to establish a plant manufacturing DRAM memory chips in Portugal. According to the firm's own estimates the investment would generate some 252 new jobs and safeguard about 596 existing ones which result in a total of 848 jobs. The cost per job is, therefore, 49,000 euros. Drawing on the literature (Haskel et al., 2002) that suggest that foreign direct investment generates productivity spillovers worth around 3,500 euros per job per year, the authors find that the project would have to continue for 25 years just to pay for itself. They, therefore, question whether decision makers follow the objective of value for money.

Wasteful spending may be a by-product of accountability, not a symptom of its absence as in by Dewatripont and Seabright (2006).[5] In numerous cases, however, wasteful spending is a consequence of ill governance (e.g. corruption). Lambert and Kosenoky (2006) cite the testimony of J. C. Mery, a City Hall official, who admitted that for ten years (1985–94) he organized and arbitrated collusion in the allocation of most construction and maintenance contracts for the Paris City Hall. In exchange, firms were paying bribes used to finance political parties. Beyond such clear misbehaviour, the authors also report cases where procurement specification can be used to favour a given party. In one case, an African country set its telephone specification to require equipment that could survive in a frigid climate. Only one telephone company from Scandinavia could satisfy this obviously worthless specification.

Ades and Di Tella (1997) illustrate the interactions between active industrial policy and corruption on the basis of the South Korean Yulgok defence procurement programme of an amount of US$9,637 million. The programme represented one-third of government spending during the 1970s and 1980s. At the heart of the programme were two policies that gave an extraordinary amount of discretion to government procurement officials. The first was the familiar request for secrecy in military procurement. The second was active industrial policy encouraging technology transfers to local companies that would later take on the supply of military equipment to the South Korean army. As these companies progressed down their 'learning curves', they enjoyed rents that the South Korean military shared through bribes. Indeed, corruption allegations led to an investigation that ended in 1993, when Lee Chun Ku, a former defence minister, was convicted for accepting a US$370,000 bribe for arranging contracts. A second former defence minister was convicted for accepting a kickback on a submarine contract. During 1993, the investigations led to no less than 39 generals being sacked, reprimanded, or thrown into jail.

The above specific cases are further strengthened when confronted with the importance of corruption in public procurement context. Following Kaufmann (2005), a conservative approach gives an estimate for annual worldwide bribery of about US$1,000 billion. Out of these, US$200 billion per year concern public procurement, corresponding to around US$1,500 billion 'tainted' procurement projects. These figures include bribes between firms and public officials or politicians in the industrialized world, between multinational corporations from industrial countries to the public sector in emerging economies, and bribery within emerging economies. Finally, the estimate does not account for the significant losses in investment, private sector development, and economic growth to a country.

5.3.2 Econometric studies

Systematic econometric analysis of the role of political economy factors in public support to industry are provided by Aydin (2007), Ades and Di Tella (1997), Hellman et al. (2000) and Hellman and Schankerman (2000).

Aydin (2007) explores domestic and international factors that determine the level of government support to industry in sixteen OECD countries over the period 1989–95. The focus is on the level of subsidies which is supposed to be determined by demand and supply factors. Demand for subsidies is influenced by unemployment, upcoming elections, and international competition, while their supply is constrained by international regimes. Subsidies are defined as public support to business of any form including direct or indirect selective financial support, such as grants, low-interest loans, and tax breaks.

The level of subsidies as a percentage of manufacturing GDP is explained in terms of the percentage of unemployed in the civilian labour force in the country, an election dummy (variable that takes on the value 1 if there was an election during that year or in the first six months of the following year and 0 otherwise), trade openness (the sum of the value of exports and imports of a country divided by its GDP), and a European Union membership dummy (takes the value 1 if the country is a member of the EU in that given year and 0 otherwise). The data are taken from the OECD Industry Committee's publication Spotlight on Public Support to Industry.

The regression results show that all independent variables are statistically significant at high confidence levels, and three of them – unemployment, trade openness, and EU membership – have signs in the expected directions. The coefficient for the unemployment variable is positive and highly significant. Governments in countries that have higher levels of unemployment, other things being equal, are likely to grant more subsidies. The coefficient of trade openness is also significant and negative. The coefficient of the EU membership variable is negative and significant at very high level. Governments of EU Member States are likely to disburse lower levels of subsidies than do non-members. Finally, proximity of elections, contrary to the theoretical expectation, is associated with lower levels of subsidies. This contradicts the well-established literature on electoral cycles. However, it is possible that incumbent governments redirect subsidy expenditures towards more direct means of increasing the likelihood of re-election (e.g. direct transfer households, voters).

Ades and Di Tella (1997) examined the extent to which corruption is higher in countries pursuing active industrial policies.[6] They estimated an equation where a country measure of corruption is explained in terms of the intensity of industrial policy in this country and other control variables. The possibility of endogeneity of industrial policy (i.e. officials may push for more intervention because they are corrupt) is taken into account in the estimation procedure.

Control variables include the country level of development (measured by the level of income per capita and the average years of total schooling), the Gastil index of political rights and the share of imports in GDP. The main source of data is the World Competitiveness Report (WCR) which consists of yearly surveys conducted amongst top managers and economic leaders in the surveyed countries. The period of observation was 1989–92.

They use two indices of industrial policy from the WCR survey section. A procurement index that measures 'the extent to which public procurement is open to foreign bidders', and a fiscal index that measures 'the extent to which there is equal fiscal treatment to all enterprises'. Both indices are measured at a scale from 0 to 100, with 100 implying that the country in question has a public procurement policy completely closed to foreign companies or a fiscal policy that treats enterprises in the most unequal way.

The regression results show that the coefficient of procurement policies is significant and positive. It indicates that a one standard deviation increase in the extent of preferential procurement practices by the government is associated with an increase in the corruption index (which ranges between 0 and 100) by 7 points, or one-third of a standard deviation. Regarding the uneven fiscal treatment to enterprises, its coefficient has the expected positive sign, and is highly significant. A one standard deviation increase in the index is associated with an increase in corruption of 11.5 points, just over 55% of a standard deviation. The size and significance of these coefficients are robust to estimation methods (Panel versus cross section regressions), corrections for possible endogeneity of the explanatory variables and inclusion of additional control variables. Policy implications are illustrated by decomposing the total effect of industrial policy into a positive, direct effect, and a negative, corruption-induced effect. In the presence of corruption, the total effect of industrial policy on investment ranges between 84 and 56% of the direct impact.

Hellman et al. (2000) present the result of a survey on how firms in transition economies have been able to shape the rules of the game to their own advantage, at considerable social cost: state capture. This is the Business Environment and Enterprise Performance Survey (BEEPS) which is a world-wide survey of firms on the obstacles in the business environment conducted by the World Bank in cooperation with the European Bank for Reconstruction and Development (EBRD), Inter-American Development Bank and the Harvard Institute for International Development. The BEEPS questionnaire for the transition economies was implemented during the period June–August 1999 in the following countries: Armenia, Azerbaijan, Belarus, Bulgaria, Croatia, Czech Republic, Estonia, Georgia, Hungary, Kazakhstan, Kyrgyzstan, Lithuania, Moldova, Poland, Romania, the Russian Federation, the Slovak Republic, Slovenia, Ukraine, and Uzbekistan. It represents the first major attempt to provide sound empirical measures of various forms of 'grand' corruption, such as 'state capture' as well as corruption in public procurement, and to measure the characteristics of firms that engage in such forms of corruption. The authors contrast *state capture* (firms shaping and affecting formulation of the rules of the game through private payments to public officials and politicians) with *influence* (doing the same without recourse to payments) and with *administrative corruption* ('petty' forms of bribery in connection with the implementation of laws, rules, and regulations).

The results indicate that some transition economies face twin problems that undermine the quality of governance: *state capture* by which powerful firms distort the reform agenda for their private gains, and *the grabbing hand* by which the state officials generate excessive regulations to increase their bribe income. State capture generates considerable performance gains to the firm, while corruption of the 'grabbing hand' variety (i.e. 'petty' forms of corruption) is associated with slower firm-level growth rates. This suggests that, while rents that are generated by state capture are shared by firms and the state, the rents from grabbing hand corruption are largely retained by public officials.

Hellman and Schankerman (2000) further investigate the relationship between enterprises and the state in transition economies. Focusing on capture, they consider two aspects: *pervasiveness* and *concentration of state capture*. Pervasiveness concerns the extent to which the economy is affected by state capture. It is measured as the ratio of firms that respond that they were significantly affected by the sale of legislation or decrees over the total number of firms. Concentration measures the extent to which a small number of firms may affect the economy.[7] Among managers who respond that their firms were significantly affected by the sale of legislation or decrees, the survey identifies those who make unofficial payments to influence the laws, decrees or regulations and those who do not make payments. Managers who make such payments are defined as 'captors'. Concentration is measured as one minus the proportion of captors in the total affected firms. Thus capture is judged to be less concentrated (i.e. affecting a more firms which are not seeking such effects) if there are fewer captor firms or if (for a given number of captors) there are more firms that are affected by capture activities. Values of the index closer to unity indicate greater concentration of state capture.

In Azerbaijan, Moldova, Russia, and Ukraine, more than 30% of the firms report a significant impact from the sale of legislation at the national level. By contrast, fewer than 10% of firms in Armenia, Belarus, Hungary, Slovenia, and Uzbekistan report such impact. While many enterprises report that they are *affected* by state capture, only a small proportion reports that they actually *engage in* making payments to influence laws, decrees, or regulations. This, of course, may reflect only the reluctance to acknowledge illegal practice.

The authors studied the relationship between state capture and the EBRD index of economic reform, and the relationship between state capture and the quality of governance. State capture has a powerfully negative impact on the quality of governance in transition economies: high-capture countries have heavier taxes and regulation, greater corruption, poorer macroeconomic management, and less effective law and order. At the same time, state capture is strongly negatively associated with progress on economic reform.

The last paper we present in this overview is Pack (2000). Although the paper had not intended to do so, we find that it provides a very interesting synthesis of the findings in the two previous chapters. It attempts to examine whether the policies pursued by Japan and Korea constitute a basis for optimism about the potential gains from a well-designed set of industrial policies.

Before going further, it is important to clarify how policies pursued by Japan and Korea are characterized in the literature. They combine both some degree of protection with an intense competition among domestic producers. According to Evenett (2005: pp. 16–18):

> While it has been commented that Japan's post-war economic development was achieved by subordinating competition policy to industrial policy...much of Japan's economic dynamism has in fact been rooted in the robust market mechanisms created through competition among firms. Industrial policy and competition policy coordinated mutually and developed an environment that allowed companies to engage in free and fair competition. The introduction of competition policy early in Japan's economic reconstruction, as well as the subsequent evolution of this in response to economic development, was a great factor in Japan's rapid economic growth in the past. Even today, it is those sectors where competition has been intensive – the automobile industry, for example – which tend to have the greatest international competitiveness.
>
> ...the Korean government's use of trade protection, selective credit subsidies, export targets (for individual firms), public ownership of banking sector, export subsidies, and price controls – all deployed single-mindedly in the service of acquisition of technological capabilities and of building industries that will eventually compete in world markets...However, a key element of the strategy was that in exchange for government subsidies and trade protection the government also set stringent performance standards. Firms were penalized when they performed poorly, as when they became subject to 'rationalization' (government-mandated mergers and capacity reduction) in the wake of over-extension. They were rewarded when

they fulfilled government objectives, as when they were awarded subsidized credit for fulfilling export targets...

Pack (2000) emphasizes the impact of industrial policies on macroeconomic TFP growth. This is assumed to be affected by the sectoral structure of manufacturing and the TFP growth rate of individual sectors. If the calculated effect is large and positive, there may be a basis for other countries to step in more intensive industrialization. If, however, even Japan and Korea, with well-designed general policies and quite efficient bureaucracies, were unable to extract major benefits from selective intervention to foster individual sectors, this would seem an unpromising path.

The author considers three scenarios to assess what the path of macroeconomic TFP growth would have been in the absence of industrial policy.

Scenario 1: It is assumed that the only effect of industrial policy was to shift the sectoral patterns of production; TFP growth in individual sub sectors was not affected by the policy. The sectoral pattern in the absence of industrial policy would have been similar to that in the benchmark countries.[8]

Under these assumptions, Korea obtained a 0.08 percentage point increment and Japan obtained a 0.32 percentage point increase in annual TFP growth in manufacturing from the policy-induced difference in sectoral structure.

Scenario 2: The second scenario assumes the reverse: that, instead of shifting the sectoral pattern of production, industrial policy only had an effect on the TFP growth rates of the sectors. The author, further, assumes that only half of the observed TFP growth rates in the favoured sectors were attributable to industrial policy. Under these assumptions, the contribution of industrial policy to TFP growth was 0.72 percentage point in Korea and 0.89 percentage points in Japan.

Scenario 3: The third calculation combines the assumptions of the first two. Industrial policy affected both the sectoral structure and productivity growth in the individual sectors. These assumptions imply that industrial policy accelerated TFP growth by 0.60 percentage point in Korea and by 0.99 point in Japan.

Given that Korea's manufacturing sector accounted for about a third of GDP at the end of the period, industrial policies that contributed

0.60 point to the manufacturing growth rate would have accounted for no more than 0.20 point of aggregate growth. For Japan, a similar calculation implies that the extra 0.99 percentage point in manufacturing would have contributed about 0.3 point to aggregate growth. Even if these figures were doubled, it would still be the case that industrial policy was a minor hormone rather than the magic elixir of aggregate growth.

Although Pack (2000) questioned the impact of industrial policy on aggregate growth, he still acknowledge that the two countries achieved impressively in term of growth rates. Were there other factors at play? The simplest explanation is that policies in both countries induced significant competition, whether by holding 'contests', as in Japan, or by linking preferential interest rates and tariffs on imported goods to success in export markets, as in Korea. Firms thus had strong incentives to improve productivity. Other countries that attempted to encourage specific sectors relied on protecting the domestic market and never credibly sought to reduce such protection. Profits and wages were never threatened, and incentives to learn were weak. Countries attempting to extract the benefits from industrial policy that Japan and Korea obtained have to possess not only an exceptionally capable bureaucracy but also the political ability to withdraw benefits from non-performing firms. Experience in dozens of other countries suggests that these conditions rarely obtain (Pack, 2000).

To conclude, there is an important body of empirical evidence that confirms theoretical arguments about the risks of government failure and importance of political economy and institutional issues for the efficiency of public support measures. In particular, most studies, both econometric model results and case study investigations, confirm that weak institutional environments and inefficient bureaucrats coupled with strong vested interests and high corruption levels entail significant inefficiency losses for an economy in terms of wasteful public spending and/or low value-for-money and fit-for-purpose outcomes.

5.4 Conclusion

The available empirical evidence (based either on case studies or on econometric analysis) on the impacts of public support to business does not cover all the existing theoretical arguments. There is a consensus that a positive relation between subsidy and private R&D expenditures exists and that such a relationship exhibits, in general, complementarity. It seems also that tax incentives are more effective than grants and research programmes in increasing private R&D. In contrast, there is little strong evidence that subsidy is able to induce a significant increase in productivity, especially in the long run. Moreover, there are cases when subsidy crowds out private investment in physical capital. Finally, the evidence also suggest that the ability of subsidy to influence firms' location or to rescue firms in difficulty is quite weak.

Various examples support the argument that in the presence of network externalities public procurements may help overcome coordination failure in the market. However, a more general conclusion depends on the assumption that the government can do better than the market, which is not always the case. In contrast, public procurement proves to be a good instrument to support R&D. It is able to give rise to private R&D expenditures and provide positive incentives to the economy as a whole.

Turning to the argument against public support, empirical analyses are quite scarce. The reviewed empirical evidence confirms the theoretical arguments about the risks of government failure, namely, the risk of corruption and the risk of capture. A weak institutional environment and inefficient bureaucracy coupled with strong vested interests entail significant inefficiency losses for an economy in terms of wasteful public spending. Even the impressive successes of Japan and Korea seem to owe at least as much to a credible and efficient bureaucracy as to industrial policy by itself.

Part II
Quantitative Assessment

6
Subsidies and State Aid

In Chapter 4, we discussed the issues raised by the multiplicity of definitions and measurements of subsidies and state aid. This section combines the various sources to try to get the more reliable data for a comparison between public supports. It also examines whether national public support reports are the best way to approach economic reality.

The international basic data sources for subsidies used here are: (1) the system of National Accounts statistics[1] (OECD source), (2) the WTO SCM notification, and (3) the State Aid Scoreboard from the European Commission. Subsidies statistics from national sources are also available and they will be discussed in the following part of this report.

These sources provide interesting views on government subsidies but they are quite different in terms of their sectoral coverage, the financial transactions covered, and the measurement basis:

- *System of National Accounts*: the SNA approach in subsidies presents shortcomings as they report only cash subsidies. Other types of subsidies, such as tax subsidy, are classified elsewhere. Also, some subsidies, such as payments to cover operational losses of state enterprises, are carried out 'off budget'. Moreover, SNA only provide information on payments to producers and exclude subsidies to consumers to obtain goods and services at below cost.
- *WTO SCM notifications*: the figures correspond to notified quantitative information on industrial and sometimes horizontal subsidies to the World Trade Organisation (WTO) under the SCM notifications requirements. The various forms of subsidy covered by the Subsidies and Countervailing measures (SCM) definition is also rather wide, as it includes direct subsidies, tax concessions, and potential direct transfers; but for the reasons explained already, the figures should

be interpreted with considerable caution: not all members fulfil the notification requirements, not all programmes are reported consistently, and the quantitative information when provided is not always clear and consistent. Moreover, services are not covered.
- *State aid scoreboard*: the figures cover only the European Union (EU) Member States and this is clearly a problem for international comparisons.

When comparing the amount of subsidies from different sources, as reported in WTO trade report 2006 (part on subsidies), for the period 1998–2002, the annual average value for the United States was US$16.3 billion in the WTO notification, less than half the value reported in National Accounts (US$43.5 billion). In Japan the WTO notification report US$4.2 billion in subsidies, compared to US$34.3 billion in the National Accounts report. For the EU (15) the WTO notification report US$96.3 billion (community and individual members combined), compared to US$109 billion in the national account, and US$80.3 billion in the EU scoreboard (see Table 6.1).

For the EU, the annual average value for the period 1998–2002 from national account is 36% higher than the same indicator from the EU scoreboard. It is not clear why the figures for the EU are so different between the different sources. Possible factors explaining these differences are:

- *Measurement basis*: In SNA, the measurement basis is the gross cost. In the EU scoreboard, the figures have been expressed in terms of aid element based on expenditure data provided by Member States on aid on which the Commission has taken a decision. The aid granted is not necessarily identical to cost to government.[2] Moreover, non notified aid on which the Commission has not yet taken a decision is not taken into account in the scoreboard statistics.
- *Sectoral coverage*: the whole economy in SNA and the EU scoreboard, compared to mainly industry in WTO notifications.
- *Treatment of general economic measures*: general economic measures are covered by SNA but are not considered as state aid in the EU scoreboard. Aids which compensate for services of general economic interest are also considered as subsidies by the SNA but are currently not included in the State aid totals under the SA scoreboard. These are possibly among major explanations for the differences observed. On the basis of certain national reports that will be presented latter on, it will be clear that in France, for example the main explanation of the

differences between the figures coming from the SNA approach and from the EU Scoreboard is the treatment of general measures which represent a large share of total sate aid.
- *Treatment of soft loans guarantees, equity subsidies and tax subsidies*: are covered by the SA scoreboard but not by the SNA. That will increase the amount of state aid in the scoreboard compared to the subsidy figures in the SNA. The SA 2006 scoreboard (COM (2006) 761 final p. 27) presents the share of each aid instrument in total aid for manufacturing and services. Grants which are the only instrument covered by the 'subsidy' approach of the SNA represented only 50% in the period 2003–5 for the EU25. Tax exemptions represented 40% of the total aid and the other instruments all together (equity participation, soft loans, tax deferrals and guaranties) only 10%.
- *Treatment of funding from Community budget*: for the EU, an important source of the difference between WTO data and the EU scoreboard is also the fact that the EU notifies Community budget funding to the WTO whereas this is of course not reported in the EU State Aid Scoreboard.

The breakdown of subsidies by industry is generally not provided in National Accounts data. Moreover, some subsidies are not specific to a particular industry but of a general nature. They are often labelled 'horizontal' subsidies. It is nearly impossible to present a clear estimate of the sectoral breakdown of global subsidies. However, WTO notifications provide information on the sectoral allocation of subsidies as Members are required to present their notifications by sector (see Table 6.2). If programmes cannot be allocated clearly to either the agriculture sector or industry, they are classified as 'horizontal'. Regional and R&D programmes are included in the horizontal category.

The WTO notification data on subsidies, even if we raise questions about its completeness; reveals that agriculture accounts for a much larger share than industry in total subsidies for the United States and Japan.

Table 6.1 Differences between data sources on subsidies (annual average value for the period 1998–2002 in US$ billions)

	EU	USA	Japan
WTO notification	96.3	16.3	4.2
SNA statistics	109.0	43.5	34.3
EU State Aid Scoreboard	80.3	–	–

Source: Data from the WTO report, 2006.

Table 6.2 Sectoral allocation of subsidies notified by WTO members: Yearly average 1999/2002 (percentage)

	Agriculture	Industry	Horizontal	Total
European Countries[a]	41	8	50	100
United States	60	8	32	100
Japan	78	22	0	100

[a] EU is EU-15 countries. However, it also includes subsidies provided by the EU institutions to agriculture. This explains why the importance of agriculture is high compared to the scoreboard.

Source: Data from WTO report, 2006.

Table 6.3 EU Member States: Rankings for average subsidy (SNA approach and State Aid Scoreboard) as a share of GDP (1998–2002)

Ranking based on SNA			Ranking based on EU SCOREBOARD		
Rank	Country	% GDP	Rank	Country	% GDP
1	Austria	3.0	1	Finland	1.5
2	Denmark	2.2	2	Ireland	1.1
3	Sweden	1.8	3	Portugal	1.1
4	Germany	1.7	4	Germany	1.0
5	Hungary	1.7	5	Denmark	0.9
6	Finland	1.5	6	Spain	0.8
7	Belgium	1.5	7	Austria	0.7
8	Netherlands	1.5	8	France	0.7
9	Portugal	1.4	9	Greece	0.6
10	France	1.3	10	Hungary	0.6
11	Italy	1.2	11	Italy	0.6
12	Spain	1.1	12	Belgium	0.5
13	Ireland	0.8	13	Netherlands	0.5
14	United Kingdom	0.5	14	Sweden	0.4
15	Greece	0.2	15	United Kingdom	0.2

Source: System of National account and EU scoreboard for total state aid, own calculations.

Table 6.3 presents the ranking for average subsidy/state aid expenditures as a share of Gross Domestic Product (GDP) (period 1998–2002) for EU Member States based on the SNA and the SA scoreboard. Even if there are clear reasons for differences between the two databases, we could expect that the two rankings will be relatively similar. Of course, that will be the case if the major explanation for the differences between the two databases played a similar role for the different countries, that is, importance of general economic measures, importance of aids to compensate for Services of General Economic Interest (SGEI), importance of tax exemption.

That is clearly not the case for certain EU Member States: Sweden (nr 3 in the SNA list and nr 14 in the scoreboard list), Greece (nr 15 in the SNA list and nr 9 in the scoreboard), Ireland (nr 13 in the SNA list and nr 2 in the scoreboard), Austria (nr 1 in the SNA list and nr 7 in the scoreboard). The United Kingdom is the only country which is considered to be low in terms of subsidy (SNA) and low in terms of state aid (EU).

6.1 Public support policies in the OECD countries (1998)

In the 1990s Organisation of Economic Cooperation and Development (OECD) undertook a major project on public support policies to increase transparency and comparability of national support policies – a project very much in line with the aim of our research.

The public support project was launched with the aim to increase transparency on support programmes, using a questionnaire to cover ten policy areas identified as priority objectives of industrial support policies. These areas were R&D, sectoral policies, crisis aid, regional development, general investment incentives, support to Small and Medium Enterprises (SMEs), labour and training, export and training, export and foreign trade, energy efficiency, and environment protection.

Within its project on public support to industry, OECD covered all types of financial government support to manufacturing industry at the central, regional, and local level. The definition which was used in this project was different from the one used in the National Accounts. The concept used for 'public support' by OECD goes beyond the concept of 'subsidies' in SNA. The definition of public support 'applies whether or not the funding results in a net cost to government' as loan programmes, venture capital funds, and equity capital infusions (OECD, 1998). However, non--financial support, such as regulatory policies and norms, did not fall within the scope of this project.

Contrary to the SNA approach, which is clearly a top-down approach, this support policy approach is a programme-based, bottom-up approach. Moreover, the public support exercise of OECD covers exclusively manufacturing, contrary to SNA which covers the whole economy. However the figures based on these two different exercises are consistent, around 1% of GDP.

The main findings of the OECD exercise on public support were as follows:

- Public support was around 1% of manufacturing GDP from 1989 to 1993.
- Only 4% of the public support programmes were limited to national enterprises. The support policies were open to domestically established firms.
- Almost 60% of public support programmes have the duration of five years or more.
- Support to regional development, exports and trade and R&D have a very prominent role in net spending, nearly 70% in 1993.
- More than 50% of sectoral programmes are concentrated on three industries (steel, shipbuilding, and textiles) which together represent only 9% of manufacturing GDP OECD.
- The policy objective of crisis aid is focused on SMEs in difficulty with funds, increasingly provided by local and regional governments.
- While most OECD governments were confronted by budget restrictions in the period 1989–95, public support programmes on R&D increased in the OECD.
- Public support programmes providing support to SMEs as primary or secondary objective constitute more than one-third of all reported programmes, in particular contributions to job creation.
- There was a shift from an interventionist to a horizontally oriented industrial policy with the growing focus on R&D, SMEs, and regional development.

Table 6.4 presents, exclusively for manufacturing, the public support calculated in terms of Net Cost to Government (NCG). The NCG measures the difference between the cost of funding a programme and the revenue generated for the public budget by the same programme in any given year.

There is considerable diversity in spending for the different policy programmes, as underlined in Table 6.4: Support to Regional Development (33.4%), R&D and innovation (18.9%), export and foreign trade (15.8%) and SMEs (8.1%) played in 1993 a predominant role in term of NCG spending, more than 75% of the total. We observe, for the period under review (1989–93) reductions in sectoral aid, export and foreign trade, investment aid, and SMEs.

The main limitations of the OECD 'public support to industry' project were as follows. First, the support policies from local and regional authorities were difficult to analyse since there was much less statistical information

Table 6.4 Reported expenditures (on manufacturing) by policy objective in OECD (NCG as a percentage of the total)

Policy objective	1989 (%)	1993 (%)	Evolution 93/89
1. Regional development	23.1	33.4	+10.3
2. R&D innovation	17.3	18.9	+1.6
3. Export and foreign trade	18.7	15.8	-2.9
4. SMEs	14.7	7.1	-6.6
5. Sectoral	12.1	7.4	-6.6
6. Crisis aid	4.4	6.9	+2.5
7. Investment	8.0	5.6	-2.4
8. Energy efficiency	1.2	3.1	+1.9
9. Environment	0.7	0.7	0.0
Total	100	100	

Source: Data from the OECD Observer n°204, March 1997.

available from region than from central government. Second, the OECD project had the goal to develop examinations of national support policies for each individual country but some governments were reluctant. Third, the OECD project, which was in a first step fact-finding, had the objective to be more policy-oriented to address the issue of the efficiency of each support programme policy, but that was very sensitive.

In fact, the OECD project was finally abandoned, since there was a very high political sensitivity on all these issues of public support policies and there was clear refusal of certain OECD member states to maintain and develop such a programme. The final report, which was published in 1998 and which covered country-specific analysis of the database, did not cover the United States.

6.2 Quantitative analysis of state aid in the EU

The State Aid Scoreboard published regularly by the Commission is the best tool to present the differences of public support policies between the Member States. However, contrary to the objective of this study, the United States and Japan are not covered. We summarize here the main conclusions of the different scoreboards published by the services of the Commission, which provide useful insights on the differences between the EU Member States.

Significant disparities between Member States

In 2006, if we consider total state aid less agriculture, fisheries and transport, Germany granted the most aid (€16 billion) followed by

France (€7.4 billion), Italy (€3.8 billion), and the United Kingdom (€3.1 billion). Total state aid for industry and services amounted to 0.42% of EU-25 GDP in 2006, but there are large disparities between the Member States. The top five countries are Malta (1.8% GDP), Sweden (0.9%), Hungary (0.9%), Germany (0.7%), Portugal (0.9%), and Germany (0.7%).

The spread is quite important between countries. Even for industry and services, sector which are quite open to competition, the level (1%) observed in Hungary, Sweden, and Portugal is around six times higher than the level observed in the United Kingdom (0.16%). The three Baltic countries, Greece, Luxembourg, and the Netherlands are the Member States with less than 0.25% GDP of state aid.

Considerable differences in the sectoral distribution of state aid

In 2006, 58% of state aid in the EU-25 was directed towards manufacturing[3] and 24% towards agriculture. The differences between Member States in the sectors to which they direct aid are partly explained by the structure of the economy (e.g. coal in Germany and Spain) (see Table 6.5).

Table 6.6 presents the share of state aid awarded to various horizontal objectives. In the mid-1990s when the volume of state aid was much higher than in 2005, the share of state aid awarded for horizontal objectives was only around 50% (p. 19 of the autumn 2006 scoreboard) for the EU against around 85% in 2006. This evolution was in line with the commitments of the European Councils and nearly all

Table 6.5 Sectoral distribution of aid by Member State[a] (2006): percentage of total aid

	Manufacturing	Services	Agriculture	Fisheries	Coal	Transport	Other non manufacturing	Total In M Euros
EU-25	58	7	24	0	5	3	1	66.723
Germany	66	3	20	0	11	1	0	20.219
Spain	49	8	18	1	22	0	0	4.879
France	65	6	23	0	0	5	0	10.389
Italy	60	9	21	1	0	8	0	5.511
United Kingdom	60	6	21	0	0	5	7	4.215

[a] The 5 countries (G, SP, F, I, UK) represents together nearly 75% of the EU-25 GDP.

Source: Data from COM (2007) 791, final, dec. 2007, European Commission.

Table 6.6 State aid for horizontal and sectoral aid in 2006 (as a percentage of total aid)

	Germany	Spain	France	Italy	United kingdom	EU-25
Horizontal objectives	85	72	97	96	90	85
R&D	11	15	23	19	18	14
Environment and energy saving	50	5	1	3	35	29
SME	3	9	26	33	5	11
Employment	0	4	19	7	1	7
Training	0	1	1	6	4	1
Regional development	19	29	19	21	19	19
Other[a]	1	9	8	6	8	4
Sectors	15	284	3	4	10	15
Manufacturing	0	0	3	0	0	2
Coal	14	27	0	0	1	7
Other	0	0	0	0	9	1
Services	1	0	0	4	0	5
Total (less agriculture, fisheries and transport bio €)	16.00	3.86	7.38	3.84	3.10	47.90

[a] Other horizontal objectives include culture, national disasters, risk capital, innovation, and social aid.

Source: Data from COM (2007)791 final, December 2007, European Commission.

the Member States have redirected aid towards horizontal objectives. This positive trend was observed to varying degrees in all the Member States.

It is important to underline, as observed previously, that state aids are classified according to their primary objective, but many Member States' programmes cover two different objectives simultaneously, such as for example R&D for SMEs. However, the data do give a good indication as to which horizontal objectives ware favoured by the larger Member States. The four main objectives were as follows:

- *Environment and Energy* saving represents the largest proportion of state aid (29% of total state aid, less agriculture and fisheries) and this is particularly the case for Germany (50%) the Nordic countries (Denmark 34%, Finland 36%, and Sweden 86%) as well as the Netherlands 68%.
- *Regional Development* represents an important proportion of state aid (19% of total) particularly in countries with important regional

disparities such as Italy (21%), Spain (29%), Greece (65%), and many of the Eastern European countries.
- *Research and Development* (14% of the total of state aid) is number three in the top priorities. This objective was favoured by countries as Estonia (28%), Finland (27%), France (23%), the Netherlands (21%), Belgium (20%).
- *Small and medium size enterprises* (11% of total state aid). State aids for SMEs were favoured in many of the large EU Member States such as Belgium (31%), Italy (33%), and France (26%).

These four main objectives represent all together nearly 75% of total state aid less agriculture, fisheries and transport. They represent the core of public policy support to industry in the large majority of Member States.

6.3 Public support policies in the EU, the USA, and Japan

To analyse international patterns and trends in government subsidies, the only international data source is the system of National Accounts. For reasons explained earlier, we thus do not compare state aid as subject to European Communities (EC) law control but a different set of public support policies that only partly overlaps with the EC notion of state aid. Table 6.7 provides SNA data on general government subsidies for different EU Member States, the United States, and Japan. The only criterion used for the EU Member States' selection was data availability for 1975–90.

The share of GDP represented by subsidies varied widely across countries, ranging from a high of 3% to a low of 0.2% in the period 1998–2002 compared to a high 7.5% to a low 0.5% in the period 1975–1990 (Table 6.8). A certain number of countries provided relatively few subsidies (less than 1% of GDP) in the period 1998–2002: the United States, Japan, the United Kingdom, Ireland, and Greece. At the opposite extreme, Austria, Denmark, Sweden, and Germany provided relatively large amounts of subsidies, more than 1.5% of GDP. A downwards trend can be distinguished in nearly all the countries, except Austria.

The EU average for the period 1975–90 was 2.73% of GDP compared to 1.28% of GDP for the period 1998–2002. The decline observed for the EU, 1.45% is also quite marked. This downward trend is particularly clear (more than 2% GDP decline between 1975 and 1990 and 1998 and 2002) for Belgium, Greece, Ireland, Italy, Portugal, and Sweden.

Table 6.7 International trends in government subsidies (as percentage of GDP)

	Average 1998–2002	Average 1975–90	Difference
Austria	3.0	2.9	+0.1
Denmark	2.2	3.2	−1.0
Sweden	1.8	4.5	−2.7
Germany	1.7	2.1	−0.4
Finland	1.5	3.2	−1.7
Belgium	1.5	3.9	−2.4
Netherlands	1.5	2.9	−1.4
Portugal	1.4	3.7	−2.3
France	1.3	2.7	−1.4
Italy	1.2	3.3	−2.1
Spain	1.1	2.1	−1.0
Ireland	0.8	7.5	−6.7
Japan	0.8	1.2	−0.4
United Kingdom	0.5	2.1	−1.6
United States	0.5	0.5	0
Greece	0.2	4.2	−4.0

Source: National account and G. Schwartz and B. Clements (1999); for the period 1975–1990, our own calculations.

Table 6.8 Trends in government subsidies (as percentage of GDP)

	1996	2004	Difference
Germany	1.98	1.31	0.67
France	1.58	1.50	0.08
United Kingdom	0.62	0.57	0.05
Japan	0.89	0.77	0.12
United States	0.44	0.38	0.06

Source: National account statistics, and our own calculations.

The country perspective for the countries selected in the country case studies (Part III) for the more recent period 1996–2004 is presented in Table 6.8. This table shows the aggregate SNA subsidy by country. In terms of the relative importance of the subsidy reductions between 1996 and 2004 the picture is somewhat different per country.

The decrease is very important in Germany (0.67% GDP), which was the country with the highest share of subsidy in 1998. This evolution is mainly explained by the influence of German reunification. However, at the other extreme, in countries with a tradition of less subsidy intervention in the economy, such as the United Kingdom and the United States, decreases are negligible. For Japan and France decreases are also limited.

The limited amount of information which can be used at this aggregate level implies that we need to look more in-depth to the orientation of the subsidy towards different objectives. The breakdown of subsidies by sector or by objective is only rarely provided in National Accounts data. Therefore, analyzing public support policies by sector or by objectives is not a straightforward exercise in National Accounts. Specific national reports on subsidies are much better fitted to get a clear and detailed picture of the different public support policies followed by the different government. However, there is the problem of comparability of the different national subsidy report. In the SNA, subsidies are current unrequited payments by the general government to resident producers with the objective of influencing their levels of production, their prices or the remuneration of the factors of production.

Subsidies are classified by functions of government (COFOG, OECD, 1997). The classification of the functions of government is a classification used to identify the socio-economic objectives of current transactions, capital outlays, and acquisition of financial assets by general government. The composition if government expenditure provides an insight into the functions provided by the government. Our proposed approach is based upon the construction of three sub-grouping of the breakdowns by division at two-digit level of the COFOG classification, with the goal of discussing the economic objectives of subsidies:

- *Efficiency objectives* represent aid to correct market failure or to pursue traditional 'industrial policy'. Justification of subsidy on efficiency grounds will be used for the following subsidy functions: general public services, environment protection, general economic affairs, and sectoral economic affairs.
- *Equity objectives* represent aid to tackle social problems. Justification of subsidy on equity grounds will be used for following functions: education, health, social protection, recreation, culture and religion, housing and community amenities.
- *Defence and public order objectives* represent aid to deal with these two sectors.

It is clear that more disaggregated information of the classification of the functions of government than the breakdown by two-digit level

Table 6.9 Classification of subsidies by functions (2004)

	F	D	UK	J	USA
Efficiency objectives					
In % of GDP	0.34	0.43	0.08	0.35	0.24
In % of total aid	22.40	32.39	13.64	45.89	64.30
Equity objective					
In % of GDP	1.15	0.88	0.49	0.40	0.14
In % of total aid	76.60	67.15	86.36	52.67	35.96
Defence/public order[a]					
In % of GDP	0.02	0.01	0.00	0.01	0.00
In % of total aid	1.00	0.38	0.00	1.43	0.00
Total subsidies (% GDP)	1.50	1.31	0.57	0.77	0.38

[a] The United States uses public procurement and not subsidy to support the defence industry.

Source: National Account Statistics, OECD, own calculations.

division will be needed to avoid some simplification in the approach proposed. In particular, general public services may cover both efficiency and equity objectives and education is also related to efficiency. However, with the present two-digit level breakdown, it is not possible to offer more in-depth analysis (see Table 6.9).

In theory, whenever subsidy pursues equity objectives, differences between countries in subsidy importance can be justified by differences in the social problems being tackled. It is interesting to note the higher share of subsidy for equity objective in the EU compared with Japan and particularly the United States. Since most subsidy programmes with equity goals aim at maintaining jobs or for the protection of poorest part of the population, the differences between the EU and the United States can be explained by the difference in the 'social model' followed by the different countries.

When subsidies pursue 'efficiency' objectives, rates of aid across countries should be relatively equal unless there are differences in the magnitude of the market failures and externalities being targeted. However, externalities are not observable and the definition of 'efficiency' objectives used here covers also traditional industrial policy, such as sectoral subsidies. The differences between countries are therefore not easily explained. However, it is interesting to note the relatively high level of subsidy for 'efficiency' objectives in France, Japan, and Germany compared with the United States (0.25% GDP) and particularly the United Kingdom (0.08% GDP). France, Japan, and Germany are also perceived as being more interventionist than the Anglo-Saxon countries and that could explain the differences observed.

6.4 Conclusion

This chapter addresses first the issues of defining and measuring subsidies, second the rules for controlling subsidies (WTO disciplines and EU state aid control, and finally an appraisal of international empirical evidence on government subsidies).

There are various definitions of subsidies and there is a multiplicity of objectives to justify subsidies programmes. The result is that there is no commonly accepted definition of subsidy and these definitions differ in the scope of policy which they consider. In the most general term, a natural benchmark for identifying subsidy is hypothetical market equilibrium without government public support policies. However, this approach is exceedingly difficult to apply in practical terms. The agreement on subsidies and countervailing measures of the WTO defines subsidy on the basis of three basic elements: financial contribution by a government or any public body which confers a benefit. The National Accounts define subsidies as current unrequited payments that government makes to enterprises on the basis of their production activities. In the EU, state aid is defined as a state intervention that effectively confers advantages or favours certain economic activities or certain undertakings and affects competition and trade. Finally, the OECD project on public support defines subsidy as any form of direct or indirect financial support, including grants, low interest rates or tax breaks that is granted selectively to a certain firms or sectors.

Many differences exist between these definitions and approaches. The WTO notification database has a much wider coverage of different forms of subsidies than the National Accounts finance statistics, in particular tax subsidies but the WTO has a much narrower sectoral coverage, as services industries are not included in the WTO notification. Moreover, certain horizontal subsidies are not necessarily included in the WTO database, as they are not 'specific' subsidies and the information collected in the notification is not always completed and precise. The National Accounts finance statistics, which defines subsidies relatively narrowly, is the only standardized international information on subsidies.

Subsidies can be useful instruments in correcting market failures but can also distort competition and trade. As subsidies are highly controversial and can be damaging, it is important to understand the relevance of WTO disciplines on subsidies and the interface with EU state aid control. The WTO and EC contain similar requirements on which constitute a subsidy from the viewpoint of benefit, but differ to a degree on the concept of specificity. Moreover in the EU, state aid will exist only where the measures entails transfer of state resources, but under WTO law, government measures that do not necessarily impose a transfer of state resources may be regarded as subsidy. The EU Commission has to assess the state aid weighting the benefits and the potential negative impact on competition before authorizing the aid, but the Commission does not assess the international trade effects of a measure. Finally, problematic subsidies in the WTO are only subject to poorly enforced notification requirement and prospective remedies, whereas EC state aid control provides for an *ex ante* assessment, *ex post* remedies (recovery) and they are subject to extensive scrutiny prior to implementation.

Comparing the data on subsidies from different sources reveals large discrepancies. Possible factors explaining these differences are (1) measurement basis (gross cost to government compared to net cost to government); (2) sectoral coverage; (3) treatment of general economic measures which are covered by certain sources but are not considered as state aid by other sources; (4) treatment of soft loans, equity subsidies, and tax subsidies which are covered or not covered depending on the source. Clearly, the last two factors play a prominent role if we focus on industry.

The only international data source is the system of National Accounts. Thus for international comparison we do not compare state aid as subject to EC law control but a different set of public support policies that only partly overlap with the EC notion of state aid. The share of GDP represented by subsidies varied widely across the EU Member States, the United States, and Japan, ranging from a high of 3% to a low 0.2% in the period 1998–2002, compared to a high 7.5% to a low 0.5% in the period 1975–1990. A downward trend can be distinguished in nearly all the countries. The decrease is very important in countries with the highest share of subsidy in 1998. However, at the other extreme, in countries with a tradition of less subsidy intervention, such as the United Kingdom and the United States, decreases are negligible. In some cases, evidence exist also of a tendency to redirect subsidies towards 'horizontal' objectives.

Subsidies in National Accounts are classified, not by sector but by functions of government. It is possible to define (1) subsidies with efficiency objectives when subsidy attempts to correct market failure as general public goods, environmental protection, R&D, etc. or to pursue traditional sectoral policies; and (2) subsidies with equity objectives when subsidy attempts to tackle social problems as education, housing, social protection, and so forth.

It is interesting to consider the higher share of subsidy for equity objective in the EU compared with Japan and particularly the United States. Since most of subsidy programmes with equity goals aim at maintaining jobs, housing or the protection of the poorest part of the population, the differences between the EU and the United States can be explained by the differences in the 'social model' followed by the different countries. On the other hand, it is interesting to note the relatively high level of subsidy with efficiency objectives (including traditional 'industrial policy') in France, Japan, and Germany compared with the United Kingdom and the United States. France, Japan, and Germany are also perceived as being more interventionist than the Anglo-Saxon countries and that could explain the differences observed.

7
Public Procurement

7.1 Divergences in assessments

Throughout Europe, the public sector and utilities, referred to as 'contracting authorities', need to purchase goods and services for a huge range of activities. Although there is some degree of uncertainty over the total size of public procurement,[1] the estimates vary significantly between the European Union (EU) Member states, ranging from 11% to 20% of Gross Domestic Product (GDP), and on average about 16% of GDP for the EU.

A preliminary comparative analysis of the importance of public procurement is conducted using data from the World Trade Organisation (WTO). Members to the Agreement on Government Procurement (GPA) report to the WTO statistics on public procurements. These statistics are not limited to procurement at central government but comprise contracts awarded by public authorities at regional and local level and also a number of utilities sectors. However, each government decides on which type of procurement to notify to the WTO. These types are specified in Annexes of the signed agreement and differ from one country to another.[2] Therefore, while comparison of public procurement over time for a given country may make sense, comparison across countries is hazardous.

The data of public procurement as a percentage of GDP are reported in Table 7.1. In the absence of a single source of information including all the countries of interest and providing harmonized statistics, the data from the WTO databases are used for the United States and Japan, and from Eurostat for the European countries.[3]

A glance at the data reveals important differences between European countries (very high percentage), the United States (medium), and

Table 7.1   Public procurement (Percentage of GDP)

	France	Germany	United Kingdom	United States	Japan
1996	17.13	17.52	20.47	6.21	–
1997	17.02	17.07	18.26	5.75	1.11
1998	16.27	16.82	17.77	5.66	1.26
1999	16.23	16.80	17.77	5.66	1.11
2000	16.24	16.76	17.43	4.85	0.94
2001	16.13	16.64	17.81	5.17	0.95
2002	16.46	16.78	18.32	5.49	1.15
2003	16.40	16.79	17.96	5.98	1.18
2004	17.70	15.48	–	–	–

Source: WTO for the United States and Japan, Eurostat for European countries.

Japan (very low). The difference between the European countries and the other two others are due to dissimilarities between methodologies of data collecting of Eurostat and the WTO one the one hand and to the fact that each government decides on which type of procurement to notify to the WTO on the other hand. The latter may explain the striking discrepancy in public procurement spending levels between the United States and Japan (both data coming from the WTO source).

7.2   Aggregate assessment using the EU definition

To bring the cross-data to a comparative ground that would allow estimating the extent to which public procurement is used as an instrument of industrial support, we employ the logic consistent with the Commission's approach to the assessment of public procurement level. The commission estimates public procurements as the sum of the three following government spending as reported in the National Account: capital formation, intermediate consumption,[4] and social transfer in kind[5] of products supplied to households. The sum is adjusted for the utilities according to Commission's own estimate.

To get an idea of the level of public procurement in the countries of interest, we calculate its amounts weighed by GDP using the data from the National Accounts in line with the definition proposed by the Commission – but without adjustment for utilities, due to the absence of access to these data.[6]

The data on public procurement obtained according to this methodology are presented in Table 7.2. There is an evident difference with previously reported data, as in Table 7.1. As far as the EU countries are

Table 7.2 Public procurement (own definition) (Percentage of GDP)

	France	Germany	United Kingdom	United States	Japan
1996	13.69	13.82	10.53	9.37	13.87
1997	13.37	13.30	9.77	9.21	13.33
1998	12.62	13.19	9.93	9.11	13.79
1999	12.72	13.39	10.27	9.34	14.02
2000	12.76	13.17	10.64	9.52	13.30
2001	12.49	13.27	11.21	9.95	13.36
2002	12.70	13.29	12.28	10.40	13.72
2003	12.96	13.18	13.16	10.56	13.74
2004	13.28	13.01	13.46	10.61	12.98

Source: OECD and authors' calculations.

concerned, the difference between our data and those in Table 7.1 may stem from the fact that, due to data availability, we cannot adjust for the utilities while the Commission does.

The cross-country difference in public procurement as a percentage of GDP is less important when the data are harmonized in accordance with the proposed methodology than when the raw data coming from different sources are reported. In fact, the harmonized data reveals that in the countries of interest there is comparatively the same level of procurement, ranging between 9% and 14% of national GDP (see Table 7.2 and Figure 7.1). However, looking at public procurements according to the functions as defined in the National Accounts reveals interesting differences across the five countries.

Before proceeding to further analysis, several remarks need to be made. When examining public procurement from the industrial support perspective, one should be cautious about the components of public procurement expenditures. In particular, expenditure in fields such as health, education, public order, and safety has an impact on industry. This impact is, however, indirect as compared to subsidy for instance. Therefore, these sorts of public interventions will not be considered as public support to industry. One exception may be defence procurements in the United States A widespread idea among economists is that defence procurements play an important role in US success in advanced technology (Ruttan, 2005).

Another pertinent remark is that there is no rigorous coherence in the definitions of the data that are reported in the National Accounts. In particular, because the United States uses different categorization from social transfer in kind, it reports zero for this component. However, to

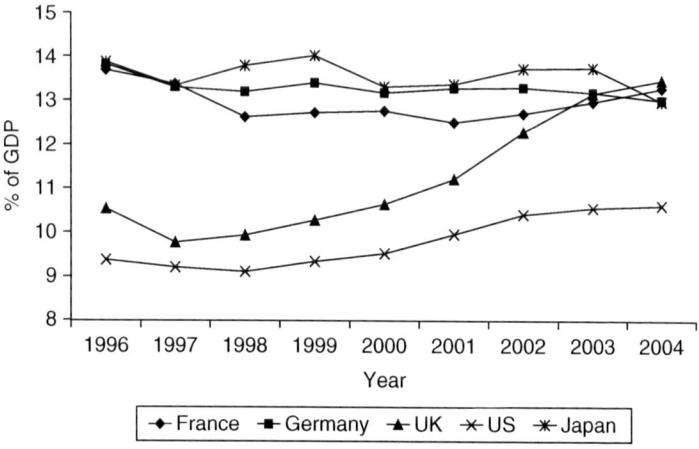

Figure 7.1 The share of public procurement in GDP
Source: OECD and authors' calculations.

some extent this is included in the intermediate consumption, which is included in our definition of public procurements. We should, however, be cautious when splitting public procurements according to the three components and stick as much as possible to our original formula. For instance, in Figure 7.2, the level of intermediate consumption is higher in the United States than other countries. However, the overall procurement level is the lowest.

A similar situation is observed with the data for the United Kingdom, which includes social transfer in kind in the amount reported for intermediate consumption. This explains the relatively high level of intermediate consumption in the UK compared with other countries. It also suggest the existence of a downward bias in the estimation of the public procurement level in this country. In fact, as it is evident from Figure 7.2 there is a gap in terms of social transfer in kinds between the United States, the United Kingdom, and the other three countries, which to certain extent may be explained by the inaccuracy in time series mentioned above.

Finally, one should keep in mind that the differences in results may reflect the countries' different strategies towards the use of public procurement to support business or other factors such as differing national accounting systems or the importance of the state's involvement in the economy (e.g. public utilities, education, social spending, etc.).

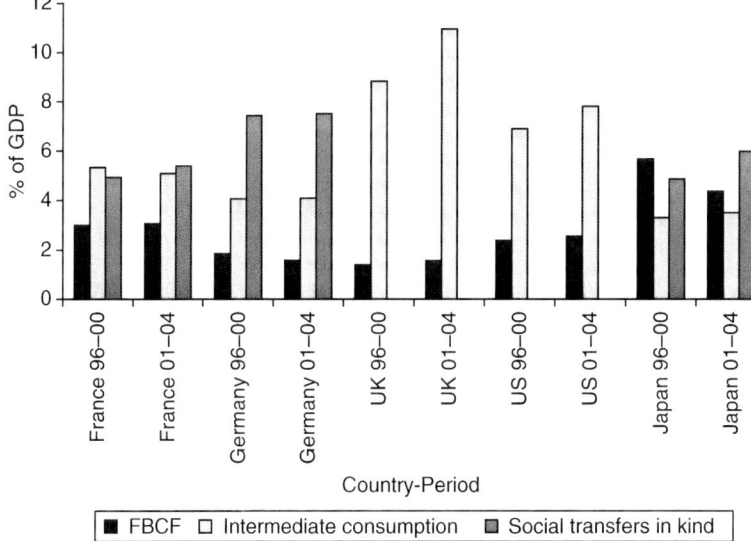

Figure 7.2 Components of public procurements as a percentage of GDP
Source: National Account Statistics, OECD.

7.3 Public procurement by functions (the EU definition)

Looking at public procurements according to function (Figure 7.3) as defined in the National Accounts reveals interesting differences across the five countries. The first striking difference between three European countries on the one hand, and the United States and Japan on the other, is in the weight of social protection[7] in procurement expenditures (see Figure 7.3). While in France and Germany 'social protection' takes on more than 60% of the total amount of public procurement, this is much less in the United Kingdom (about 14%), though this is still significantly higher than in the United States and Japan, which do not exceed 4% and 3% respectively. This means that shares of other components of public procurement are much more important in the United States and Japan than in the European countries. In particular, the United States spends a quite significant part of its public procurement on education (19%) and defence (20%),[8] followed by the United Kingdom with 11% and 13% for education and defence correspondingly and Japan with 8% for education and 9% for defence. Meanwhile the relative shares of public procurement in France and Germany does not exceed 4% and 3% correspondingly for education, and 3% and 2% for defence.

106 *Industrial Policy in Europe, Japan and the USA*

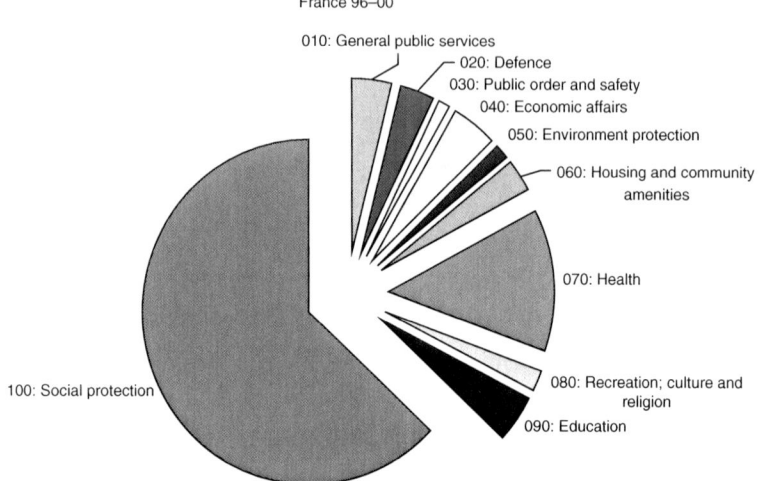

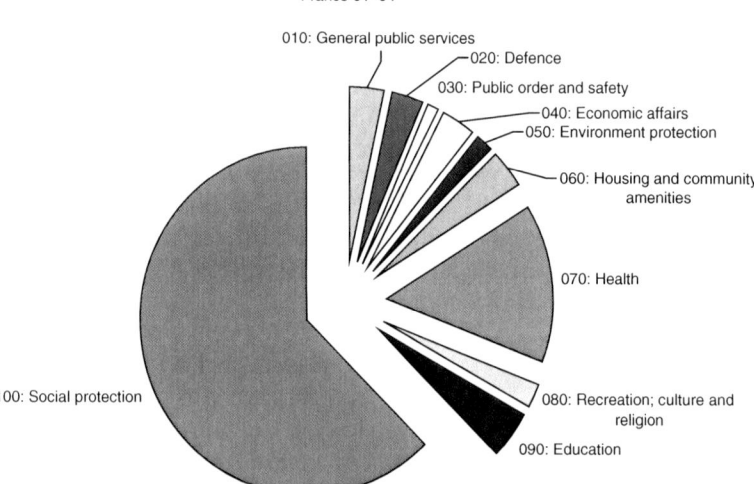

Figure 7.3 Public procurement by function (Percentage of total)
Source: National Account Statistics, OECD.

Public Procurement 107

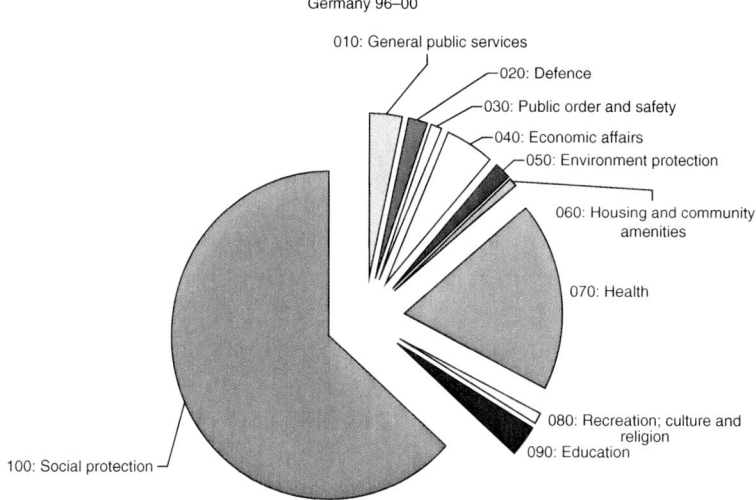

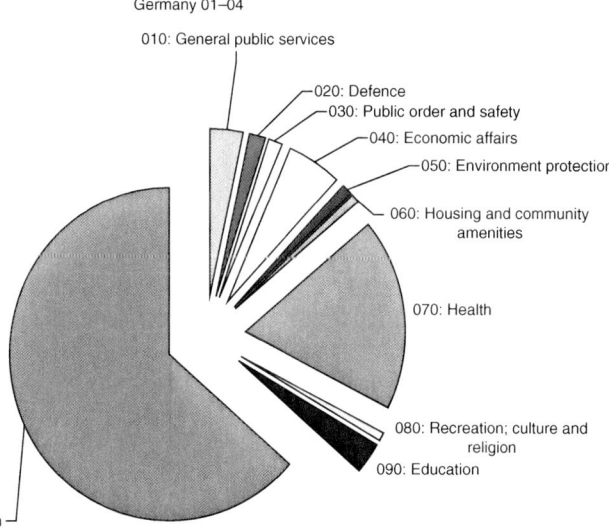

Figure 7.3 Continued

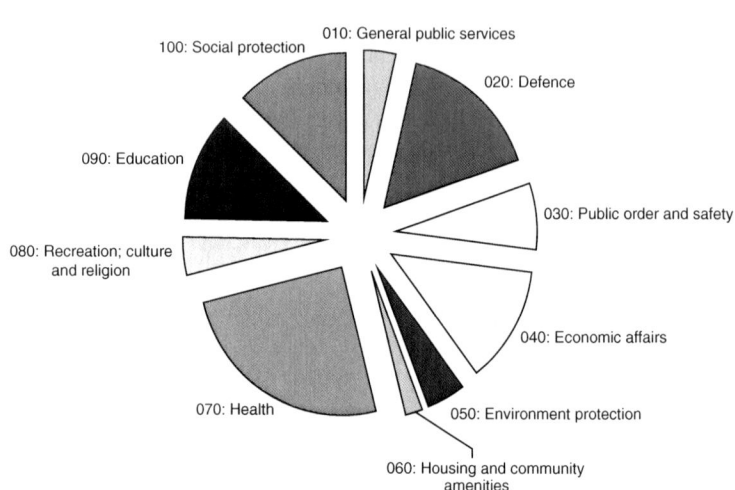

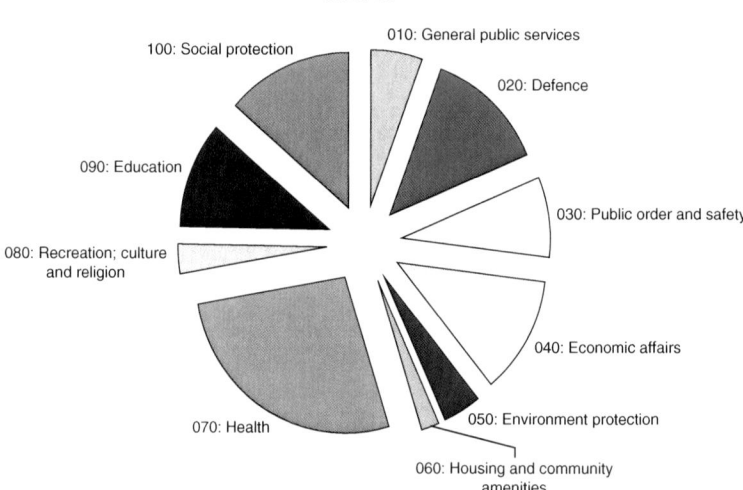

Figure 7.3 Continued

Public Procurement 109

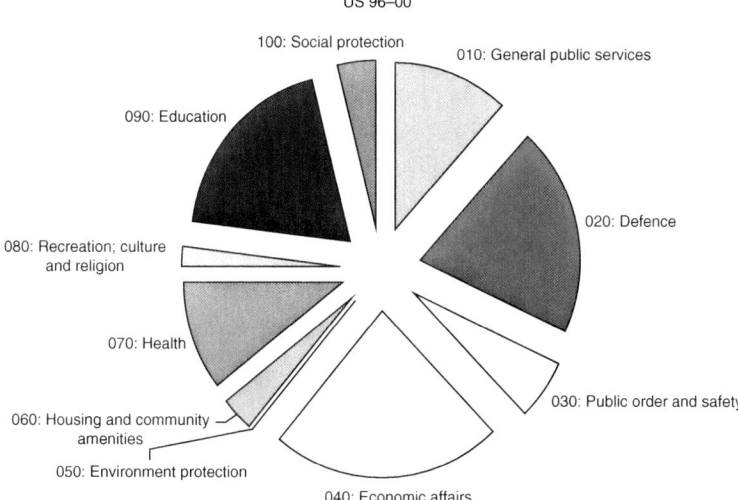

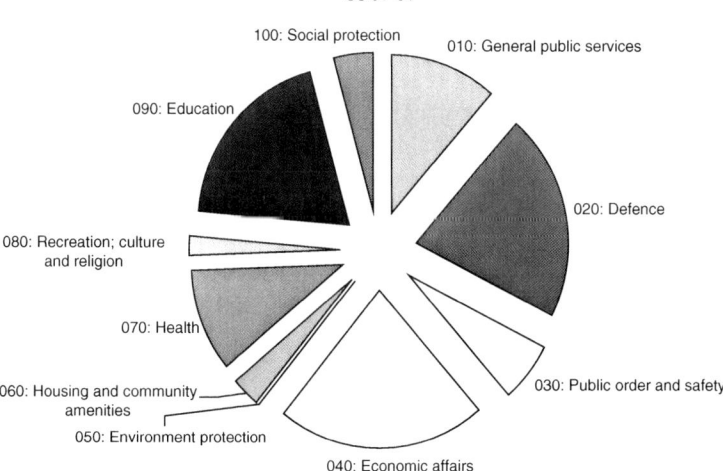

Figure 7.3 Continued

110 *Industrial Policy in Europe, Japan and the USA*

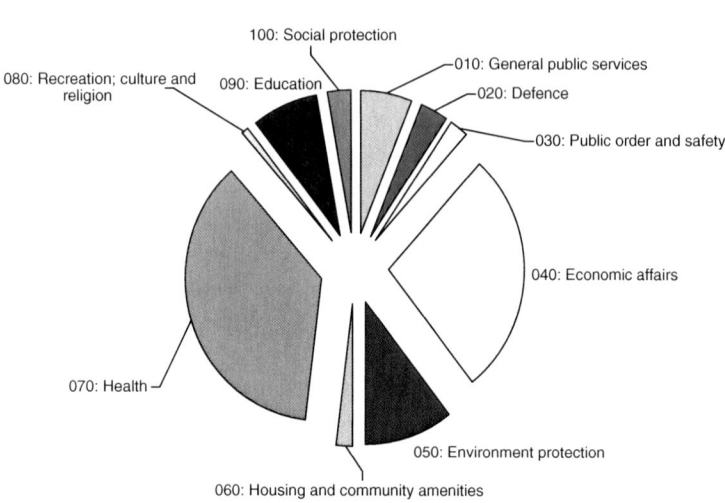

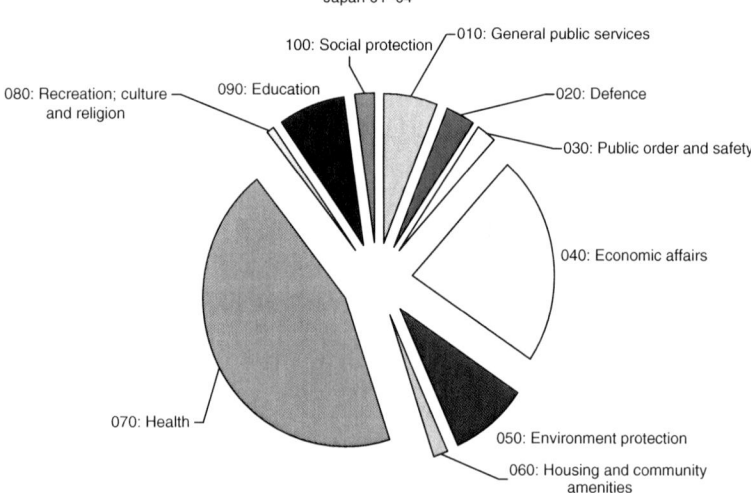

Figure 7.3 Continued

Public procurement devoted to health is relatively important in all countries, with 44% in Japan in head, followed by the United Kingdom – 19% of public procurement, and France with 15%. The United States spends 11% of its procurement on health.

Significant differences between countries are observed with respect to expenditures on environment protection, with Japan in the leading position, with up to 9% of its total public procurement. allocated to this sector. The United Kingdom spends more then two times less (4%), France 2%, and Germany 1%. The United States does not foresee any public procurement expenses for this sector.

Public order and safety[9] has a much more important place in the United Kingdom and the United States, with 8% and 6% respectively of their total procurement, but has a more modest place in the other countries –1% in France and Germany and 2% in Japan.

One public procurement function that is likely to be associated with public support from an industrial perspective is economic affaires.[10] There are striking differences between the five countries in financing this procurement function. In particular, the United States and Japan (each one assigns 23% of the total) spend more than four–fives times the amounts spent in France and Germany on economic affaires (respectively 4% and 6%), and nearly twice as much as the United Kingdom (12%) devotes to this sector. In terms of the percentage of GDP, the figures are 1.1% in France, 1.84% in Germany, 1.54% in the United Kingdom, 2.30% in the United States, and 3.18% in Japan. Although the differences are less impressive, they remain very important.

There is less of a discrepancy in the allocation to general public services, which includes in particular basic research, with the United States in the lead, devoting up to 11%, the United Kingdom and Japan 6% and France and Germany only 3% of their total public procurement.

7.4 Conclusion

The assessment of the importance of public procurement across the five Organisation of Economic Cooperation and Development (OECD) countries (France, Germany, the United Kingdom, the United States, and Japan) proves difficult due to differences in data definitions and availability. In this chapter, the definition, based on National Accounts data, used by the Commission services was adopted in order to secure as much comparability as possible. In spite of this, one should keep in mind that the differences in results may reflect the countries' strategies towards the use of public procurement to support business or other factors such as differing national accounting systems or the importance of the state's involvement in the economy (e.g. public utilities, education, social spending, etc.).

The analysis shows that public procurements as a share of GDP are broadly similar across the five countries (especially since 2001). This is striking given the well documented reliance of the United States on public procurements as an instrument of industrial policy. However, looking at public procurements according to the functions as defined in the National Accounts reveals interesting differences across the five countries.

The first difference between the three European countries on the one hand, and the United States and Japan on the other, is in the importance of the social protection function in procurement expenditures. The share of this function in total procurement is more than ten times higher in France and Germany than in the United States and Japan.

One public procurement function that is likely to be associated with public support from an industrial perspective is economic affairs. As a percentage of total public procurements, the United States and Japan spend more than four–fives times the amounts spent in France and Germany on economic affairs. A similar conclusion holds if one looks at public procurements in economic affairs as a percentage of GDP. This suggests that the European countries use procurement as an instrument of public support for industrial policy much less than the United States or Japan.

Part III
Country Studies

8
Public Support in Germany*

A report on the specific characteristics of public support for industry in Germany was published by the Organisation of Economic Cooperation and Development (OECD) in the late 1990s (OECD, 1998).[1] The report emphasized that the reunification of Germany in 1990 was the exceptional event that dictated the priorities of all governmental decisions in Germany. This event led to important changes in industrial policy, or, more precisely, a dual system of industrial policy: continuity of the industrial policy for West Germany ('alte/old Länder') and policies directed towards East Germany ('Neue/new Länder').

According to the report, changes necessary for the preparation for the Economic and Monetary Union (the Maastricht criteria), which should have led to a significant decline of public support, could only be pursued in the old 'Länder' and was overshadowed by support for the new 'Länder'. Indeed, Germany was one of the few European Union (EU) nations with an increase of total public industry support, from about €36,000 million in 1985 (West Germany only) to about €60,000 million in 2000 (reunified Germany). By 2005, public support has been reduced to €55,000 million (Subventionsbericht der Bundesregierung 2006). However, different sources show different results for public support. While at one extreme the European Commission comes up with much smaller figures because, not accounting for tax relieves (about €20,000 million according to the EU scoreboard), the Kieler Subventionsbericht arrives at a total amount of €110,000 million (Boss and Rosenschon, 2006). The wide range of estimates accounting for about 0.8% to 7.4% of Gross Domestic Product (GDP) are due to different interpretations, the inclusion of different support measures and actors, making it difficult to interpret the German support policy unanimously. Policies directed towards the new 'Länder' have remained an important issue to date. The federal government claimed to have mobilized €250,000 million in direct aid between 1990 and 2006, and mobilized a further €150,000 million between 2006 and 2019.

A major shift in German industrial policy took place in the mid-1990s: by 2005, public support for environment, energy, and energy saving accounted for 47% (up from only 3% in 1995) of total support compared to 2% in France or 28% in the United Kingdom (another country with a strong increase in this activity).

In general, German politics is more oriented towards horizontal measures and the creation of an overall positive economic climate than the creation of national or European champions. One major exception is the support of the coal (and mining) industry as a social measure to preserve employment.

8.1 Objectives of public support

The objectives of public support policy in Germany concern economic growth and employment, environmental aspects, and regional differences.

8.1.1 Continuous development of Eastern Germany

Germany was characterized during the 1980s by an industrial policy that focused horizontal aids to the industry and rejected specific sectoral policies. This approach to improving overall economic framework conditions remained unchanged in the period from 1989 to 1993 for the 'old Länder'. In order to foster rapid economic development the policy measures for the 'new Länder' concentrated on three main goals: first, the creation and development of strong Small and Medium Enterprises (SMEs) through investment in new fields regardless of sectors (manufacturing and services); second, the reorganization of the industry through the privatization of former nationally owned firms under the guidance of the Treuhand Gesellschaft; third, different labour market and social policy measures necessary to facilitate the period of adjustment and to assist in the restructuring process. Besides these measures mention should also be made of the heavy investments into the general infrastructure (roads, railways, and telecom).

These measures were partially financed by shifting regional aids from the old to the new 'Länder', through the equalization procedure between all 'Länder' and additional tax measures and borrowings. The necessary investments in infrastructure were also initially underestimated and partially explain the substantial aids granted to railways and transportation throughout the 1990s.

8.1.2 Green energy

As stated in the Introduction, a major shift in German industrial policy took place in the mid-1990s: by 2005, public support for the environment, energy, and energy saving accounted for 47%, up from only 3% in 1995. Two main factors can explain this strong change in public policy. Besides a strong general awareness of environmental concerns, Germany is a country poor in natural resources and the need for alternative resources is considered to be critical. The increase also coincides with the Schröder government and the Green Party, which was for the first time part of the federal government. Two main decisions were taken by the federal government that increased the need for alternative energies and energy saving: an ecological tax on fuel that led to a 10% increase of fuel prices and the decision in 2000 to close down all nuclear energy plants and therefore phasing out nuclear energy production by 2020. Depending largely on external energy resources such as oil and gas, and renouncing nuclear energy, the search for other energy sources such as renewable resources became a natural consequence. If one considers that horizontal objectives accounted for 81% of state support and that 18% of the remaining 19% of sectoral aid was directed toward the coal sector in 2005, it becomes clear how important energy policy has become in Germany. The restructuring and revitalization of the coal sector is a primary concern and comprises goals such as emission-free coal plants. State support is driven by the conviction of market failure for green energy which today is not competitive with traditional energy resources: measures therefore include price subventions for the production of renewable energy as well as the obligation for energy providers to feed in alternative energy.

8.1.3 Public support for R&D

A third pillar of public support is R&D and education. The Federation and the Länder have laid great emphasis on high-tech industries since 2000. R&D had been stimulated in biotechnology, communication technologies, and especially environmental technologies and energy-related fields.

8.1.4 Public support for start-ups and existing SMEs

A fourth area of public debate is the support of SMEs that comprises three distinct areas: the creation of high-tech start-ups, increasing innovation, and support for existing SMEs, usually called Mittelstand.[2] Policy around and even research about the Mittelstand has a long-standing tradition in Germany. The institute for research of the Mittelstand (ifM) was founded in the 1950s. In this sense, Germany has been named the home of the 'hidden champions' (Simon 1996, 2007): large medium-size companies (up to 1,000 employees), privately held, virtually unknown to the public with owners shy to appear in the public that dominate in global niches with global market shares between 40% and 90%. Recent studies have underlined the continuing importance of these 'hidden champions' (Vernohr & Meyer, 2007).

The German Mittelstand is considered the backbone of the German economy. According to the IfM definition (500 employees), they were 99.7% of all German firms that were subject to value-added tax (VAT), realized 43.2% of all sales, employed 69.7% of all employees, were responsible for the training of 83% of all apprentices and 48.8% of the GDP in 2000 (IfM, 2007).

Since the beginning of the new millennium, there is a clear focus on two issues of SME support in Germany: they concern the innovative power of SMEs and the creation of high-tech start-ups, which became part of the politic agenda. In accordance with the Lisbon objectives, the measures were widely targeted towards education and research, regions, and favouring start-up activities in general. Bridging the lack of Venture Capital (VC) was also a major objective.

8.1.5 An overview of public support in Germany by objective and its estimates

The total amount of public aid to companies is estimated at almost €56,000 million in 2005. These estimates are given by the German state and are published in the 'Subventionsbericht der Bundesregierung' (2006). This sum includes the federal and regional level. The total aid of the Federation amounts to about €22,000 million. The 'Subventionsbericht der Bundesregierung' (2006) presents a global overview of subsidy by objective in Germany (Tables 8.1 and 8.2).

The German state considers for public support both subsidies (direct financial aids in the form of effective payment) and tax reliefs. Public support concentrates on specific benefits for private enterprises and industries. This means that it does not include aids to state-owned enterprises or semi-public institutions. A more critical distinction might be the public funding of research: the German state does not consider funds for basic research as public support since a priori its possible application does not specifically favour a given private enterprise or

Table 8.1 Total aids of the Federation (in €thousand million) in 2006

	Total	%
Industry support	11.3	50
Housing	5.3	24
Other tax relief	1.8	8
Aid for private savings and wealth creation	1.7	8
Transport	1.2	5
Agriculture & consumer protection	1.2	5
Total	22.4	100

Source: Subventionsbericht der Bundesregierung (2006).

Table 8.2 Industry support of the Federation (in €million) in 2006

	Total	Financial aid	Tax relief	%
Industry support (General)	7.821	432[a]	7.389[b,c]	69
Coal industry	1.719	1.708	11	15
Regional objectives	1.104	486	618	10
R&D grants	313	313[d]	–	3
Energy saving	229	228	1	2
Other sectoral aid	82	82	–	1
Total	11.269	3.250	8.019	100

[a] €424 million that is almost the entire sum of financial aids are directed to SMEs.
[b] €480 million of the tax relief benefits SMEs.
[c] €1.5,000 million of the tax relief concerns support for biological fuel.
[d] €310million that is almost the entire sum specifically targets SMEs.

Source: Subventionsbericht der Bundesregierung (2006).

sector. The distinction is, however, somewhat discretionary: application or sector-oriented non-private research institutions that play a major role in Germany are therefore excluded from the official public support statistics. Institutes such as the Frauenhofer, Max Planck, Leibnitz, and Helmholtz are not counted even if active in research fields such as atomic energy, aerospace, and the environment. Max Planck has a yearly budget of about €1.4,000 million of which more than 80% is financed by the Federation and the Länder; the Fraunhofer Gesellschaft has a budget of about €1.1,000 million of which 50% is financed by the state; Leibnitz has a budget of €1.1,000 million of which about 70% of public financing and the Helmholtz Gesellschaft receives 70% of its €2.3,000 million from the Federation and the Länder. The Kieler Subventionsbericht, which is also a highly regarded source in Germany, arrives at very different estimates. The total amount reaches about €110,000 million (Boos and Rosenschon, 2006). In addition to different interpretations, the Kieler Subventionsbericht includes measures that are not contained in the Subventionsbericht der Bundesregierung such as public support of the agency for employment mainly through wage subsidies in the case of hiring, part of the aids to the education system. In addition, the Kieler Subventionsbericht includes measures such as the support to hospitals, theatres, the Church, and so forth. Most importantly, it includes the municipalities. As a consequence, the financial aids of the Federation become less than one-third of the total aids. If one considers the total public support according to the Kieler Subventionsbericht, the total amount in 2004 was about €146,000 million by excluding the support to public or semi-public institutions, we arrive at a sum of about €110,000 million that includes the Federation, the Länder and the municipalities on the actor side and both financial aids and tax relief (Boos and Rosenschon, 2006).

A critical issue in interpreting the public support is the appropriate use of the data, which partially depends also on the access to the data and the quality of the data. In the German federal system, the Federation, the Länder (the regions), and the municipalities have different weights than in other countries. The role of the Länder and the municipalities is particularly important but not for all possible means and instruments (Sachverständigenrat, 2006). We will follow the data published by the official institutions.

The above figures do not particularly reveal the objective of fostering the 'New Länder' nor the support for SMEs. The German reporting system is objective-driven and not regionally based; the federal statistics therefore do not reveal to which particular regions these aids were directed. In addition, the federal statistics do not account for the specific measures of the Länder and the equalization system, as will be explained in the section about actors. Most of the items of regional objectives concern the 'New Länder' as well as many items in general industry support.

As stated in the footnotes, the SME support is not obvious in the official statistics but the individual items of the 'Subventionsbericht der Bundesregierung' (2006) lead to the following results shown in Table 8.3 (see also footnotes 1, 2, 4 of Table 8.2):

Table 8.3 SME support in (€million) 2006

Total	Financial aids	Tax relief
1.214	734	480

Source: Based on data from Subventionsbericht der Bundesregierung (2006).

This global sum of SME support accounts for 10% of total industry support and, excluding the specific aid to coal, amounts to about 15% of general industry support. Most of the remaining measures in industry support are targeted towards all companies with only a few items specifically targeted to large firms.

The R&D grants seem to be rather small; it should, however, be noted, that the financial aids listed do not contain any contribution to the general education system (including higher education such as universities). Basic research is therefore also excluded (which is usually undertaken at universities). Also excluded are financial aids to non-university institutions such as the Max Planck or the Fraunhofer Gesellschaft that are important actors for research and development (e.g. the mp3-format was originally developed at the Fraunhofer Gesellschaft) as well as for technology transfer.

8.2 Actors

8.2.1 The role of Bund (federal government/state) and Länder (regions)

The particularities of the Germany industrial policy are linked to the particularities of the federalism that favours strong regions (Länder). The basic (theoretical) rule is that the Federation and the Länder 'shall be autonomous and independent of each other in their budget management', but that they shall on the other hand 'have due regard...to the requirements of overall economic equilibrium' (Article 109/1-2 of the Constitution). Rights and responsibilities are divided between the Federation and the Länder even if more and more rights are allocated at the federal level. However, the Länder have strong authority in matters of education, research and development, and regional industrial policy. Germany's tax revenues are divided between the Federation, the Länder, and local authorities according to a mixed system of both separate and shared taxes. Shared taxes are the most important ones and comprise income and corporation taxes (amounting to approx.

45% of all revenue), which are shared equally between the Federation and the Länder. Most important for the working of the federal system is the role of the shared VAT. VAT revenue is approximately shared 55% to 45% between the Federation and the Länder. The ratio is subject to biannual negotiations. In addition, there is a very complicated system of financial equalization (Finanzausgleich): one important function is reallocation of funds between the Länder themselves. Similar to the EU equalization system, there are net contributors and net receivers. Payments from net contributors amounted in 2005 to €6.9,000 million. While the financial equalization could be seen as a measure of regional aids, it does not figure completely in the official statistics. In addition to the financial equalization system, the Federation grants additional funds to particularly underdeveloped regions, which was mainly the case for the new Länder. Table 8.4 illustrates the financial equalization system.

The revenues of the Länder and the aids of the Länder to industry are merged in the national and international statistics. However, 60% of all aids derive from the Länder that spend these aids on the regional level. Of the €15,000 million of German public support to the industry

Table 8.4 The financial equalization system between the Länder (in €million)

Land	1990	1995	2000	2005
Baden-Württemberg	−1.264	−1.433	−1.957	−2.209
Bayern	−18	−1.295	−1.884	−2.219
Brandenburg[a]		442	644	581
Hessen	−739	−1.101	−2.734	−1.593
Mecklenburg – Vorpommern[a]		394	500	428
Niedersachsen	985	231	568	359
NRW	−32	−1.763	−1.141	−487
Rheinland-Pfalz	250	117	117	292
Saarland	187	92	167	112
Sachsen[a]		907	1.182	1.007
Sachsen-Anhalt[a]		574	711	580
Schleswig-Holstein	308	−72	185	145
Thüringen[a]		521	670	573
Berlin[a]		2.159	2.812	2.441
Bremen	327	287	442	366
Hamburg	−4	−60	−556	−377
Total equalization volume	2.057	5.724	8.273	6.885

[a] New Länder; positive values indicate funds received, negative values funds given.
Source: Statistisches Bundesamt, Statistisches Jahrbuch 2006.

only €6,000 million come from the Federation and are truly part of the industrial policy of Germany while €9,000 million are funds of the Länder.

Despite the equalization system, there are striking differences between the Länder in terms of economic growth, unemployment rates, public debt, and investments, which reinforce themselves.

The Figures (8.1, 8.2 and 8.3) illustrate these differences.

In essence, the Länder are a powerful engine for economic development. The Federation plays only a partial role in public support of the industry. Strong differences in revenues and industrial policy between the Länder partially explain the regional economic development and additional funds provided by the Federation to the Länder. The complex system also means that the interpretation of Germany's industrial support policies is highly complicated.

8.2.2 The role of the municipalities

The municipalities in Germany seem to play a decisive role in public support in Germany. The Kieler Subventionsbericht that disaggregates only the financial aids between the Federation on one hand and the Länder together with the municipalities on the other estimated that

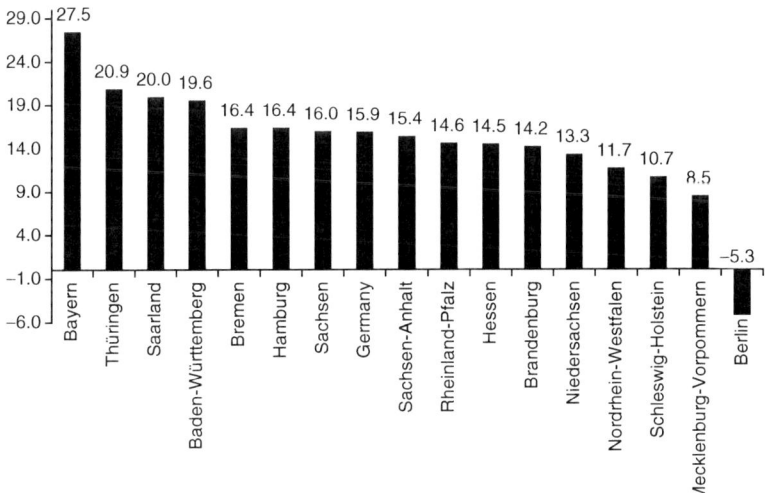

Figure 8.1 Economic growth in the Länder (in %)
Source: BSF 2007.

124 Industrial Policy in Europe, Japan and the USA

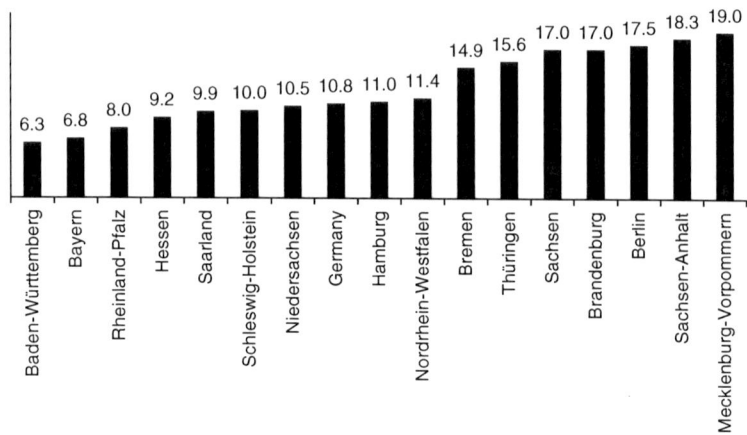

Figure 8.2 Unemployment rate in the Länder in 2006 (in %)
Source: BSF 2007.

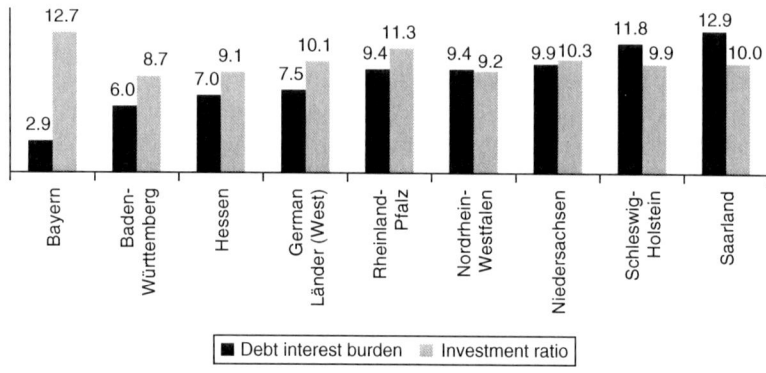

Figure 8.3 Debt interest burden and investment ratio of the Länder in 2006 (in %)
Source: BSF 2007.

the financial aids of the Federation accounted in 2005 for about €25,000 million while the Länder and municipalities accounted for about €57,000 million (Boos and Rosenschon, 2006). Unfortunately, the data at municipality level is not especially transparent (Sachverständigenrat, 2006). If we apply the 40–60 split that emerges from the Subventionsbericht der Bundesregierung to the data of Boos and Rosenschon, then this split would lead to remaining financial aids coming from the municipalities of about €20,000 million. In this sense, the relative power of the Federation to implement an effective support policy or even to establish a support agenda seems to be somewhat limited.

8.2.3 The particular role of the banking sector

Concerning public aid, the banking sector in Germany is also significant. Besides the Federal Bank (Deutsche Bundesbank), there are also state-owned Landesbanken (regional banks). In addition, the Kreditanstalt für Wiederaufbau (KfW) – the former bank for the rebuilding of Germany – that is owned by the Federation (80%) and the Länder (20%) plays an important role. The KfW has been managing the ERP (European Recovery Plan) funds of the Marshall Plan. With the partial debt remission by the United States, these funds are used almost exclusively for the support of SMEs.

8.2.4 Innovation and SME policy

In Germany, clear attempts are being made to reduce the complexity of public support for innovation and SMEs. The main actors are the Federal Ministry for Education and Research (BMBF) and the Federal Ministry for Economics and Technology (BMWi) on the federal level, the corresponding ministries on the regional level, and the public bank and VC sector. The federal ministries work closely together as do the federal and the Länder ministries. The different ministries usually publish all relevant information, for instance, publishing their own activities as well as the activities of the other ministries on the federal and regional level. There is a relatively small number of actors involved since the ministries directly promote the support programmes. In a worst-case scenario, an entrepreneur would deal with four institutions: the Federal Ministry, the Regional Ministry, the Regional Public bank or VC institution, and the KfW. However, programmes are usually organized in concert between the federal, the regional level, and the finance sector.

8.3 Instruments

The total amount of public aid to companies is estimated at nearly €56,000 million in 2005 (excluding soft loans). The following table shows the development between 2000 and 2005. The figures include tax reliefs and ERP financial aids. Since tax reliefs accrue to all firms, they are usually not included in the European statistics. ERP financial aids

Table 8.5 Total aids by instrument and source (in €thousand million)

	1990	1995	2000	2001	2002	2003	2004	2005
1. Financial Aid								
Federation	7.3	9.4	10.1	9.5	8.1	7.5	6.7	6.0
Länder	7.2	10.7	11.2	11.1	10.5	10.4	10.1	9.9
Communities	1.1	1.5	1.6	1.6	1.5	1.5	1.5	1.4
2. Tax reliefs								
Federation	7.9	9.1	13.1	13.3	14.3	16.4	17.0	17.0
Länder & communities	9.2	12.9	12.0	10.5	10.6	12.2	12.0	11.5
3. ERP aid	2.9	5.9	5.7	4.3	3.2	2.4	2.5	3.2
4. EU	4.9	5.4	5.6	5.9	6.2	5.9	6.0	6.5
Total	40.5	54.9	59.3	56.2	54.4	56.3	55.8	55.5

Source: Bundesregierung Subventionsbericht, 2006.

can be financial subsidies, interest-free grants or subsidies for R&D. The ERP financial aids are extraordinary funds that derive originally from the Marshall Plan for German recovery after the Second World War. These funds are exclusively directed towards SMEs. They amounted to €3.2,000 million in 2005.

The Subventionsbericht of the Bundesregierung (2006) presents a breakdown of aid by type of instrument, as shown in Table 8.5.

Table 8.5 also shows a steady decline of the federal subsidies from €10,000 million in 2000 to €6,000 million in 2005.

Table 8.6 lists the top ten aid mechanisms in 2006, ranked in descending order of budgetary cost. They only include aid mechanisms of the Federation.

These ten mechanisms alone represented 74% of total federal state-funded aid in 2006. Four out of the ten items concern transfers to households and individuals and can therefore be considered only an indirect support. The most important item is, for example, the home owner's allowance. The effects on the housing sector are therefore mainly achieved through stimulation of 'consumption'. The heavy impact of the energy policy also emerges from the statistics. Four out of the five most important items can be considered environmental issues. It is interesting to note that large parts of this support are actually counter-measures to the ecological fuel tax introduced by the Schröder government: they concern various tax reliefs from these very energy taxes.

Two main issues emerge from these statistics. First, tax reliefs increase and financial aids decrease. Tax reliefs have become the preferred instrument in public support policy. Second, most of the tax reliefs are linked

Table 8.6 Aid mechanisms, ranked in descending order of budgetary cost (Federation)

	Billion
Home owner's allowance, incl. ecological allowance (**Tax relief**)	€3.9
Energy tax reliefs for firms (**Tax relief**)	€3.6
Financial aids to the coal and steel industry	€1.6
Mineral oil tax reliefs for firms (**Tax relief**)	€1.5
Support for biological fuel (**Tax relief**)	€1.4
Tax exemption for capital gains (**Tax relief**)	€0.9
The reduced VAT rate for cultural entertainment services (**Tax relief**)	€0.7
Tax relief on salary supplements (work on Sundays, holidays, night) (**Tax relief**)	€0.7
The reduced VAT rate for local public transport (**Tax relief**)	€0.6
Premiums of the housing programme	€0.5
Total Top-10	€15.4

Source: Bundesregierung Subventionsbericht, 2006.

to renewable and fired energies. However, there are still doubts regarding the effectiveness of these measures given that some of the tax reliefs are countermeasures to tax increases for the same energy sources.

In general, state monopolies and tariff monopolies cannot be considered as industry support. In an era of decreasing state monopolies through deregulation and privatization, tariff monopolies, or minimum wages for specific industries can benefit specific firms and reduce the entry of new competitors. The recent discussion of minimum wages in the postal service industry and the reaction of the potential competitors show how the minimum wage could protect the former monopolists to the detriment of consumers.

8.4 Industry sector and structure

Table 8.7 presents the breakdown of support to particular industries. The figures presented are, however, misleading since in the cases of transport and home building they do not perfectly account for sectoral aid in the sense of sector support. The measures for housing are very broad and include renovation, new house building, as well as social aid for individuals with little effect on the sector. Most of the aid in transport is tax reliefs, which concern mainly fuel tax exemptions for public transport, aviation and shipping. Part of these tax reliefs is used to exempt enterprises that would be particularly concerned by ecological

Table 8.7 Total aids of the Federation (in €million) in 2006

	Total
Housing	5,258
Transport	1,155
Agriculture & consumer protection	1,169
Coal industry	1,719
Ship building	47
Aeronautics	35

Source: Data from Subventionsbericht der Bundesregierung, 2006.

fuel tax. The financial support for transport amounts to about €60 million and is exclusively dedicated to training measures in the shipping industry. The benefits for aviation and shipping concern fuel consumption on German ground independent of nationality and cannot be considered as sector support. For aviation the tax relief amounts to about €400 million and for shipping to about €130 million.

The overall picture is a policy of horizontal aids, with the exception of the coal industry. For decades, there has been public support for the coal industry to maintain employment as a social measure. During the 1990s, the public support doubled, but employment went down by a half. If employment is the goal, then the per capita spending for the 38,000 coal workers amounts to about €60,000. Extracting one ton of coal in Germany costs €160 compared with €60 on the world markets (Bund der Steuerzahler, 2007). It should, however, be noted that Germany intends to phase out production subsidies for coal by 2017.

8.5 Public sector structure and public procurement

In Germany, at the end of 2006, the state had important direct holdings (defined as more than 25%) in 33 enterprises and overall participations in 112 firms. These figures had been constantly declining since 1991 when the state had 214 holdings (of which 136 large ones). One interesting fact is the reduction of the holding in the Deutsche Telekom under 25% and of the Deutsche Post under 40% by 2006. These figures do not account for the holdings of the Länder and the municipalities, for which the statistics are insufficient (Mühlenkamp, 2003), even if there is a general trend towards increasing privatization.

In any case, state participation cannot be considered as a strong measure of industrial policy, but the contrary might be the case for the last

15 years. The Länder in particular were using the receipts from reducing their participation as a policy measure. The Land of Bavaria has estimated receipts of about €10,000 million from privatizations between 1992 and 2007. About half of it had been used for venture capital and public support for innovation and the economy in general (Bayrische Staatsregierung, 2007).

As poor as the statistics are at regional level are for public participation in private enterprises, the above example of Bavaria shows that the regions might play a similar major role in public participation as for public support in general. The most recent case concerning a possible takeover of Volkswagen (VW) highlighted also this position; it was the Land and not the Federation that held the participation in the firm. Unfortunately, the lack of data does not allow for an appropriate analysis (Mühelnkamp, 2003).

It is clear that public procurement, like public support policy, is likely to be conditional on the importance of the public sector. Public procurement in Germany is organized under the supervision of the Ministry of the Economy and Labour. The Federal Ministry of Economics and Labour is responsible for the principles, regulations, and laws regarding public procurement. Figure 8.4 presents the major organization of public procurement in Germany.

Three Federal Public Procurement Regulations detail the procedures of public procurement. These regulations are binding at federal and regional level. The selection of the suppliers remains, however, the only responsibility of each public organization. One important factor for efficient public procurement is competition. Competition is a function of access to calls for tenders. Germany has been increasing its electronic commerce activities. On the one hand, public procurement has moved on an electronic platform (e-procurement), on the other, there are attempts to centralize: an electronic shop has been created from which different public organizations can buy online. The move to e-procurement and commerce as a form of innovation aims at economies in the public procurement.

The figures presented account only for the published public procurement according to EU principles, which remain the most reliable statistics for public procurement. Concerning the overall public procurement, the German system (partially due to its decentralized organization) is not very transparent. Public procurement in Germany was estimated at €360,000 million which represents €17 % of the BIP. Germany is one of the countries with the lowest publication rate in public procurement (Sachverständigenrat, 2006) (see Tables 8.8 and 8.9).

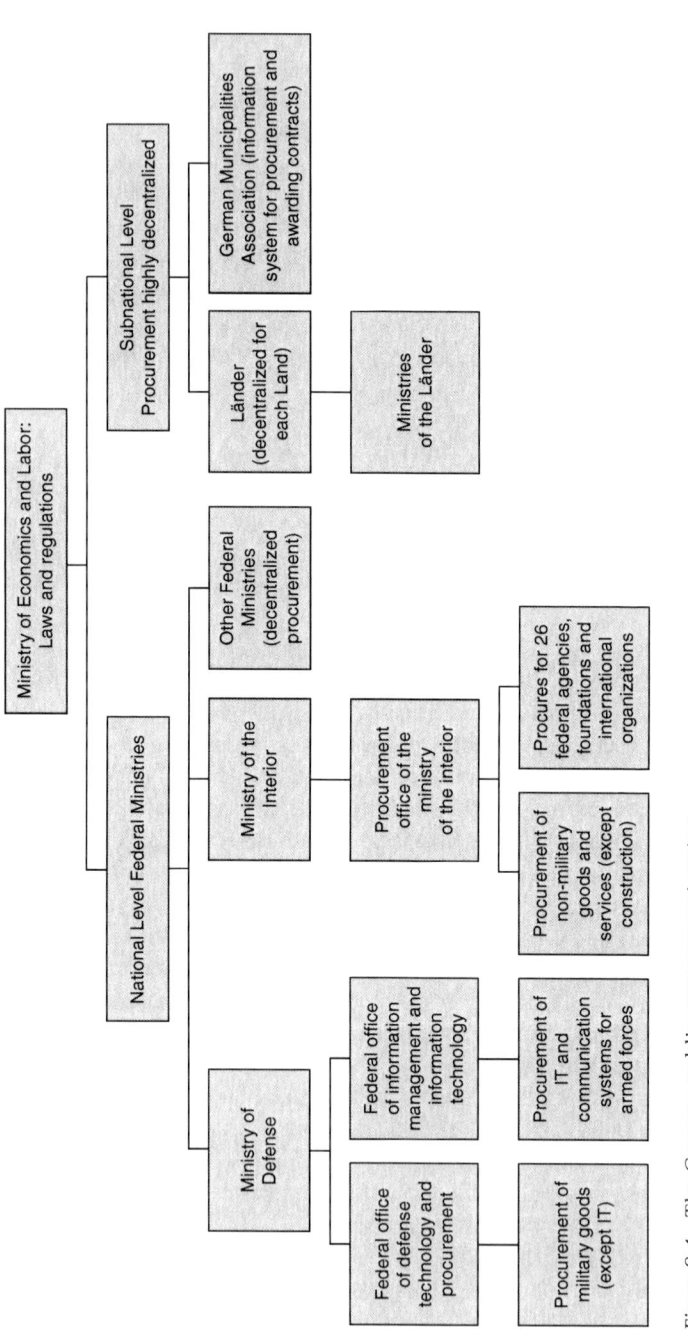

Figure 8.4 The German public procurement system
Source: http://www.bescha.de

Table 8.8 Public procurement in Germany in 2005

(in million €)	Federation	Länder	Total
Supplies			
under threshold value	1,308	NA	
over threshold value	1,459	1,482	2,941
Services			
under threshold value	605	NA	
over threshold value	966	2,463	3,429
Construction			
under threshold value	1,308	NA	
over threshold value	1,459	2,672	4,131
Total	7,105	6,617	13,722

Source: BMWi, 2007 – EU-Vergabe-Statistik.

Table 8.9 Federation public procurement in 2005

Most important actors	(in €million)
Ministry for Education and Research	84
Independent research institutes	226
Ministry of internal affairs	235
Finance Ministry	409
Employment Agency	442
Ministry for Transport, Construction and Urban Development	1,724
Defence	1,821

Source: BMWi, 2007 – EU-Vergabe-Statistik.

Again, the data is very poor at regional and local level. If we assume the same split between the Federation and the regions together with the municipalities (1/3 to 2/3), we can only make the hypothesis that the municipalities in particular play a major role in the promotion of local enterprises.

In general the objective of public procurement in Germany is economic efficiency. The inclusion of other objectives is subject to debate since they may be in conflict with the cost-efficiency goal. With the exception of transport, construction, urban development, and defence, there are no major procurement actors. The defence budget, is, however, minimal compared to that of France and cannot be considered a major driver for innovation or other possible objectives.

Two objectives of German procurement are regularly cited in Germany: environmental concerns and support to SMEs. Environmental concerns can be included in calls for tenders in order to favour environmental friendly enterprises: call for tenders can prescribe the usages of certain materials, accept only companies that were awarded environment protecting quality labels, and similar. About 30% of calls for tenders in Germany include environmental criteria (Sachverständigenrat, 2006). One of the arguments for the inclusion of environmental criteria is that the state should internalize part of the negative external effects. Another argument is the stimulation of environmentally friendly technology. To what extend this objective can be better obtained through public procurement is difficult to measure.

The support of SMEs through public procurement is also difficult to estimate. The state aims to facilitate access to calls for tenders by creating electronic platforms, introduce reforms to simplify the tender processes, and present recommendations to split larger procurement in smaller work packages that are accessible for SMEs.

8.6 Evaluation and efficiency of instruments

8.6.1 The strange situation of SME funding and support

- According to EU statistics, SMEs receive only 3% of total public aid, which translates into less than €500 million in clear contradiction to governments' declared political priority. The majority of aid benefits all companies, irrespective of their sector or size. Given the importance of the Mittelstand in Germany and a priority act passed in 2004, general aids should be of greater benefit to SMEs. However, as already noted, specific measures for SMEs within general industry support account for more than €1,200 million.
- SME aid does not account for the different size definition of the Mittelstand in the German understanding).
- Support for SMEs does not include the €3.2,000 million of ERP financial aids that are directed to SMEs (European definition).
- In the past the various Länder had created some form of VC firms (Beteiligungsgesellschaften) in order to fill the VC gap in Germany. These firms co-invest in the case of the presence of a professional VC lead investor. For example the Bavarian Kapitalbeteiligungsgesellschaft (BayBG) had an active investment portfolio of about €270 million and new investments of €40 million in 2005. The total amount of

Länder VC is unknown but can be conservatively estimated at €200 million for Germany. In addition the Federation had also created a VC fund with the KfW-Bank, not included in the official aids. This fund had invested about €250 million in 2000.
- In addition, there are a series of soft loan programmes that are not included in the official statistics. In 2006, the KfW had given about €6,000 million of soft loans to SMEs (entrepreneurs' credits).
- As a consequence, the support of SME's in Germany is supposed to be much higher than shown in official figures. If we include soft loans, public VC, and the official aids, the support to SMEs can be estimated at about €10.9,000 million.

8.6.2 Fostering the spirit of enterprise

The aim of fostering the spirit of enterprise is implemented on four levels: education, financing, innovation, and cluster development. Starting at the end of the 1990s, a series of measures was undertaken to foster the entrepreneurial spirit and favour spin-offs from universities. About 25 entrepreneurship chairs had been founded at German universities since 2000. The Exist programme launched by the Ministry of Education and Research (BMBF) initially awarded five regions, with specific support to enable high-tech start-ups from universities. Private and public business plan competitions spread throughout the country.

SME support in Germany is focused on innovation and technology. As stated before, R&D grants are almost exclusively directed towards SMEs. The names of specific programmes signal also this focus, for example, 'High-Tech Offensive'.

In terms of financing, as already mentioned, Germany put in place a 'mosaic financing' to overcome a lack of VC financing. A classical co-financed deal consisted of a private VC lead investor, the KfW as co-investor and a Landes-KBG as additional co-investor. This model went well until 2000 when the Internet bubble drained VC funding, and not only in Germany. Germany was particularly hit by the withdrawal of private VC from seed and to a lesser extent from early-stage financing. The following figures (8.5, 8.6 and 8.7) illustrate this phenomenon.

As a consequence, the KfW through the initiative of the Federation, created a new ERP start-up fund to cover the seed financing gap in 2005. In 2006, already €250 million had been invested to which additional co-financing of the Landes-KBG needs to be added. In addition, there are soft loans and specific support for innovative SMEs (ERP).

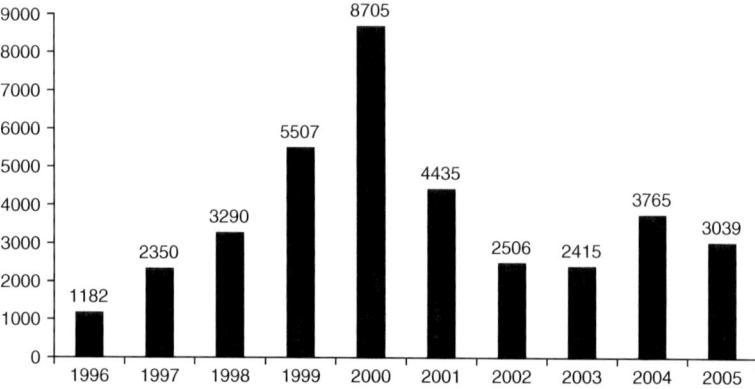

Figure 8.5 Total private 'private equity' in Germany (in € million)
Source: BVK, 2006.

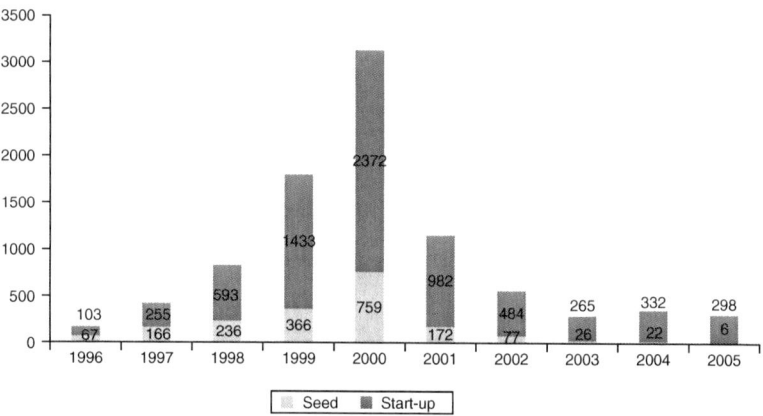

Figure 8.6 Seed and start-up financing provided by private 'private equity' firms (in € mio)
Source: BVK, 2006.

Another important instrument for entrepreneurship was the general goal of favouring cluster development. A series of regional competitions for centres of excellence had been organized by the BMBF such as BioRegio (first started in 1995) and, subsequently, the more general InnoRegio. The idea of these competitions was to bring together firms, institutions, research, and VC in order to strengthen regional clusters.

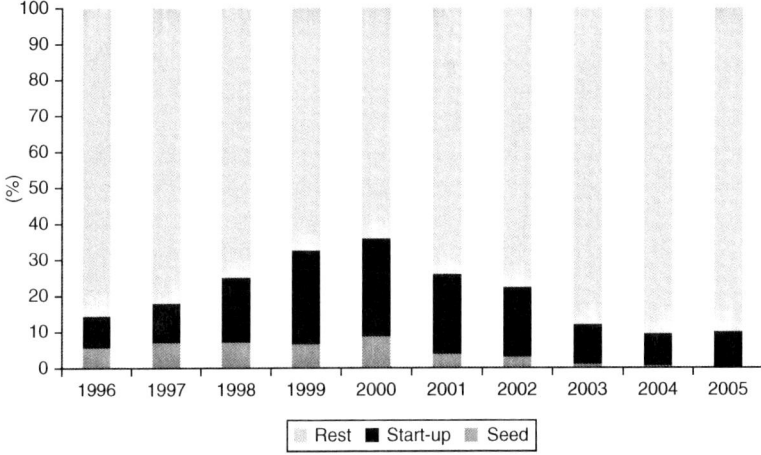

Figure 8.7 Seed and start-up financing vs all remaining private 'private equity'
Source: BVK, 2006.

While the statistics show relatively little support for SMEs, most measures are actually targeted on SMEs. As already stated, a large part of the financial support is not integrated in these statistics but it is also true that many measures aim at facilitating entrepreneurship without excessive spending. The latest programme of the Federation for fostering entrepreneurship comprises the following goals: reducing bureaucracy for starting and managing SMEs, strengthening the innovative power of SMEs, improving education, attracting SME financing, and creating a favourable environment by reducing the tax burden for SMEs (Bundesregierung, 2006).

The overall results of these activities, however, have been mixed. The GEM (Global Entrepreneurship Monitor) that traces entrepreneurial activity in many countries shows that the start-up rate in Germany has been decreasing constantly since 2000 (Bosma and Harding, 2006). While Germany was, compared with other industrial countries, still a rather entrepreneurial country, it had fallen behind France by 2006, which was traditionally a low entrepreneurship country. Even if the actual start-up activities are low, Germany remains a country with relatively high business ownership (Bosma and Harding, 2006).

8.6.3 Eastern Germany remains a problem

The New Länder remain the problem children of the nation with an unemployment rate of 18%. Given these figures the effectiveness of public support can be highly questioned. While part of the support to stimulate competitiveness of the firms might be considered rather ineffective, the major part of support to the New Länder was a necessity to allow for decent economic conditions and social measures. The ineffectiveness of the transfer payments to the New Länder can be summarized in the following way. Most of the transfers were directed to spending. In 2003, about 45% of the support was spent on unemployment benefits and pensions. About 20% was undirected support via the equalization system between the Länder, which did not necessarily have to be spent in public support. Public investment and support to companies accounted for only about 20% (Jansen, 2004). Moreover, the initial productivity differences combined with increasing wage convergence inevitably made investments in the New Länder less effective (Jansen, 2004).

Development in basic infrastructure (roads, railways, and telecom) is a precondition for economic development; some inherited problems needed to be internalized by the German state and could not be avoided because there was no market for these types of problems: pollution of the soil sometimes combined with the necessary closure of firms is one example. It is therefore also difficult to measure to what extent the support to New Länder could have been reduced (Boss and Rosenschon, 2006).

8.6.4 Reforms do not go far enough

The reports of the German Council of Economic Experts (Sachverständigenrat, 2006) were very critical about Germany's policy. The German Council of Economic Experts advises the German Government and Parliament on economic policy. The independent academic body was set up by law in 1963 with a mandate to periodically assess overall economic developments and to inform policymakers and the general public. Its main instrument is the publishing of an annual report. By reviewing the policy in the 1990s, the experts criticized the continuous failure to address employment problems, consolidation of the state's finances, and the lack of an effective tax reform for enterprises. A major problem of the German tax system was, according to the experts, the difficult distinction between the entrepreneur (as owner) and the enterprise in an economy in which SMEs (Mittelstand) a dominant factor (Sachverständigenrat, 2000). At the beginning of

2000, the experts saw a strong necessity for broad reforms concerning industrial policy, R&D, and the tax system. They criticized the lack of effort to create more competition between universities. The following years up to 2003 were characterized by a weak German economy, rising unemployment, and increasing state debt. To deal with the rising problems, the experts required substantial changes in Germany's policy and requested among other things to further cut taxes, to heavily reduce the state's share of more than 50% in 2003, and to shift public expenses towards investments, to reduce public debt, to create more flexibility in the labour market (Sachverständigenrat, 2003). The 2006 report is titled 'Missed Opportunities'. While the experts see some positive trends on the labour market and welcome the decreasing state share (down to 47%), they focus on the increasing problem of long-term unemployment (51.8% of total unemployment) and the high unemployment rate of low-skilled labour (20.5%) at a general unemployment rate of 9.5%. The respective figures for France are 41.6% (long-term unemployment), 12.1% (unemployment rate of low-skilled labour) and 9.6% (general unemployment rate) and, for the United Kingdom, 21.4%, 6.6%, and 4.7%. The experts take a rather positive view of the measures undertaken to favour entrepreneurship (Sachverständigenrat, 2006).

8.7 Conclusion

German reunification has without doubt had a major impact on public support in Germany. While most European countries reduced the amount of their public support, Germany witnessed an increase of total public industry support from about €40,000 million in 1990 to about €55,000 million in 2005.

A major shift in public support occurred during the 1990s: Germany has heavily emphasized a green energy policy. Support increased from about 3% in 1995 to 47% in 2005. The lack of natural resources as well as the decision to phase out nuclear energy are at the heart of the country's energy policy.

The German support system is a logical consequence of the German political system. The federal system with a division of competences between the Federation and the Länder, strong competences of the Länder and an equalization principle between the Länder leads to a coordinated but decentralized system. As a consequence, the German support system is highly decentralized, with the great majority of public support coming from the Länder. The support to industries is mainly regionalized.

As a result, the potential of industry support depends more on the regional policies and the regional situation of the Länder than on the Federation. In Germany, there are strong differences in terms of entrepreneurship, innovation, and amount of support to companies.

In this sense, the potential of a centralized public support policy driven by the Federation appears to be limited. In Germany, public support is strongly driven by the Länder that often act in concert with the municipalities. They are responsible for the majority of funding for public support to business.

The question as to whether federalism eventually leads to more or less subsidy can not be answered. Regional interests to foster public support are, however, mitigated by the German equalization system.

In any case, federalism will negatively affect the support for national champions since public support is mainly realized at the regional level. Potential state intervention is most likely at the regional level and the intervention of the Federation to promote national champions through public support appears to be limited.

Overall, there is a relatively small number of actors involved in public support. While it is difficult to obtain and effectively interpret the data, access to public support is rather transparent. Over the past 5 years, there has been a series of attempts to facilitate access to public support. E-procurement, the reduction of the complexity of calls for tender procedures, one-stop-shop solutions for firm creation, and cross-publications of available funds at the different ministries are a few examples.

The most important regional support has been directed towards the New Länder. These have a strong negative impact on the German economy and employment status, with an unemployment as high as 18%. Given the figures, the effectiveness of public support is highly questionable. Reasons for the ineffectiveness of public support to the New Länder are: wage convergence but different productivity levels, most of the support spent on consumption and only a small fraction of total support effectively spend on public investment and company support.

While part of the support to stimulate competitiveness of the firms might be considered ineffective, the major part of support to the New Länder was a necessity to allow for decent economic conditions and social measures.

More than half of sector-specific support goes to agriculture, coal, transport, and housing, while the value creation of these sectors compared to the whole industry is very low. There are few incentives to reduce support for agriculture given the European Funding (Boss and Rosenschon, 2006). There is, however, some agreement that the strong support for housing is not justified (Boss and Rosenschon, 2006; Sachverständigenrat, 2006). The support to the coal (and mining) sector is hotly disputed; while little effective it is considered rather a social measure for employment preservation even if the jobs were halved during the 1990s. Basically all German governments retained the support as necessary. The coal and mining sector in Western Germany is highly concentrated in one of the most densely populated areas, which was the early engine of industrial development; thus the region is strongly based on heavy industries. It may, however, be argued that both the federal and the regional policies have missed the opportunity for structural changes.

Overall, German's support policy is largely focused on horizontal measures that benefit firms most. Specific sectors are hardly fostered.

Participation of the state in enterprises is difficult to judge. The only reliable statistical sources are those of the Federation. Given the decentralized nature of Germany, these figures might be misleading. It seems, however, that state participation has lost its strategic importance. Since the late 1990s, it seems rather that the receipts from the reduction of firm participation by the state are used to increase other forms of public support.

Germany is among the leading innovators in the EU. There are few market failures among the innovation activities of the large firms; public support for innovation is almost exclusively directed towards the SMEs.

Support for start-ups and existing SMEs, while not emerging from the general statistics, is quite important and remains a historical objective of public support. The total support to SMEs can be estimated at almost €11,000 million. While experts make positive evaluations on the entrepreneurship support, the results since 2000 are still modest.

9
Public Support in France

Since the late 1990s, industrial policy has remained a very sensitive issue in France and has been very much present in economic and political debate, despite the fall in the volume of funding. Thus, the Economic Analysis Council set up by Prime Minister Lionel Jospin in July 1997 to provide decision support for the government on economic issues, devoted one of its first reports to 'industrial policy' (Cohen and Lorenzi, 2000). The report came in the wake of the recognition that Europe had fallen behind the United States in terms of R&D, innovation (number of patents), and industrial renewal, and it was produced in the perspective of the main Lisbon Summit resolution, to make Europe 'the most competitive and dynamic knowledge economy in the world'. This report highlighted, within a historical perspective, certain specificities of French industrial policy.

The heart of French industrial policy lies in the public sector, 'national champions', where the state can take action in its role of shareholder, regulator, and strategist. The big French government projects, focused on investment programmes in the infrastructure and energy sectors (railway transportation, telephony, nuclear energy), were borne by the national champions (powerful operators such as EDF, Gaz de France, AREVA, and France Télécom); these projects constituted an important level of French industrial policy.[1] Moreover, when mergers and acquisitions take place, the role of the state in a country with a mixed economy can be very significant.

The 'grands projects' were the core of industrial policy and certain of them were considered to be successful as the nuclear 'grand project' launched in 1969, the high-speed railway 'grand project' launched in 1976, and the telecommunications 'grand project' launched in 1974. These 'grand projects' implied a huge procurement policy aimed at serving the national market. Other 'grand projects' led to major failures as the 'plan calcul' (Cohen, 2006). This high-tech Colbertism French model ends in the mid-1980s with the financial constraints, well described in the OECD report focused on public support in France at the end of the 1980s, beginning of the 1990s.

This report on the specific characteristics of public support for industry in France was published by the OECD in the late 1990s (OECD, 1998). The report highlighted a number of changes in industrial policy beginning in the late 1980s, changes due to economic constraints related to a high level of debt and public deficit problems. This new orientation was clearly the result of macroeconomic measures aimed at budgetary consolidation in preparation for Economic and Monetary Union (the Maastricht criteria). There was a marked decline in the amount and structure of public support for industry between 1989 and 1995. According to the OECD, the amount of public support for industry dropped from FF21.5 billion in 1989 to FF12 billion in 1995. Over this period, France was one of the three countries of the OECD members that had reduced their public support by 50%. This sharp drop in the volume of funding for public support of industry was accompanied by drastic cuts in export promotion and sectoral support, and by a reorientation of aid towards horizontal objectives (R&D, regional development). In 1989, sectoral and export aid accounted for 50.8% of public spending on industry, whereas in 1995 it represented only 21.8%. Conversely, horizontal spending in support of R&D, regional development and SMEs represented 46.6% in 1989 versus 72.9% six years later, in 1995. Another specific characteristic of public support for industry in France noted by the OECD is that of extreme centralization. Only 10% of total public spending on industry was funded by regional or local authorities, the remaining 90% being funded directly by the central government.

The report 'Politiques industrielles pour l'Europe' published after the OECD report (Cohen and Lorenzi, 2000) was pessimistic on French public support to industry. For the authors, the French vision of industrial policy, the 'Colbertist model', was concretely abandoned. The triangle formed by competition policy, trade policy, and industrial policy is seriously imbalanced, since competition policy occupies 'a dominant, almost constitutional place'. Industrial policy is only a policy of spreading funds too thinly, funds which are in any case very insufficient. The authors take up the arguments of economic theory that justify state intervention only when it is undertaken to correct market failure, or when it results in the creation of positive externalities for the whole industry. However, they consider that these principles of market failure and externalities are 'not very operational in practice'.

'Industrial policy, strictly defined, is sectoral: its aim is to promote specific sectors which, for reasons of national independence, technological autonomy, failure of private initiative, decline of traditional activities, or territorial or political balance deserve aid' (Cohen and Lorenzi, 2000).

9.1 Objectives of public support

In 2004/2005, faced with the challenges of globalization and worrying reports on the competitiveness of the French industry,[2] major changes in the approach to public support took place in France. This new approach called 'new French industrial policy' was first based on the recommendations of a report prepared at the request of the President of the French Republic by Jean-Louis Beffa (Beffa, 2005). The proposed measures had the objective to undertake a redefinition of the set of objectives, instruments, and means of public support to industry in order to create new industrial development and services to firms, anchored and sustainable within France and in sectors of high added value (Commissioning letter from the President of France, annex document Beffa, 2005).

9.1.1 Funding of major industrial innovation led by companies

The Beffa report recommended the government reorient French industrial policy towards a determined public effort at effective support of high-tech industries. This renewal of industrial policy was to be organized around the promotion by the state of long-term industrial technology programmes. The report emphasized the necessity for the public authorities to conduct a determined, proactive industrial policy 'as close as possible to industrial or *pre-competitive* development'.

Beffa proposed a partnership between private-sector companies and public authorities, in which the latter would commit to financing, in the form of subsidies and repayable advances. The partnership would enable an optimal circulation of information, and the involvement of public authorities would encourage risk-taking by the private sector companies. The programmes of aid to companies proposed in the Beffa report were meant to last from five to ten years.

A new 'Agency of Industrial Innovation' was proposed with the aim to support this project. All the missions were to be grouped together in this new structure. This French initiative to promote industrial innovation could be coordinated with similar initiatives in other EU countries. Beffa recommended a European intergovernmental framework for this new industrial policy. European cooperation projects would then be constituted, and their selection and financing would be done jointly by the countries involved.

9.1.2 Public support to powerful regional centres of competitiveness

A second pillar of the 'new French industrial policy' after the industrial innovation agency was unveiled by the French Prime Minister J. P. Raffarin in 2004: the launch of the new regional industrial policy with the announcement of the creation of 'centres of competitiveness'. The objective was to build powerful regional business clusters to improve competitiveness. Centres of competitiveness were not really a new concept since France had some limited examples of this kind, such as Cosmetic Valley in Eure-et-Loire. The 'centre of competitiveness' was defined by the Inter-ministerial Regional Planning and Development Committee (CIADT) as a 'group of businesses, training centres and research units in a given area involved in a partnership approach designed to general synergies for shared innovative projects and with the critical mass necessary for international visibility'. Competitive clusters policy is based mainly on Michael Porter's cluster theory (M. E. Porter, 1999) which has inspired many public policies to support innovation. The experience of competitive clusters in Sweden and Denmark provide indications of the advantages of the public support policies: increase in public-private research partnerships, improved dissemination, and assimilation of high technologies within industry.

9.1.3 Public support to SMEs on innovation project

The third pillar was directed towards small and medium size enterprises. The objective was to improve the economic environment of SMEs: lack of equity finance, market access, and regulatory burden. OSEO was created in December 2004 to support SME for innovation projects with a technology component and real marketing potential. To encourage small and medium businesses and industries to engage in R&D, the Minister for Economy, Finance and Industry set a goal of 25% small business participation in the programmes financed by the Agence pour l'innovation industrielle by mid-2005.

9.1.4 An overview of public support in France by objective

The total amount of public aid to companies is estimated at nearly €65 billion (4% of GDP), which is a sum significantly higher than the national education budget and double that of the defence budget. The 'Rapport sur les aides publiques aux entreprises' (2007) presents a global overview of subsidy by objective in France (Table 9.1). When we look to the amount of subsidy and public aid to enterprises by objective, a large amount of public money aims at employment, in practice reducing costs, in particular for low-skilled employees.

The total amounts of public aid focused on the 'knowledge economy' represents around only 3% of the total (R&D). Public support to SMEs (mainly investment aid and creation of firms) represents 9% of the total. Sectoral aid (mainly operating aid and public enterprises) represents 36% of the total. The majority of aid (55% of the total) benefits all companies, irrespective of their sector or size. They include, in particular, employment aid and a large part of investment aid. This investment aid includes a portion aimed at facilitating investment via share ownership, which, according to the report, almost exclusively benefits big companies.

Table 9.1 Breakdown of aid[a] by objective (€million)

	Total	%	No. of budget headings
Employment	19.303	34	14
Investment[b]	11.863	21	61
Operating aid[c]	11.670	20	51
Public enterprises[c]	6.102	11	9
Regional aid	2.596	5	34
R&D	1.926	3	45
Training	1.301	2	12
Creation of firms[b]	1.181	2	17
Environment	631	1	4
Export	56	0	5

[a] A significant share of the aid mentioned here does not correspond to the classical definition of state aid usually adopted in industrial policy discussion.
[b] SMEs are mainly subsidized via Investment aid and creation of firms.
[c] Operation aid and public enterprise are mainly sectoral aid (85% of all sectoral aid).

Source: PLF 2005.

9.2 Actors

Figure 9.1 presents clearly the different positioning of the French agencies with responsibility to provide public support to enterprises, depending on the size of projects, large versus small and the nature of research (fundamental research or research oriented towards the market). However, the Prime Minister announced in September 2007 the merger of the OSEO and Agency for Industrial Innovation, both providing funding for innovation in the private sector.

The French government put in place new structures to modernize the system of public funding for R&D and innovation. The new approach is defined as 'mobilizing programmes for industrial innovation' (MPIIs). These programmes are organized on a medium- to long-term basis to enable a sustainable contribution to the improvement of French industrial specialization. They aim to bring together private enterprises from the elaboration of the projects and correspond to an expected demand in the European and global market. Finally, the choice of sectors and products is based on economic arguments and in a way that makes possible a clear evaluation of the programme's.

The public sector is a catalyst and public procurement will be only one of the components in the creation of new demand. The MPIIs

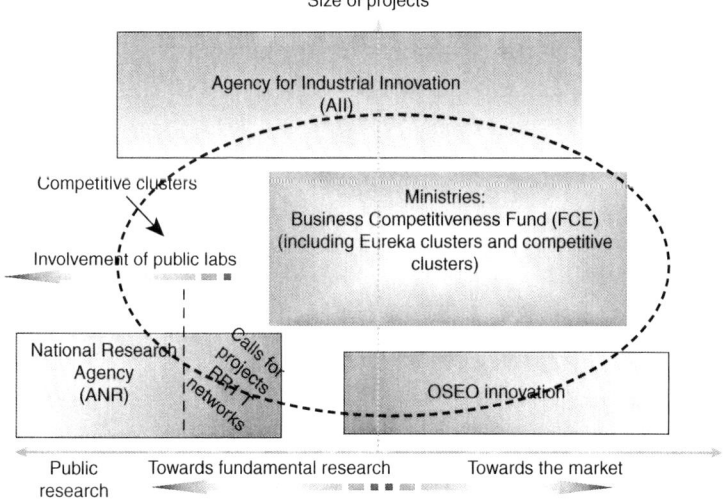

Figure 9.1 Presents the main actors of public support for R&D and SMEs in France

has to push the synergy between firms, research, and market developments. New agencies were created in 2005 for the implementation of new industrial policy.

- *Agence Nationale de la Recherche* (ANR) has a twofold mission: creating new knowledge and encouraging interactions between public and company research laboratories via partnerships. Its aim is to focus the majority of public funding on a limited number of research projects. The projects will be selected on the basis of public tendering addressed to public laboratories and enterprises laboratories. The ANR has to support enterprises and public laboratories for the most promising research fields. The budget was around €700 million in 2005.
- *Agence de l'Innovation Industrielle* (AII) had a threefold role: the definition of the MPIIs, the organization of the contractual relation between the different stakeholders and, finally, the monitoring and evaluation function. The AII is in charge of supporting, in particular, major industrial innovation programmes led by companies. The AII selects and supports projects whose aims are to design and produce new and innovative products focusing in disrupting technologies and involving technological spin-offs. In its calls for projects, the AII considers participation in a competitiveness cluster to be a positive favour in its evaluation process. The budget of AII is around €2 billion in 2005–7. The French government expects R&D investment of comparable magnitude from the industrialists participating in the project and public funding. The majority of the first PMII to be financed in 2007 were presented by a consortium with a clear leadership of a major enterprise, with the involvement of certain high-tech SMEs for a specific part of the innovation project. Public funding contributes up to 50% of the programme budget and may be a grant or repayable advance. By sharing the inherent risks of R&D, the AII aims to support the French effort necessary to couple with the Lisbon Agenda which requires for France an annual effort of €15 billion. The AII aims to support 15 to 20 different PMII per year.
- *Oseo* is the result of the combination of ANVAR and BDPME, existing French institutions. Oseo's specific remit is to support SMEs for the different critical steps of their developments through incremental innovation. Oseo's budget to support innovation is around €190 million for 2007, of which 90 million coms froma budgetary grant. A decree issued on 20 November 2007 dissolved the AII into the OSEO. This operation aims to better target financial support to SMEs and

not to change the general approach of the AII. The reasons behind such a move is that the new government research policy stressed the need to distribute public funds on the basis of R&D projects instead of traditional R&D structure and to redirect public policy on SMEs rather than large enterprises.

- *Pôles de compétitivité*: the establishment of regional competitiveness clusters is another important component of the new French approach to industrial policy The objective is for public authorities to support networks of regional industries, universities, research institutions, SMEs, that can create a dynamic competitiveness process, all the components of each *pole de compétitivité* being located in the same area. Some 66 *poles de compétitivité* are being promoted to increase regional industrial specialization in order to compete more efficiently. These clusters can be broken down into three categories: global clusters (6), clusters with global visibility (9) and national or regional clusters (51). Rhône-Alpes has 3 global clusters, 1 chemistry-environment, 1 Nanotech and 1 Biotech, Aquitaine and Midi-Pyrenées has 1 global cluster, Aerospace (see Table 9.2).

The 'Fonds de compétitivité des entreprises' (FCE) under the supervision of the Minister of Industry has launched public tendering of projects The global funding of the programme 'Pôle de compétitivité' has a total budget of €1.5 billion over three years, between 2006 and 2009. The R&D project funding of the clusters with a global dimension is presented in Table 9.3.

The number of competitive clusters is clearly excessive. The French government initially planned for only 15 clusters, changed in the end to 62 clusters. Annual funding per cluster is only 50% of what was expected.

Finally, the Ministry of Industry is responsible for deciding on the strategic industrial priorities and targeting public support towards these priorities according to technology changes and international competition. Clearly, the French system is also very centralized since 90% of this amount is provided by the state and only 10% by regional or local authorities. An inter-ministerial fund ('Fonds Unique interministériel') also finances the collaborative R&D projects carried out by competitive clusters. The objective of this fund is to support applied research products. The fund cover the 2006–8 period (€720 million) and is under the responsibility of the Ministry of Economy, Finance and Industry. The fund's contributors are the Ministries of Industry, Defence, Infrastructure, Agriculture, Health and Spatial Planning. Half

Table 9.2 Breakdown of competitiveness clusters by sector and type[a]

	Sectors concerned	Global	Global visibility	National or regional
High technology[b]	Electronics/communication	3	2	4
	Pharmaceutical industry	2	1	3
	Aerospace	1	–	–
	Scientific instruments	–	–	2
Medium–high technology[b]	Chemicals (excl. Pharm. Ind.)	–	2	2
	Electrical machinery	–	–	3
	Automobile industry	–	–	6
	Railway equipment	–	1	–
	Machinery and equipment n.e.c.	–	–	1
Medium-low technology[b]	Refined oil products and nuclear combustibles	–	–	2
	Plastic and rubber products	–	–	1
	Naval construction	–	2	–
	Processed metal mineral products	–	–	4
	Non-metallic mineral products	–	–	1
Low technology[b]	Agribusiness and food	–	1	10
	Textiles and clothing	–	–	5
	Construction	–	–	2
	Wood	–	–	1

[a] 4 competitiveness clusters are included in the service industry classification.
[b] OECD classification.

Source: FOCUS, February 2006.

Table 9.3 R&D project funding: Clusters with a global dimension

Sector concerned	Total amount of R&D investment budgeted (€m)	Funds allocated by ANR[a] in 2005[a] (€m)
Electronics/communication	1,293	84.02
Pharmaceutical industry	479	35.33
Aerospace	480	NA
Chemicals (excl. Pharm. Ind.)	240	12.35
Railway equipment	145	NA
Naval construction	240	9.65
Agribusiness and food	125	NA

[a] ANR the French National Agency for Research. The agency funds research projects and in 2005 had at its disposal a EUR 700m commitment capacity for research projects lasting for a maximum of three years.

Source: ANR, call for project documents.

the beneficiaries were small businesses who received 28% of the allocated fund from the inter-ministerial fund.

Instruments

The 'Rapport sur les aides publiques aux entreprises' (2007) presents a breakdown of aids by type of instrument, as shown in Table 9.4 below.

More precisely, when we look at aid mechanisms, ranked in descending order of budgetary costs, Table 9.5 can be referred for the top ten aid mechanisms.

Table 9.4 Public support by instrument[a]

Instrument	Amount	%
Reduction in cost of labour (employee contribution)	24.118	42
Tax aid (lowering tax paid by firms)	8.348	15
Aid to investors (incentives to invest in equity)	6.452	12
Under-taxation of sales (lower VAT rates)	6.320	11
Subsidies	6.258	11
Aid for purchase of intermediate goods (oil products for specific consumers)	4.033	7
Aid to buyers (mainly for real estate)	420	1
Repayable advances (gross amount)	406	1
Total	56.355	100

[a] Aid representing less than 1% is not reported here such as loan guarantee, lower interest rate etc.

Source: PLF 2005.

Table 9.5 Aid mechanisms, ranked in descending order of budgetary cost

Reduction in employer contributions: nearly €17 billion
Reduced VAT rate of 5.5% for certain work: €4.2 billion
Tax credit: €4 billion (mechanism now abolished)
Funding of retirement costs for the national railway (SNCF): €2.5 billion
Reduced tax rate on long-term capital gains: €1.8 billion
VAT rate of 5.5% for hotel catering : €1.5 billion
Reduced corporate tax rate: €1.4 billion
Reduced TIPP (domestic petroleum products consumption tax) for home heating oil used as fuel: €1.3 billion
TIPP exonerations for air transport : €1.3 billion
Contributions to cover railway infrastructure costs: €1.2 billion

Source: PLF, 2005.

These ten mechanisms alone represented 63% of total state-funded aid in 2005.

This global overview of the use of the different instruments has also to be analysed for each specific agency at the core of public support to industry.

- *Oseo* innovation supporting SMEs on innovation projects with a technology component and real marketing potential. Preferred instruments are repayable advance, up to a maximum rate of 50% and additional support, grants during the feasibility phase. The budget of €190 million includes €90 million from budgetary grants.
- *The agency for industrial innovation* supports large-scale, long-term R&D projects by contributing up to 50% of the programme budget in repayable advances and subsidies.
- *The competitive clusters* received in 2006, €536 million in financial support, but the breakdown of funding services is the following: OSEO (€83 m), AII (€88 m), ANR (€172 m) and inter-ministerial fund (€153 m). The funding of competitive clusters which was set at €1.5 billion over three years (2006–8) is earmarked for R&D projects. Companies in the cluster are eligible for tax breaks and subsidies from the intervention funds but local administrations may offer additional support to clusters.

In September 2007, the French Prime Minister announced also that the research tax credit for enterprises would soon be dramatically amended so as to cover 100% of research expenses. Up to September 2007, tax credit was limited to about half of these expenses. The rate was to be 30% up to €100 million and 5% beyond that.[3] The cost was expected to be €800 million in 2009 and €2.7 million after to support business in their R&D projects.

9.3 Industry sector and structure

In France, 36% of total aid is targeted to specific sectors, which is a significant amount (over €20 billion); it breaks down as illustrated in Table 9.6 below.

Some 61% of total aid is devoted to transportation and housing. Together with agriculture, the figure rises to no less than 80% of total sectoral aid. Whether such sectoral aid is useful or effective is a question the authors of the report raise, but they do not offer any answers.

Table 9.6 Sectoral aid by sector

Sector	Amount (€millions)	%
Transportation	8,140	39
Housing	4,621	22
Agriculture	3,941	20
Tourism	2,175	10
Audiovisual	703	3
Press	420	2
Aeronautics	268	1
Space	165	1
Commerce	154	1
Defence	118	1
Total	20,705	100

Source: PLF, 2005.

The Beffa report (2005) provided a clear overview of the French system of R&D public support and their sectoral and industry structure allocation. The sectors receiving the majority of R&D public support correspond to the sectors involved in large-scale programmes. Public financing of corporate R&D represented, in 2005, 45% of total R&D of enterprises in aeronautics, 32% in measurement instruments, 28% in machine and equipments, but only 1% in pharmaceutical products and in the car industry. If we focus exclusively on public funding, excluding defence and large-scale programmes such as space, aeronautics, the nuclear and nano-electronic sectors, the proportion of R&D expenditures of enterprises financed by public funding represented 18% for enterprises with more than 2,000 employees but only 5% for enterprises between 500 and 2,000 employees. This shows clearly that French support policy in 2005 helped mainly large firms, especially in a limited number of sectors, even after one excludes defence and large-scale programmes, which are naturally the preserve of large enterprises. If we look more precisely to the agencies in charge of industrial policy, we find the following sectoral allocation of budget:

The logic of the Agency for Industrial Innovation (AII) is sectoral specialization since this agency aims focuses on a limited number of disruptive technologies. In 2006, the AII approved 12 projects and 45% of the approved aid went to SMEs. The breakdown by sector was the following: ICT (45%), chemicals and biotechnology (30%), transport-energy (25%).

In 2006 the 'competitive clusters' received, €536 million in financial support for 663 R&D projects. SMEs received 28% of the allocated funding. The sectoral breakdown of projects financed by the inter-ministerial fund was the following: software (21%), biotech (15%), transport (13%), microelectronics (12%), network and multimedia (11%).

The French National Agency for Research (ANR). In 2006, 49 calls for proposals were launched. Each of the 1,600 projects supported had duration of around three years, based on the cooperation of three stakeholders. The total budget for 2007 was €825 million, but part of this budget was dedicated to competitive clusters funding (€176 million in 2006). Allocation per sector is not meaningful for fundamental research.

In the case of SMEs, there is the perception that there is only a limited number of SMEs which make an important contribution to innovation and increase in employment. General measures, such as tax reduction or reduction of labour costs, are not targeted towards these high-tech SMEs but to more traditional sectors with large representation of SMEs (construction, hotel, catering, and so forth). General measures are more likely to create an environment with low-quality, low-wage employment in SMEs with little prospects. Public support policy towards SMEs, outside direct financial transfers, are important, as simplification of administrative procedures for start-ups. The best SMEs do not have so much difficulty in finding private funds (business angels), and special public equity funds to finance high tech SMEs is important but less so than the simplification of the administration burden.

The 'new industrial' policy is more focused on innovative start-up than the previous one. Small- and medium-sized businesses less than eight years old and which focus on a new activity and 15% of whose expenditure is dedicated to research are provided with numerous tax breaks as a result of the status of innovative start-up company.

According to the European Commission's Community Innovation Survey (CIS) the French economy stands out by the low percentage of SMEs that carry out industrial R&D. In particular, innovation is extremely low in the case of SMEs with less than 50 employees. SMEs are adapting their products without carrying out their own research. Moreover, only 9.3% of innovative SMEs in France have cooperated with other enterprises on research projects (Community Innovation Survey), well below the levels reported in Scandinavian countries. The low level of partnership of SMEs in international projects is another characteristic of French industrial companies.

9.4 Public sector structure and public procurement

At the end of 2004, the French state was the majority shareholder of around 1,300 enterprises in France, which represented 4% of total employment. The ten largest enterprises of the public sector represented 75% of the enterprises of public sector. La Poste, SNCF, and EDF alone represented two-thirds of employment in the public sector (INSEE). However, the French state is also a minority shareholder of a certain number of private firms (e.g. Renault.) which are not public enterprises since they belong to the private sector.

It is clear that public procurement as public support policy is likely to be conditional on the importance of the public sector. Public procurement in France is organized under the supervision of the Ministry of the Economy, Finance and Industry. Figure 9.2 presents the organization of public procurement at the national level in France.

A 'Public Procurement code' defines in detail the procedures in accordance with the law while the selection of suppliers remains the responsibility of each public organization. It is interesting to note that the Public Procurement code provides for the possibility of forming purchasing groups to allow economies of scale and the pooling of procurement procedures, especially for small buyers whose procurement activities constitute only a minor part of their activity.

Moreover, the Public Procurement code explicitly refers to innovation as award criteria. The implementation manual of the code explains that purchasers have to make the balance in the award criteria between cost and innovation, but the extent this approach is applied remains at the

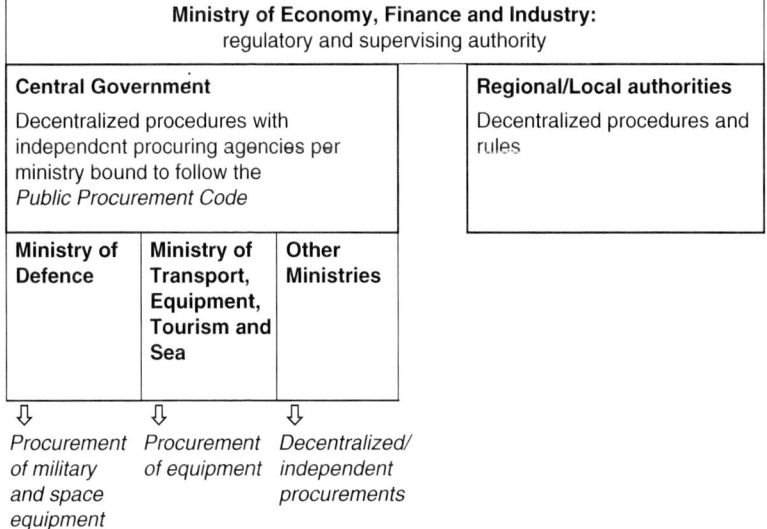

Figure 9.2 Organization of procurement at the national level

discretion of the procuring agency. The Ministry of Defence accounts for the largest part of public procurement budget in France. It is the only Ministry that makes an extensive use of the innovation criteria mentioned above, and invests systematically in R&D. The Délégation Générale pour l'Armement manages public procurement for the French Ministry of Defence with an annual budget of about €10 billion for the purchasing of military equipment.

The Ministry of Economy, Finance and Industry is responsible for the regulatory and supervising conditions governing the public procurement system. It also carries out its own procurement programme, which reaches around €2 billion per annum covering property, information technology, provision of services, and so forth.

The Ministry of Transport and Equipment is also responsible for an important public procurement annual budget. It is responsible for the implementation of public works projects and procurements in the areas of transport and equipment.

La 'Commission des Marchés Publics de l'Etat' (CMPE) assists the different stakeholders in awarding and monitoring a contract of public procurement. The CMPE is only mandatory for public procurement contracts of more than €6 million. In 2006, the CMPE received 644 different files for an amount of €18 billion.

The figures presented in Table 9.7 cover only the public procurement contracts managed by CMPE (those over €6 million and managed by the central state Ministries).

To a certain extent, public procurement can be used to promote innovation but the Public Procurement code allows only limited degrees of freedom in respect of the criteria imposed, the choice of the most economic advantageous tender (MEAT). The possibility exists for tenderers to submit variants based on alternative technology innovations because 'a new product can be expensive at the first right but finally be cheaper if its durability is taken into account' (code) but only the Minister of

Table 9.7 Public procurement in France (2006)

Sectors	Amount (M€)	Share (%)
Defence	7,993	44.3
Property, public works	1,974	10.9
Information Technology, telecommunication	2,488	13.9
Supplies (energy, water, etc.)	5,574	30.9
Total	18,029	100.0

Source: CMPE.

Defence has explicitly incorporated innovation-favouring criteria in its procurement policy.

For SMEs the situation is less clear. Only 21% of public procurement market in value comes from SMEs. The government of François Fillon favours the introduction of the US 'Small Business act' model and philosophy in French public procurement policy. In 2004, the Ministry of Defence decided to promote the participation of innovative SMEs, provided they could prove they were about to produce innovative technology. Innovating SMEs can even directly conclude an R&D contract with the Ministry of Defence without having to face the usual procedures, even if it is at the expense of competition.

9.5 Evaluation and efficiency of public support policy

In terms of innovation, the European Innovation Scoreboard developed at the initiative of the European Commission under the Lisbon strategy placed France in 8th position among the EU-15 countries. The summary innovation index picks out a group of leaders in the EU (Sweden, Finland, Denmark, and Germany), and France belongs to the group of innovation followers with the United Kingdom, the Netherlands, Belgium, and Austria. According to the European Innovation Scoreboard the fact that France is lagging behind in terms of innovation can be largely attributed to the small number of innovative companies, the non-existence of public–private partnerships and the low R&D productivity with respect to innovation that can be used by industry.

As highlighted in the Council of Economic Analysis 'Education and growth' report (Aghion and Cohen, 2004), France can no longer be only a follower of initiation technology already available on the market, but must produce its own innovation to improve its productivity.

It is possible to measure R&D productivity as the rate of return with respect to innovation of corporate sector R&D via a ratio comparing the number of triadic patents[4] with industrial R&D spending expressed in dollars and adjusted for PPP (OECD) (European Commission, 2005). This ratio has remained stable in France since the early 1990s and it has increased by only 3% in France compared with a 36% increase for the EU-15; 67% in Germany and by 60% in the United Kingdom; the low productivity of French R&D is confirmed by the low number of French patents filled with the European Patent Office compared to Germany (less than half of the score of Germany). The weakness of France in term of innovation is also confirmed by the technology sub-component of the World Economic Forum ratings, France lagging behind the technological leaders.

9.5.1 Great complexity of aid mechanism

According to the *Inspection des finances* report, there are at least 6,000 mechanisms of public aid to companies in France, and these different mechanisms fall under the responsibility of hundreds of different economic actors: the state, local governments, public organizations, and the different Chambers of Commerce. The report highlights the fact that there are dozens of mechanisms that 'compete for the same objective, such as the 42 mechanisms that aim at promoting recruitment through specific reductions in employee contributions'. Other examples in the report clearly show the incredible complexity and opacity of French public aid mechanisms. For instance, there are 120 aid mechanisms for starting a company in France, but only 10% of new business ventures actually benefit from any of them.

Several inventories of public aid have been made in France. The one conducted by the Chambers of Commerce and Industry is the most complete: over 6,000 aid mechanisms are identified in a database known as 'Semaphore'. This database distinguishes financial aid from technical aid. If we focus on the 360 national financial aid mechanisms, 287 different mechanisms out of these 360 are inventoried by the Ministry of Finance, but there are also aid measures from national state organizations such as the Energy Conservation Agency, and even from national non-state organizations like the Chamber of Commerce network or the *Agence pour la Maîtrise de l'Energie*, another energy conservation structure.

The complexity of aid mechanisms has led certain consultants to become specialists in 'public aid consulting'. These firms' service propositions to companies is to identify the aid mechanisms that may be available to the firm, to prepare their application, and file it with the appropriate authorities, and to follow up the process, assuring communication with the authorities.

9.5.2 Absence of evaluation of the effectiveness of public aid

Faced with the multiplicity of aid mechanisms, with their complexity, and opacity, we note that there are no reports devoted to evaluating the real effectiveness, from an economic standpoint, of public aid. Moreover, the cost of gaining access to relevant information on available aid is particularly high, which constitutes a major barrier to entry for SMEs–the very companies governments have declared should be the primary recipients of public aid.

Furthermore, the incredible profusion and complexity of aid mechanisms makes it almost impossible to clearly identify the intended effects on any particular mechanism. There are numerous potential interference effects between the different mechanisms, and it is impossible to separate out the respective economic impact of each one.

The demand for *ex post* control of aid mechanisms is increasingly being made, mainly because of the debate on 'delocalization'. The case of companies that have received aid and have then chosen to go offshore (usually to Asia) – whereas the public authorities have provided them with aid to set up operations in a French region – has prompted a demand for stricter control, as well as for certain *ex post* reimbursements of the aid that was granted.

Even in a domain such as that of public aid for R&D, where there is a relative consensus between the savings on the beneficial effects linked to positive externalities, there are still today no real studies in France on the effectiveness of aid mechanisms for France. The *Inspection des finances* report has noted, moreover, that public support for corporate R&D has not produced any clear positive effect on the intensity of R&D undertaken in the private sector.

The fundamental question is thus to determine to what extent mechanisms of public aid to companies produce only 'windfall effects'. Companies are granted aid with the idea that they will be able to engage personnel, make investments in R&D, or develop new activities; but the aid received is said to have had no influence on their actual behaviour, since they would have made the same decisions even in the absence of aid.

Any serious economic evaluation of public aid in France will also have to take into account the cost for the public authorities of launching, processing, and following up the aid measures. Given the very high number of aid mechanisms, one can legitimately raise questions about the number of civil servants, the time spent on aid development and administration, and the overall cost for the public sector of aid in France. Finally, given the complexity of current mechanisms that have led certain consultants to specialize in public aid, there is a real cost of access to information, and thus a barrier to entry, that any real cost-benefit analysis of French aid mechanisms must evaluate.

9.6 Conclusion

Public support to industry in France has substantially changed since the late 1980s. From the 1990s, in particular because of budget deficits and public debt, traditional French industrial policy approach (support to 'grand projects' as sectoral policies, public enterprises as national champion) has given way to a new horizontal approach in line with European policies.

In 2004/2005 following major reports on new industrial policy and faced with the challenges of globalization and following worrying reports on the competitiveness of the French economy, changes in the approach to public support took place in France. This 'new industrial policy' represents a determined public effort at effective support of major industries through the creation of the 'Agency of Industrial Innovation', National Research Agency, public support to SMEs on innovation with OSEO, Centres of Competitiveness.

When we look at the total amount of subsidy and public aid to enterprises by objective in France, we find that most aid benefits all companies and that a primary objective is employment, in particular reducing the cost of labour for low skilled work. In 2005, the amount of public aid focused on R&D or on SMEs represented only 3% and 9% respectively of total aid. Moreover, if we look only at aid targeted to specific sectors, transportation, housing and agriculture represent no less than 80% of total sectoral aid.

French public support policy is a very centralized system: 90% of public support is provided by the state and only 10% by regional or local authorities. The Ministry of Economy, Finance and Industry is responsible for deciding on the strategic industrial priorities.

Traditionally, public authorities in France are highly involved in corporate research, above the EU average. However, government support clearly focused on a few key sectors (aerospace, nuclear used defence) and helped mainly large firms. In France, cooperation between the government and industry was limited to a few strategic sectors and mainly large firms; SMEs did not get clear public support.

France lags behind in terms of innovation and its R&D is not sufficiently productive. This is confirmed by a large number of reports and indicators, as the number of patent applications filed with the patents office per million inhabitants, the ratio of triadic patents, the industry finance of R&D and the indicator of the European Innovation Scoreboard. There are various explanations for this: the small number of innovative companies, the low level of specialization of the French economy in the high-tech sector, and the difficulties of public-private partnerships. One of the main problems is that the public research capabilities (Universities, CNRS) are under-exploited by companies. Further, there is a lack of cooperation between public research and industrial companies.

France is characterized by an over-complex funding system with too many actors as public economic agents (AII, ANR, OSEO, Ministries, government agencies) and the result is that the system of funding lacks visibility. There are too many mechanisms competing for the some objective. A recent report clearly show the incredible complexity and opacity of French public aid mechanisms; 120 different mechanisms for starting a company in France, but only 10% of new business ventures actually benefit from any of them. Faced with the multiplicity of public support mechanisms with their complexity and opacity, there is a lack of reports devoted to evaluation of the real effectiveness, from an economic viewpoint, of public subsidies.

French SMEs are characterized by the low percentage of them carrying out industrial R&D. They adapt their products without carrying out their own research. This is particularly the case for SMEs with fewer than 50 employees. French SMEs have cooperated with other enterprises on research project at a much lower level than is the case with innovation leaders in the EU. One of the benefits of competitive clusters will be to facilitate the pooling of technological information and so the SMEs involved will get greater access to technological innovation and resources. However, SMEs' involvement in competitive clusters seems to be too low at the time of writing, mainly because of the timescale of the projects, which is too long and the technological implications, which are too complex. In principle, the expected results of competitive clusters are well adapted to the structural weaknesses of France in terms of innovation, the small number of innovative SMEs, the low level of cooperation between public and industrial research, and the low level of productivity of R&D.

10
Public Support in the United Kingdom

In the United Kingdom, public support to business, supervised by the Department of Trade and Industry (DTI),[1] was for a long time dominated by regional development concerns. Indeed, regional policy has been the mainstay of industrial policy in the United Kingdom postwar, based on a recognition of the need to reduce regional disparities in employment, earnings, and the cost of living. Regional policy itself has undergone a number of incarnations but to date its most enduring feature has been the Regional Selective Assistance (RSA) scheme, which was introduced in 1972. Designed as a discretionary capital subsidy linked to the creation and safeguarding of employment, it operates in Assisted Areas only and is primarily directed towards manufacturing (often foreign-owned) companies. Although RSA is explicitly designed to assist certain regions of Great Britain, it also implicitly helps to build up the science and technology base of industry in those regions. A significant proportion of aid goes to small firms (Harris and Robinson, 2004). In contrast to the RSA scheme, two programmes (SMART, SPUR) are explicitly aimed at encouraging innovative activity in the Small and Medium Enterprise (SME) sector. They were launched in 1986 but became fully operational in 1988, and since then have undergone various transformations and amalgamations.

10.1 Objectives of public support

The priorities for UK industrial policy are international competitiveness, innovation, competition, and skills formation. These are the same as those in the 1960s (Beath, 2002). The main difference between the 1960s and the 2000s is that there are new instruments of policy and two areas benefit from further attention: competition policy and technology policy. The view of the UK authorities on industrial policy is that 'the government cannot stand in the way of change but that change itself needs to be managed so that its consequences are not traumatic or so disruptive that they actually hold back economic growth' (Byers, 2000).[2]

Reviewing the main components of the British industrial policy, Wren (2001) suggested the following characterization. The policy is essentially microeconomic, has a distributional role (through it has a strong regional policy), and gives a priority to the development of small and medium enterprises (SMEs).

UK industrial policy has three additional characteristics. It is 'soft' (i.e. consisting of advisory support, gateway services, the dissemination of best practice and so on), decentralized (i.e. it is provided by agencies that are funded by central government but outside its direct control), and monitored (i.e. programmes that were not bringing value for money are abandoned and funding is concentrated in few schemes).

10.2 Actors

UK industrial policy is an important part of the country's competitiveness policy. Between 1983 and 2007, the Department of Trade and Industry (DTI) was in charge of the policy. In 2007, reorganization split the tasks of the DTI between the Department for Business, Enterprise & Regulatory Reform (DBERR) and the Department for Innovation, Universities and Skills (DIUS). Moreover, Scotland, Northern Ireland, and, to a lesser extent, Wales, enjoy a certain degree of autonomy in industrial policy. Until now, this has not affected the guiding principles, priorities, and structure of the policy. However, the 2007 election of a Scottish Nationalist executive may lead to some divergence.

The DBERR is helping every region of the United Kingdom to have sustainable economic development. It is working with Regional Development Agencies (RDAs) and other regional bodies to raise national and regional economic performance by working to promote regional regeneration, investment, skills, training, employment, efficiency, and competitiveness. The DBERR is also in charge of small business. The former 'Small Business Service' was renamed the 'Enterprise Directorate'. The new Directorate retains specialist expertise in policies to both strengthen the enterprise environment for small businesses and to enable more people and communities to pursue entrepreneurial opportunities.

The DBERR works closely with the Department for Innovation, Universities and Skills. The DIUS is intended to deliver the Government's long-term vision to make Britain one of the best places in the world for science, technology, research, and innovation. This new department brings together functions of the Office of Science and Innovation from the former DTI with further and higher education and skills, previously part of the Department for Education and Skills. In particular, it is in charge of the Foresight programme, which seeks to identify possible 'needs, opportunities and threats to UK national wealth' and develop links between business and the science base in order to address these issues.

The United Kingdom's Office of Government Commerce (OGC) supports procurement by central government agencies and other public bodies. The OGC's mission is to work with the public sector as a catalyst to achieve efficiency, value for money in commercial activities and improved success in the delivery of programmes and projects. To promote procurement for innovation, OGC has produced advice in the form of a booklet entitled 'Capturing Innovation' (European Commission, 2005).

10.3 Instruments

For a long time government support to business in the United Kingdom had been primarily limited to the provision of funds to finance some R&D activities in private industry. In 2002, the government introduced an R&D tax credit (Becker and Pain, 2003). The use of public procurement is also becoming an important tool to promote innovation. The Government's Innovation Report of 2003 proposed a series of measures aimed at increasing the research and innovation impact of public procurement.

Table 10.1 presents figures for selected government expenditures. The first panel concerns total procurement of goods and services and subsidies as reported in the nations' budget. Part of this is targeted toward industrial policy but it is not possible to have the exact split among the different uses. The second panel provides expenses on industrial policy measures (drawn from Wren, 2001) and mainly covers spending in England. The figures do not include expenditure on space, defence and aerospace programmes, or on the general science budget. In the case of small firm policy it gives government pump-priming for Business Link and expenditure on local competitiveness measures, such as the Small Business Service (SBS), while for the RDAs it gives spending on the competitiveness functions. Expenditure on central government administration is also excluded.

Table 10.1 shows that expenditure on industrial policy measures in England was at about £400 million per annum between 1997 and 1999.

Table 10.1 Selected government expenses (£ million)

	1997–8	1998–9	1999–2000	2000–1	2001–2
			All purposes		
Procurement of goods and services		84,667	89,826	98,077	106,453
Subsidies		7,250	7,150	7,456	8,377
			Industrial policy measures		
Science and technology	121.9	118.2	139.3	170.0	167.7
Knowledge transfer/collaboration	39.3	45.5	47.2	56.9	50.1
Innovation[a]	78.0	61.2	79.5	109.2	117.2
Sector challenge	4.6	11.5	12.6	3.9	0.4
Small firms	171.3	152	180.3	225.2	202.9
Business link	31.2	14.3	1.2	0.4	0.0
Small firm services	98.0	103.2	124.8	132.2	138.1
Enterprise fund	41.3	33.9	48.5	73.5	56.5
Other initiatives	0.8	0.6	5.8	19.1	8.3
Regional policy	128.2	126.4	127.3	147.2	147.6
Regional selective assistance	114.2	112.2	110.0	116.3	110.3
Enterprise grant	0	0	0	9.0	15.0
RDA competitiveness fund	0	0	2.0	5.2	5.2
Regional development organizations	10.4	11.0	11.2	11.0	11.6
Invest UK	3.6	3.2	4.1	5.7	5.5

[a] Includes the Smart scheme and its predecessors SMART, SPUR and RIN, Enterprise Centres, Local Support Centres and some sector initiatives.

Source: Wren (2001) and http://www.hm-treasury.gov.uk/media/4/9/excel_pesa04_chap3_tables.xls

It increased to more than £500 million per annum between 2000 and 2002. Over the whole period the split between the three components slightly favours 'small firms' but remained almost unchanged. The main sources of growth in expenditures are innovation, small firm services and, to a lesser extent, knowledge transfer. The rest of this section is devoted to a detailed discussion of the main programmes of UK industrial policy: science, technology, research, and innovation, small firms' development, and regional policy.

10.3.1 Science and technology

A key part of science and technology policy is the Foresight programme, which seeks to identify possible 'needs, opportunities and threats to UK national wealth' and develop links between business and the science base in order to address these issues. It works primarily through thematic and sector panels, which are composed of representatives from business, science, the voluntary sector, and the government. The panels attempt to anticipate trends and develop policy initiatives. There are three schemes: LINK, TCS, and SMART.

The LINK scheme aims at encouraging pre-competitive collaborative projects between industry and the research base. It supports projects of two to three years duration which have good potential for commercial exploitation. The latest scheme involved around 1,500 companies and 200 research base organizations.

The TCS scheme is a mechanism for promoting technology transfer. It seeks to form industry–academia partnerships. It funds graduates to carry out projects in companies, and increasingly it is used to take forward to market the results of LINK research. In 1998 the LINK and TCS Boards were merged.

The SMART/SPUR family programmes represent the largest share of the science and technology funds. SMART is aimed at encouraging innovative activity in the SME sector and began in 1986 (although this was a pilot and the full scheme started in 1988) and since then has undergone various transformations and amalgamations. A similar scheme, SPUR, started in 1991 but was aimed at larger companies initially, although in 1994 it was also restricted to SMEs. In 1995, SMART stage 2 was incorporated into SPUR while in 1997 SMART, SPUR, SPURplus and the Regional Innovation Grants scheme were merged into a single SMART programme, which was extended in 1999 and expanded slightly. Throughout, the various programmes have been focused on helping SMEs to research and develop new products and processes themselves, or to acquire new technologies developed or adapted for them by technology providers.

Firms in receipt of SMART/SPUR awards get different levels of assistance depending on their size and whether the project is in the form of a feasibility study (available only to small firms who then receive up to £45,000 at 75% of their eligible costs with a minimum project cost of £30,000) or a development project (maximum grant is then around £150,000 at 30% of eligible costs).

10.3.2 Regional policy

UK regional policy distinguishes three types of Assisted Areas. Tier 1 areas are those with per capita Gross Domestic Product (GDP) below 75% of the European Union average. They are eligible for Objective 1 support under the European Union (EU) Structural Funds, and include West Wales and the Valleys, Cornwall, Merseyside, and South Yorkshire. Tier 2 areas are those with 'acute labour market need', which are determined by the UK government but the funding needs to comply with the requirements of the RAG. The third tier of areas differs across the UK regions and concerns areas with 'identified special need'. Firms in the latter category are not eligible for the RSA scheme.

The RDAs, which were formally launched in the eight English regions in April 1999, with a ninth in London a year later following the creation of the Greater London Authority, are the key agents for the implementation of the competitiveness programme at the regional level in England. Their role is to encourage the exploitation of the science and engineering base; develop links between business and higher education; coordinate the development and implementation of innovation and technology programmes; and to disseminate best practice.

The RDAs' strategies provide a framework to coordinate development work and serve as a basis for establishing detailed plans of action. They have a number of specific roles, including reviewing the business support in their regions, such as the Business Link partnerships, helping to establish the Regional Venture Capital Funds, facilitating the development of clusters and improving supply chains.

In their regions the RDAs take a lead role in attracting and retaining mobile investment projects, including assembling packages of support for individual investors. This work is coordinated by Invest UK which has responsibility for promoting the UK overseas and filtering enquiries to the RDAs or other agencies. Invest UK focuses on high-value projects (those which support the development of sector or technology-based clusters) and on RSA.

The RSA scheme is the most important domestic policy instrument in terms of regional industrial policy (Wren, 2001). Since its introduction in 1972, RSA has been recognized for its simplicity as a policy tool. Its chief aim is to safeguard and create employment opportunities in designated Assisted Areas, through offering a discretionary subsidy to plants in the form of a capital grant. That is, RSA provides money towards capital investment projects that secure employment opportunities.[3] A sub-aim of RSA is to increase foreign inward investment into Assisted Areas, since this should avoid problems of displacement, but also because of the assumed better economic performance exhibited by foreign firms. Thus it also aims to improve overall competitiveness in the regions. RSA is primarily directed at supporting manufacturing in assisted regions, though increasingly it has been available to non-local service sector industries.

In addition to offering some sort of commitment to safeguard or expand employment, firms that wish to apply for RSA funding (to perhaps expand or modernize) must meet a set of four criteria. First, in order to be eligible, firms must be located in an Assisted Area. Second, the firm must demonstrate that the project to which the grant is to be directed is itself viable (within a three-year period). Third, the project must be shown to be 'additional', which means that the investment would not have taken place in the way that it did without government support. Fourth, it is also a requirement that any award of RSA funds does not result in displacement within the Assisted Area; so that, by providing funding within a region to a firm, the government is not causing other competing firms to close or cut employment.[4]

Whilst the aim of RSA has traditionally been to safeguard or create employment, the scheme now clearly has an explicit obligation to make sure that firm performance is improved, that is, that RSA positively impacts on firm efficiency and thus improves aggregate efficiency in UK manufacturing.

Under the decentralization policy, the Treasury has responsibility for allocating funds to Scotland, Wales, and Northern Ireland within the overall framework of public expenditure control. The decentralized administrations have the freedom to formulate policy and to make their own spending decisions on matters which are 'not reserved', including economic development, industry, education, and training.

10.3.3 Small firms

The SBS aims to simplify and improve the government support offered to small business. It was established in April 2000, and its main roles are: to monitor and advise on small firm regulation; promote business-support access and take-up in disadvantaged communities; and provide a gateway service for business information and advice from a range of suppliers in the public, private, and voluntary sectors. It is linked to other initiatives, so that the SBS manages small-firm TCS and SMART technology measures, and the national network of Business Link, which is the main publicly funded source of information and advice for smaller enterprises. The SBS is also expected to form close links with the RDAs.

Business Link comprises 85 locally based partnerships covering England and handles around 400,000 enquiries a year. Similar organizations operate in other parts of the United Kingdom. The government provides ongoing funding for core services, which is in addition to the

Business Link own fee income. The Business Link partners have been invited to put forward proposals to run the SBS local services, which will work through 45 local franchises. Business Link has been criticized for being too localized. Hence, in 1998 arrangements were set for access to expertise at the regional level through 22 Centres of Expertise where it is not cost-effective to supply this locally. These provide specialist services in the areas of ceramics, aerospace, defence, and printing.

Local Support Centres offer a range of advice in the use of the information and communication technologies. These promote electronic business and commerce, with £25 million set aside over three years to connect around 650,000 small businesses to the Internet. In addition, the government seeks to build up a customized advisory service to support 10,000 innovative start-ups a year.

Enterprise Fund is dealing with finance for small business. It received £180 million from the government (over three years) to help fund early-stage high technology firms. This comprises £40 million a year for Small Firms Loan Guarantee Scheme and £500,000 to offer equity investment supporting early-stage high technology firms through the UK High Technology and the Regional Venture Capital Funds. The latter seek to establish a Regional Venture Capital Fund in each English region, with similar initiatives being established in Scotland and Wales.[5]

10.4 Outcomes of public support in the United Kingdom

The effectiveness of public support to industry can be examined with respect to its main priorities. These include job creation, foreign direct investment (FDI) attractiveness, productivity improvement and R&D.

Regarding employment, the exact effect is still controversial among the UK institution (ranging form 84,000 to 6,000 jobs created over the four-and-a-half-year period 1991–95). Wren (2005) suggests that the difference among estimates comes from the way adjustments are made for the displacement of jobs elsewhere in the Assisted Areas, for multiplier and linkage effects in supplier firms, and for permanent net job equivalent. Correcting for these shortcomings, the author proposes an estimate of 12,000 net jobs created per year. Wren also assessed the costs of the created jobs and concludes that industrial policy is at least as cost-effective as measures designed either to reduce or to alleviate unemployment.

A recent study by Harris and Robinson (2004) examined the impact of UK government industrial support schemes on manufacturing plant level Total Factor Productivity (TFP). The empirical analysis suggests that RSA plants had below-average levels of productivity, with overall

TFP 4.7% less than the average. Following assistance, RSA plants improved their TFP by an average of 2.5%. However, when allowing the assistance effect to differ across regions, only Scottish plants seemed to have benefited in a major way; the average improvement in TFP here being some 4.8%. There is little benefit in other regions for RSA-assisted plants when compared to non-assisted plants. Regarding SMART assisted plants, they were better than the average (nearly 8% more productive), but assistance seems to induce little significant change in TFP.

Devereux et al. (2007) focused on the effect of government grants on the location of domestic and multinational firms new plants in Great Britain. They find evidence that firms are more likely to locate greenfield plants near larger markets and that plants within the same industry tend to co-locate. More importantly, they find that on average greenfield entrants are less likely to locate in Assisted (compared with non-Assisted) Areas and that grant offers have a greater effect on location incentives in areas where there is more existing economic activity in the entrants' industry. Put differently, the results imply that higher grant offers are needed to attract greenfield entrants to locations where industry agglomeration or natural resource benefits are weaker.

In contrast to the above results, a recent study (OECD, 2006; a chapter of which is devoted to the United Kingdom only) suggests that public support was very effective in terms of R&D. Focusing on the behavioural additionality of grants in the context of a firm's total portfolio of assets, the study suggest that even projects that had not led to exploitation nonetheless contributed towards capabilities that were exploited in the context of other projects. In particular, people recruited as a result of one grant were subsequently key contributors to later work, technological knowledge, and skills enhancements during one grant were applied subsequently, and networking partners form one grant formed the basis of subsequent collaborations.

In sum, it seems that the effectiveness of public support to industry is highly debatable in terms of job creation and disappointing in terms of FDI attractiveness and productivity improvement. It appears, however, strong regarding R&D.

It is also worth noting that the UK administration performs regular evaluations of the effectiveness of the subsidy programmes and adopts a 'value-for-money' approach. Recently they have reviewed all the subsidy programmes, including the functioning of the relevant office/department in the central administration, abandoned those programmes that were not bringing value for money and concentrated funding in selected schemes.

10.5 Conclusion

Regional policy has been the mainstay of industrial policy in the United Kingdom post-war. At present, the priorities for UK industrial policy are science, technology, research, and innovation, small firms' development and regional policy. These are the same as were in place in the 1960s. The main difference is that two areas benefit from further attention: competition policy and technology policy. UK industrial policy has three additional characteristics. It is 'soft' (i.e. consisting of advisory support, gateway services, the dissemination of best practice and so on), decentralized (i.e. it is provided by agencies which are funded by central government but outside its direct control), and monitored (i.e. programmes that were not bringing value for money are abandoned and funding is concentrated in selected schemes).

In pursuing industrial policy, England spends more than £500 million per annum. The split between the three components slightly favours 'small firms'. For a long time government support to business in the United Kingdom was limited to the provision of grants and advisory services. From 2002, the government introduced an R&D tax credit and has used public procurement to promote innovation.

Three institutions are the main actors in the field of industrial policy: the Department for Business, Enterprise & Regulatory Reform (DBERR), the Department for Innovation, Universities and Skills (DIUS) and the Office of Government Commerce (OGC). The latter's mission is to achieve efficiency of programmes and projects and to promote procurement for innovation.

There is no relation 1 for 1 between specific programmes and objectives (i.e. R&D, SMEs, and regional policy). A given programme may target more than one objective at the same time. The SMART/SPUR family programmes are aimed at encouraging SMEs to research and develop new products and processes themselves, or to acquire new technologies developed or adapted for them by technology providers. The RSA scheme is the most important regional policy instrument. Its chief aim is to safeguard and create employment opportunities in designated Assisted Areas, through offering a discretionary subsidy to capital investment projects especially foreign inward investment.

Studies of the effectiveness of public support to industry show that such effectiveness is highly debatable in terms of job creation. It is disappointing in terms of FDI and productivity improvement but strong regarding R&D.

11
Public Support in the United States

'We don't do industrial policy,' asserted John Sununu, former White House Chief of Staff and now member of the US Senate (Fong, 2000). This statement illustrates the difficulties one has to face when studying public support (to use a softer term than industrial policy) to industry in the US.

According to Ketels (2007), one cannot easily challenge the assertion that the 'United States does not do industrial policy' if this is understood in a narrow sense, namely 'an interference in the market process with the objective of fostering an industry that would otherwise not succeed'. But adopting a broader definition that includes economic policies with an industry-specific impact, the United States clearly has an industrial policy. This is a horizontal policy that has differential effects across industries. Therefore, the discussion of whether or not the United States engages in industrial policy is relevant only in terms of politics; it provides little guidance to understanding actual policies.

Although the point could be taken for granted, the issue of identifying the various industrial policy's stakeholders, their exact tasks, and the amounts involved remains a formidable challenge. While very detailed data on various aspects of the American economy are available publicly, one fails to find a single source (or at least limited number of sources) allowing to set the stage of public support to industry in the United States (see Bianchi and Labory, 2006 for further discussion). The task is further complicated by the multiplication of authorities that can support business: federal, states and local governments in addition to the Congress and a multitude of agencies (Markusen, 1995).[1] Moreover, no explicit legislation on states' aid to business seems to exist in the United States. Only antitrust law can be used (Martin and Valbonesi, 2006). However, antitrust law does not mention subsidies provided by the different levels of government. States appear to have therefore a large amount of freedom in implementing state aid to business.[2]

Regarding expenses, the federal budget should, in principle, be informative about the amounts of public support at the federal level. Section no. 40 regarding grants and fixed charges, of which number 41 is grants, subsidies and contributions give reasonable approximation. However, no distinction is made according to the precise destination of these grants, subsidies, and contributions. Moreover, information on public procurements, which many specialists (e.g. Ruttan, 2005 and Montani, 2005) consider as an important instrument of support to industry in the United States, does not provide their precise destination.

11.1 Objectives of public support

It is hard to understand the rationale behind the US support to industry independently from the importance granted to military concerns (Smith, 1985). The United States has always been preoccupied by its military capabilities and its ability to stand well in face of any foreign threats. The period of the Cold War illustrates markedly the importance the United States gave to these issues and, hence, the amounts of funds it spends to achieve its objective.

The policy (including both subsidies and procurement), organized in the Pentagon, encompassed every aspect of industrial policy as practised in Japan and Europe: research and development commitments, long-term procurement contracts, investment guarantees, and bailouts for failing corporations (Markusen, 1995). It seeks to stimulate and support vigorous domestic competition and innovation and to establish and sustain cost-effective industrial and technological capabilities that assure economic competitiveness and military readiness and superiority.

Science and technology are clear priorities for the United States. The science and technology efforts are stronger than in the average Organisation of Economic Cooperation and Development (OECD) country but they are not exceptional when compared to those of Japan or the Nordic countries. Rating the generosity of R&D tax incentives using the B-indexes, the OECD (2001) ranked the US (B-index=0.934) among the moderate incentive providers; far behind Denmark (B-index=0.871) which was ranked among the generous incentive providers (see also Ketels, 2007).[3] Regional development does not seem to be a top priority at the national level. Efforts in this field are not results of deliberate national programme but rather the outcome of the balance of power between lobbies and representatives from various regions and states (Markusen, 1995).

Military and defence-related expenses have been a major source of commercial technology development across a broad spectrum of industries that account for an important share of United States industrial production (see Ruttan, 2005). However, these benefits seem to be the result of the country's concerns about its military supremacy and its role as the first political superpower in the world, rather than purposeful industrial policy (Ketels, 2007).

11.2 Actors

The institutional structure of the United States differs from that of other OECD countries in many respects. A first particularity of economic policymaking in the United States is the balance of influence between the President and Congress. A second particularity is the strong role of individual states in many economic policy areas. Finally, economic policymaking in the United States is characterized by a high level of cooperation between government and the private sector.

In the presidential system of the United States, the President can set the political agenda and has a good chance to implement his or her views in a few high priority areas by investing the political capital of the Presidency. But Congress members have to make sure that they can report direct benefits for their respective constituencies.

This makes a sustained national push on behalf of a specific industry hard to sustain, as it will inevitably raise demands or protests from others. For instance, the American Competitiveness Initiative (ACI) announced at the 2006 State of the Union address makes significant commitments to science and technology policy while the budget consolidation has led to proposed spending cuts in many programmes (like the Advanced Technology Program and the Manufacturing Extension Partnership program) not specifically identified as a Presidential priority. Congress has overruled the President's decisions, concerning the Advanced Technology Program, based on individual political or constituency interests.

Individual states have also a strong role in many economic policy areas and enter intense competition to develop their area. The US states use a broad set of policy tools to strengthen the competitiveness of their communities. These include higher education and transportation infrastructure. Although they do not involve money transfer, they may be powerful supports to business.

It is worth noting here that the federal government has no mechanism for controlling or coordinating the aids by the individual states. The Constitution grants Congress the power to regulate commerce 'among the several states'. Under a legal theory known as the negative commerce clause, the Supreme Court can cancel down state taxes and regulations that have the effect of taxes when it finds them to be protectionist, favouring businesses within a state and thus discouraging national commerce. However, there is no recent evidence that subsidies have ever led to interstate litigation.[4]

On all geographic levels, business leaders are regularly involved in policy discussions and strong institutional platforms exit that formulate the position of industry. In comparison to other countries, lobbying for market interventions is much less dominant than elsewhere and there is a broader coalition of private sector leaders willing to get engaged in formulating and executing initiatives.

The above specificity of the institutional structure of the United States makes the precise identification of the various industrial policy stakeholders, their exact tasks, and the amounts involved very difficult. Even limiting itself to the federal level, one has to devote a lot of time to identify the actors and their respective roles. It is necessary to go through the composition of the executive and its sub-branches to identify the main player regarding public support to industry. The US executive departments that seem to be the most involved in supporting business are the Department of Defence (DoD), the Department of Energy (DoE), the Department of Health (DoH), and the Department of Commerce (DoC). Interestingly, only the DoD has a Deputy Under Secretary for Industrial Policy. His mission is to ensure that 'the industrial base on which the DoD depends is reliable, cost-effective, and sufficient to meet DoD requirements'. Since many multilateral agreements (e.g. the WTO) do not cover defence matters, this may give the United States a lot of autonomy in pursuing an industrial policy.

11.3 Instruments[5]

Table 11.1 reports the main federal expenses related to public support to business. The data are the most recent available. They concern direct support to R&D, advice to business, and trade adjustment assistance. The table also reports expenses in public procurements since these constitute, at least in part, an indirect public support to business; mainly for R&D.

Direct support to R&D takes the forms of grants and tax provisions. The latter include special exclusion, exemption and deduction from

Table 11.1 Selected Federal expenses (in millions of dollars)

	2003	2004	2005
	All purposes[a]		
Grants of all kinds	441,037	460,152	–
Procurement of goods and services	327,413	339,680	–
	Industrial policy measures[b]		
Science and technology	96,631	105,691	109,457
of which			
Small Business Innovation Research	1,759	2015	–
Small Business Technology Transfer Program	102	209	–
Advanced Technology Program	154	155	–
Manufacturing Extension Partnership	106	39	108
Trade Adjustment Assistance	10	12	11

[a] These figures are not comparable to those in Chapters 6 and 7 because on the one hand they concern the federal government only and on the other hand they cover other expenses than public support to business.
[b] This figure includes both subsidies and public procurement.

Sources: Budget of the United States Government, Fiscal Year (FY) 2005, Table 18.1. National Science Foundation, Survey of Federal Funds for Research and Development: FY 2003, 2004 and 2005. NIST/Technology Administration Budget Summary FY 2003 and 2005. Hornbeck (2007). US Census Bureau, Consolidated Federal Funds Report: FY 2003 and 2004.

gross income and special credit, preferential rate of tax and deferral of liability. It is reported in the federal budget under the title 'tax expenditures'. Inspection of the budget shows that the largest component of 'tax expenditures' targeted toward business is 'accelerated depreciation of machinery and equipment' (62% of total) and that R&D represent an important share (12% of total).

The most important structured programmes targeted toward science and technology are the Advanced Technology Program (ATP), the Small Business Innovation Research (SBIR) and the Small Business Technology Transfer program (STTR). These are explained in detail below.

The main expenses targeted toward advice to business concern the Manufacturing Extension Partnership (MEP). Its purpose is to provide small- and medium-sized manufacturers with the services they need to succeed through advice and tap into the expertise of knowledgeable manufacturing and business specialists all over the United States. These specialists are people who have had experience in manufacturing and in plant operations.

The Trade Adjustment Assistance (TAA) program represents the main expenses of the Economic Development Administration (EDA) directed toward business. It is part of a broader programme that also provides assistance to workers and farmers. To benefit from this programme, a firm must demonstrate that imports have contributed importantly to declines in its employment (or to the threat thereof), and in sales or production. Once accepted, the firm has two years to develop a business recovery plan which should be approved by the EDA.

Table 11.1 shows that science and technology are clearly the most important concerns of public support to business in the United States. The amount of support for R&D is almost 100 times higher than for the other programmes.

President Bush made science and technology a central plank of his ACI announced at the 2006 State of the Union address. The ACI proposes to increase basic research funding by US$50,000 million over the next decade and to make the R&D tax credit for companies permanent with an amount of US$86,400 billion over the next decade (Ketels, 2007). At the same time, the President repeatedly targeted for elimination of the TAA and MEP programs. For instance, while the budget for the MEP was around US$106 million in 2002 and of a similar amount in 2003, the President proposed to put it at US$12 million in 2004. Finally, the budget was US$40 million in 2004 and US$108 million in 2005 as a result of tough negotiation between Congress and the White House. In what follows, we will, therefore, focus on support to R&D.

Regarding the split of the US federal R&D budget by performer, about one-third is used to finance research in government agencies or federally funded research institutions, 50% goes towards research conducted by companies, and the rest is used to finance R&D at universities and non-profit organizations. It is worth noting that the DoD is the source of almost 50% of the total funding and 84% of the R&D performed by industrial firms (NSF, 2006).

Although science and technology are clear priority for the United States, the extent of structured programmes targeted toward their development is limited (ATP, SBIR, STTR) as Table 11.1 shows. The government relies much on funding for specific research purposes.

11.3.1 Structured subsidized programmes

Advanced technology program

The ATP is a part of National Institute of Standards and Technology (NIST) which is an agency of the US Commerce Department. It offers partnerships with the private sector's (including academia and independent research organizations) early-stage investment in innovative technologies that promise significant commercial payoffs and widespread benefits for the nation. In sharing the risks of technologies that potentially make feasible a broad range of new commercial opportunities, the ATP fosters projects with a high payoff for the nation as a whole, in addition to a direct return to the innovators.

The ATP differs from other government R&D programmes in various respects. It focuses on the technology needs of the American industry, not those of the government (research priorities are set by industry), has strict cost-sharing rules (companies working together must pay at least half of the project costs),[6] and does not production, marketing, sales and distribution costs.

ATP awards are selected through open, peer-reviewed competitions. All industries and all fields of science and technology are eligible. Selection is based on the innovation, the technical risk, potential economic benefits to the nation and the strength of the commercialization plan of the project. ATP awards are for specific time periods, specific goals, specific funding allocations, and completion dates are established at the outset. Projects are monitored and can be terminated for cause before completion. Finally, the ATP accepts proposals only in response to specific published solicitations. Notices of ATP competitions are published in Commerce Business Daily.

Small Business Innovation Research (SBIR)

The SBIR program funds early-stage R&D projects at small technology companies. It is the largest source of early-stage technology financing in the United States. It is a highly competitive programme that encourages small business to explore their technological potential and provides the incentive to profit from its commercialization. Congress required that each year, 11 federal departments and agencies reserve a portion of their R&D funds for SBIR.[7] Small companies retain the intellectual property rights to technologies they develop under these programmes.

To qualify for the programme, the company must be American-owned, for-profit and employing less than 500 workers. The principal researcher should be employed by the company. The awards criteria are small business qualification, degree of innovation, technical merit, and future market potential. The programme has three phases:

- Phase I awards of up to US$100,000 for approximately six months' support exploration of the technical merit or feasibility of an idea or technology.

- Phase II awards of up to US$750,000, for two years, expanding Phase I results. During this time, the R&D work is performed and the developer evaluates commercialization potential. Only Phase I award winners are considered for Phase II.
- Phase III is the period during which Phase II innovation moves from the laboratory into the marketplace. No SBIR funds support this phase. The small business must find funding in the private sector or other non-SBIR federal agency funding.

The programme is coordinated by the Small Business Administration (SBA); an independent agency of the federal government. The SBA reviews the progress of the projects, and reports annually to Congress on its operation. Funding is awarded competitively.

Small Business Technology Transfer (STTR)

The STTR programme is similar in structure to SBIR but funds cooperative R&D projects involving a small business and a research institution (i.e. university, federally funded R&D centre, or non-profit research institution). The purpose of STTR is to create an effective vehicle for moving ideas from research institutions to the market, where they can benefit both private sector and government. Congress required that each year five federal departments and agencies reserve a portion of their R&D funds for STTR.[8]

To qualify for the programme the small businesses must meet eligibility criteria similar to those of the SBIR. The partner must also be located in the United States and meet one of three definitions: non-profit college or university, domestic non-profit research organization, or federally funded R&D centre (FFRDC). Like the SBIR, the programme has three phases and is coordinated by the SBA.

11.3.2 The use of public procurement

Although many specialists argue that public procurement (e.g. Ruttan, 2005 and Montani, 2005) is an important instrument of support to industry in the United States, it is very difficult to infer from available data the precise destination of procurements and, hence, the extent of their use as industrial policy instruments.

The Government Procurement Agreement (GPA) is implemented in US law at the federal level primarily through the TAA of 1979. This provides authority for the President to waive discriminatory purchasing requirements (such as the Buy American Act), designate eligible countries, and ban procurement from non-designated countries. At the state level, the GPA is implemented through laws and regulations in each state.

Procurement at the federal level is decentralized, through the various executive agencies' procurement systems. The Office of Management and Budget (OMB) oversees and coordinates federal procurement, and reviews proposed regulations for compliance with policy guidance, through the Office of Federal Procurement Policy (OFPP). The Federal Acquisition Regulation (FAR) regulates all federal executive agencies' acquisitions of supplies and services with appropriated funds. Agency-specific procurement regulations supplement the FAR. The FAR system allows individual executive agencies and their sub-agencies to develop specific internal guidelines.

Procurement policy provides preferential access conditions to small businesses, veteran-owned small businesses, small disadvantaged business (SDBs), and women-owned small businesses. The DOC determines annually the authorized SDB procurement mechanisms and application factors (percentages). The Small Business Act (P.L. No. 85–536) requires, in principle, each contract with an anticipated value greater than US$2,500 but less than US$100,000 to be reserved exclusively for small business concerns.

With certain exceptions, federal government agencies are required to publish notices of proposed procurement opportunities in excess of US$25,000 in the online federal-government-wide point of entry (GPE), Federal Business Opportunities (FedBizOpps).

Potential contractors are simply required to register online in the Central Contracting Registration (CCR), the primary vendor database for the US Federal Government.

At the sub-federal level, procurement is governed by state or other sub-federal government laws and procurement regulations. In some cases, where procurement is funded with federal money, states must comply with certain federal statutory requirements. Local governments have their own procurement agencies, as well as their own procurement policies. In some states, preferences are granted to local suppliers, and local content requirements are applied under certain conditions. Reciprocal preferences are used among states.

The United States maintains a number of domestic purchasing requirements for procurement not covered by its multilateral or bilateral agreements. For instance, the Buy American Act of 1933 restricts the purchase of supplies and construction materials by government agencies to those defined as 'domestic end-products'. However, the President can waive the Buy American Act and other procurement restrictions.

Access conditions for procurement at the state level vary according to the state. Not all American states participate in the GPA. Among these one finds Alabama, Alaska, New Mexico, Indiana, and South Carolina.

11.4 Outcomes of public support in the United States

Empirical analysis seems to lend support to the US strategy favouring support to R&D. The majority of the empirical studies suggest a positive relation between subsidies and public procurement on one hand and private R&D expenditures on the other. The surveys by Hall and Van Reenen (2000), Jaumotte and Pain (2005), and OXERA (2006) not only support this conclusion regarding subsidies but also found a complementarity between government and private expenditures on R&D. Studies focusing on public procurement (Ruttan, 2005 and Cozzi and Impulitti, 2004) suggest that public procurement in military and defence related research contributed markedly to the technological success of the US industry.

A part of subsidies is structured into specific programmes. Regarding these programmes, Lerner (1999) examined the long-run performance of high-technology firms receiving funds from the SBIR programme. This is the most important programme in term of funds as shown in Table 11.1. The author compared the growth of awardees to a set of matching firms which mitigates potential sample bias. The SBIR awardees appeared to enjoy substantially greater employment and sales growth. This pattern, however, was not uniform. The superior growth of SBIR awardees was confined to firms based in areas with substantial venture capital activity. Moreover, no increase of performance was associated with larger subsidies. The awards seem to play an important role in certifying firm quality but higher amounts do not add much to this signal.

However, as Lerner acknowledged, the analysis did not assess the social benefits of the programme. The social rates of return to R&D could be much higher or much lower than the private returns that the firms performing the research enjoy. In addition, some academics feared that the SBIR led to a reduction in funding for academic research, which may have even greater social benefits. A subsequent analysis by Audretsch (2003) addressed these aspects.

Audretsch (2003) evaluated the impact of the SBIR on the commercial activities of Small and Medium Enterprises (SMEs) based on a comprehensive survey undertaken by the US National Academy's division on Science, Technology, and Economic Policy (STEP). The analysis was complemented by case studies based on detailed interviews with the founders, owners and employees of over fifty firms that had received SBIR assistance. They are dispersed across the United States and span a broad range of technologies, products, and industries.

The results suggested that the benefits of the SBIR extend beyond the impact on the individual recipient firm. The social rate of return, which incorporates external positive impacts, exceeds the private rate of return. There was no evidence of a negative rate of return associated with the SBIR. In particular, the results for firms in the US biotechnology industry showed that the survival and growth rates of SBIR recipients have exceeded those of firms not receiving SBIR funding. Moreover, the SBIR awards provide a source of funding for scientists to launch start-up firms that otherwise would not have had access to alternative sources of funding.

Regarding the impact of ATP, Sakakibara and Branstetter (2003) focused on the effects of participation in ATP-funded consortia on the research productivity of consortia members. The authors developed a data set for one group of firms that participated in ATP-funded research consortia, and for a second control group that was never involved. Innovative output was measured using patent data. The findings revealed a positive relationship between the firms' intensity of participation in research consortia and their overall research productivity. Participation in one additional ATP-funded consortium per year would increase a firm's patenting that year by as much as 8%.

Nail and Brown (2006) sought to assess technology spillovers from the ATP. The analysis combined the North American Industry Classification System (NAICS) and the industry classification data used by ATP online Business Reporting System. This allowed assigning a six-digit NAICS code to each ATP project participant's own-industry and to its customer-industry. Such linkages were identified for any commercial applications reported by project participants. The results of the study demonstrate that ATP projects exhibit certain factors that suggest high spillover potential, such as multi-use innovation, infrastructural technology, and licensing the technology inter-industry. Another finding was that a majority of the ATP participant's industries are characterized as primary technology generators, while approximately one-third of the use-industries are characterized as either primary or secondary technology generators. This suggests that ATP project selection enables technology to be developed in a more sophisticated technology sector, which may then flow to less sophisticated technology sectors.

Shipp et al. (2006) examined behaviour additionality in ATP joint venture projects. The paper is based on results from the Survey of ATP Joint Ventures. The survey shows that companies form an ATP joint venture to benefit from complementary R&D expertise, to pool resources with other firms, and to address a technical problem that is common to their industry. One clear behavioural effect evidenced was that the formation of a joint venture project fosters trust and cooperation among partners. The analysis also showed persistent collaborative links among ATP partners and between ATP firms and their non-ATP technology subcontractors.

Hall et al. (2003) focused on the importance of industry–university research partnerships for US innovative capacity. The industry motivations for industry–university partnerships are access to complementary research activity and research results and access to key university personnel. The university motivations are largely financially based. The paper reports the results of a small survey of such partnerships that focuses on their performance rather than the reasons underlying their formation. The authors selected a sample of 192 projects funded by ATP. The results showed that partners agreed that projects had experienced difficulties acquiring and assimilating basic knowledge necessary for progress toward completion. Prior experience working with a university as a research partner or as a subcontractor is a significant factor in decreasing the difficulty of acquiring and assimilating basic knowledge. Projects with larger for-profit lead partners or non-profit lead partners have experienced more difficulties acquiring and assimilating basic knowledge. Despite such difficulties, and taking the results with caution due to the limited sample size, it seems that universities create research awareness among the research partners in the ATP-funded projects and that projects with larger research budgets undertake research of broader scope, as opposed to researching narrower projects. The authors concluded that universities are important to US innovation.

Turning to public procurements, Ruttan (2005) provides various examples of their role in military and defence-related research that contributed to the technological success of US industry. The examples concern in particular military and commercial aircraft, nuclear energy, computers and semiconductors, Internet, and space industries.

Although not recent examples, the way in which military concerns favoured the development of commercial aircraft is illustrative. The US has employed two principal instruments to support the development of the aircraft industry: state support for aeronautics R&D, and procurement of military aircraft. Before the beginning of the First World War there was substantial concern within the aviation community that the US was lagging in institutionalizing aircraft R&D capacity compared with the major European countries. The perspective of US participation in the First World War speeded up the efforts to fill this gap and gave a birth to the National Committee on Aeronautics (NACA). Until the 1920s, the NACA primary efforts were directed to the development of research facilities and high-skilled personnel formation. During the 1930s, research efforts focused on the domain of the aerodynamics of high speed: to fly higher and at greater speed. The production of the first jet engines in the US during the Second World War was financed by the Air Force. However, when in the late 1940s engineers began to consider the possibility of a commercial jet airliner development, doubts arose that initial sales could break even with development costs. The problem of financing was solved by an Air Force contract to build a military jet tanker designed for the in flight refuelling of the B-52 bomber. This allowed the building of the first US commercial jetliner, the Boeing 707, which set the design standard for the modern commercial jet airliner.

Apart from these examples, Cozzi and Impulitti (2004) attempt to estimate the impact of public procurement on R&D using econometric methods. The authors focused on the impact of the US Government dramatic shift in procurement choices in favour of high-tech sectors in the 1980s and 1990s. Public investment in equipment and software (E&S), which consisted 20% of total government investment in 1980, rose to about 40% in 1990 and to more than 50% in 2001. The private demand also switched towards E&S but more than a decade later. The authors also investigated the impact of the introduction of the Research and Experimentation tax credit in 1981 in stimulating private R&D. Companies that qualified for the credit could deduct or subtract from corporate income taxes an amount that in the period 1981–2004 has been in the range of 20 to 25% of qualified research expenses above a base amount.

The results showed that government policy, indeed, played a non-negligible role in a surge of innovations that hit the US economy since 1980s. It confirms, therefore, the theoretical argument put forward earlier, that public procurement could have a 'pull-off' effect. The latter plays an important role in providing producers of new investment goods with the appropriate market size in an early stage of development.

11.5 Conclusion

This chapter has examined the industrial policy framework in the United States. The analysis shows that it is not possible to dissociate industrial policy from the importance of military concerns in the United States. Military and defence expenses are very large and have a major impact on commercial technology development across sectors that account for an important share of the country's production. US policy seeks to stimulate and support vigorous domestic competition and innovation and to establish and sustain cost-effective industrial and technological capabilities that assure economic competitiveness and military readiness and superiority.

Industrial policy in the United States is the outcome of interplay between four actors: the President, Congress, individual states, and the private sector. The executive departments that seem to be the most involved in supporting business are the Department of Defence, the Department of Energy, the Department of Health, and the Department of Commerce. Interestingly, only the Department of Defence has a Deputy Under Secretary for Industrial Policy.

US industrial policy is mainly horizontal but has differential effects across industries. Science and technology and development of SMEs are clear priority for the United States. Regional development does not seem to be a top priority at the national level.

The private sector receives around 50% of the US federal R&D budget. The direct support to business R&D takes the forms of grants and various forms of tax exemptions. Indirect support (hard to estimate) comes from public procurements. Only a part of the allocated 50% is devoted to structured recurrent programmes. The latter include ATP, the SBIR, and the STTR programs.

Empirical analysis seems to lend support to the US strategy favouring support to R&D. The majority of the empirical studies suggest a positive relation between the various forms of aid schemes and private R&D expenditures. Regarding the specific programmes, available evidence also suggest that they were very effective in stimulating private R&D, that their benefits extend beyond the impact on the individual recipient firm and that they reinforce fruitful collaborations between business and universities.

12
Public Support in Japan

The OECD report on public support to industry (OECD, 1998) presented specific features of industrial policy in Japan for the period 1989–93. Japanese industrial policy, in this period was based on the principle of providing incentives to firms to strengthen their economic performance. The focus of public support policies was on promoting 'technological fundamentals', such as advanced information and telecommunication systems and 'intangible fundamentals' as education and training.

In this period Japan was one of 15 OECD member countries in which public support to manufacturing industries increased the most, even if public support to manufacturing industry measured as a share of manufacturing GDP was below OECD average in each year of the period covered by the survey. In 1991, which showed high spending on public support in Japan, the Japanese public support rate amounted to less than one-third of the OECD average rate. Spending on SME programmes, R&D and export promotion represented around 88% of total expenditure in the period.

Spending on SME had a leading role in total public support to manufacturing industry, representing 50% of the total. With R&D, they represented 70% of total expenditure in 1993. Export promotion, which represented 20% of total public support expenditure in 1993, was in reality a large export credit insurance programme which accounted for around 90% of such support. Enterprise and sector-specific support represented a limited percentage of total public support, except energy which represented 3.7% of the 5.8% in 1993. The computer industry and shipbuilding were the main beneficiaries of sector-targeted programmes. Under the policy objective of R&D, spending remained relatively stable and horizontal programmes in support of technological developments absorbed more than 70% of the total R&D expenditure, the remaining 30% being focused on technology-specific programmes. The policy objective of regional development remained limited, below 5% of the total, and sub-central levels of government were mainly involved in providing such supports. At that time, expenditure on export was mainly focused on a large export credit insurance programme, which represented about 90% of such support (see Table 12.1).

It is interesting to underline that a large part of public support programmes are administered by regional governments, particularly the promotion of SMEs and local industries. Of the 235 programmes of public support to industry in the 1990s, the majority were managed and financed by local governments. Only 37 of the 235 programmes were carried out under the responsibility of the central Japanese government.

The bursting of the economic bubble at the beginning of the 1990s and the economic recession that ensued convinced the Japanese population and political elites that their economic system needed liberalizing reforms. That particularly affected the thinking about the role of state and public support policies towards industry.

The creation of the Deregulation Subcommittee in 1995 was the start date of a decade-long process of regulatory reform. This deregulation subcommittee was directly attached to the Prime Minister's office. It proposed every year, new deregulation which may be implemented as

Table 12.1 Expenditure by policy objectives (amount in Bio Yens and %) in Japan

		1993	1989
SME	Yen	143.7	152.7
	%	50.0	56.5
R&D	Yen	48.5	47.4
	%	16.9	17.5
Export	Yen	57.7	40.7
	%	20.0	15.0
Sector (inc. Energy)	Yen	16.6	12.3
	%	5.8	4.6
Regional	Yen	9.5	9.9
	%	3.3	3.7
Others	Yen	12.1	7.4
	%	4.1	2.7
Total	Yen	288.1	270.4

Source: OECD, 1998.

the government's regulatory reform plans. This deregulation subcommittee was replaced by the Council for Regulatory Reform.

Deregulatory measures in the 1990s include public utilities such as electricity and gas, transportation, telecommunications, and financial services These deregulation measures have enhanced competition and neo-liberal scholars and business leaders continue to ask the government to pursue the process of liberalization. For example, in July 2003, new telecommunications common carriers filed a suit against the Ministry of Public Management, Home Affairs, Posts and Telecommunications, to force it to cancel approval given to NTT (Nippon Telegraph and Telecom corp.), the incumbent telecom company in Japan, to raise interconnection charges.

M&A was in Japan very rare in the 1980s, but it is more and more considered as a mean for restructuring and spending business transformation. The total M&A was less than 1,000 at the beginning of the 1990s compared with over 3,000 in 2003 (Nezu, 2007). More M&As are particularly needed in Japan, since compared with other industrialized countries, the number of firms in one sector was generally much larger, as in the car sector (8 enterprises) and the electronic industry (12 enterprises). Moreover, with the economic stagnation of the 1990s, many companies in financial trouble were forced to sell out, even to foreign companies – as did Nissan in the car sector. It is interesting to note the changing stance of METI in the debate over M&A, since, in the past MITI was considered to be against M&A. In 2006, with an amendment to the corporate law, M&A by foreign companies targeting Japanese enterprises through the swap of stocks became possible (Nezu, 2007). Finally, in the field of competition policy, new guidelines by the JFTC also are making M&A easier.

The banking sector has been less affected by deregulation. With the collapse of Japan's asset bubble, Japanese banks were confronted with massive non-performing loans. Japanese governments have not been aggressive in forcing banks to write off non-performing loans and have instead used public funding to avoid widespread bankruptcies and to manage a soft-landing with limited impact on the labour market. With a truly liberalized banking system and without public support, many of the indebted small and medium firms would go out of business. To a large extent, sustained low interest rates and the Japanese government policy of avoiding bankruptcies had a major impact on enterprises survival and constituted a key element of public support policy to industry in Japan.

However, the public support policy marked an important change from the 1990s. Sectoral policies became less important and the change of this philosophy was reflected by the change of the basic structure of the MITI. In 2000, MITI was changed into METI and became responsible for the macro economy. The horizontal bureau of the METI became more important (more responsibilities and staff) than the vertical bureau in charge of sectoral policies (Nezu, 2007).

12.1 Objectives of public support

During its rapid growth period, the Japanese government undertook a variety of public support interventions, such as the encouragement of research consortia between firms, capital channelled to preferred sectors through direct or indirect subsidies through state-owned banks, preferential tax breaks, accelerated depreciation allowed under the tax system (Goto and Wakasugi, 1988). A variety of economic arguments for activist industrial policies have been involved with respect to Japan (see Part I).

However, since the mid-1980s, the traditional approach to industrial policy and their instruments has been confronted with changes in the domestic and international environment for Japanese economic performance and growing budget deficit. Japan now faces significant challenges. 'Today, at the technological frontier, with demographics that put an increasing premium on raising productivity, Japan faces significant challenges in encouraging innovation and entrepreneurship' (Noland, 2007). Emerging innovation in emerging sectors or activities and entrepreneurship, start-up, and SMEs are the pillars of the new industrial Japanese industrial policy.

The Japanese government is determined to continue its strong support for those technologies they believe are essential to maintaining Japan competitiveness. Investment in Japan's science and technology infrastructure continues to be an essential element of Japan's economic industrial policy. The council for Science and Technology Policy (Council for S&T): chaired by the Prime Minister includes 15 permanent members, in particular the Ministry of Education (MEXT), the Ministry of Economy Trade and Industry (METI), and academics. Its functions are to establish the basic policy planning in promoting S&T, to examine resources (budget, personnelm and others) allocated to S&T and finally to review national S&T projects.

Small and medium enterprises (SMEs) have always played a very important role in Japanese industry, in particular as suppliers to large firms.[1] The long-stranding relations between SMEs and large enterprises were negatively affected by economic stagnation, since due to lack of competition between suppliers, outsourcing prices for large enterprises became too high. The pressure on cost implied the breaking up of the traditional relations between SMEs and large groups. Throughout the period of the bubble economy, SMEs were big sufferers. In 2006, looking back, the METI underlined that 'the past 20 years can be redefined as an unusual period in which the Japanese economy deviated from the norm in that the presence of major companies and banks were overstated' compared to SMEs. In Japan, the percentage of closures of enterprises was systematically higher than the percentage of new business launches in the period from 1991 to 2004.

It is widely accepted by economists that high-growth SMEs contribute to economic wealth; but in Japan, as shown in Figure 12.1, business start-up rate for all types of business in Japan had been stable and the rate of business closings gradually had been increasing. In 1999 a change in the philosophy behind SME policy was implemented, as Japan was confronted with a decreasing number of start-ups and innovative SMEs. The basic philosophy of the new public SME policy was the development of diverse and vigorous growth of independent SMEs to revitalize the Japanese economy. The main public policies were to support business creation and management reforms in existing SMEs, to encourage partnerships between SMEs, universities, and government, to implement new government organizations for SME financing, and to support industrial concentration of SMEs and local and regional revitalization.

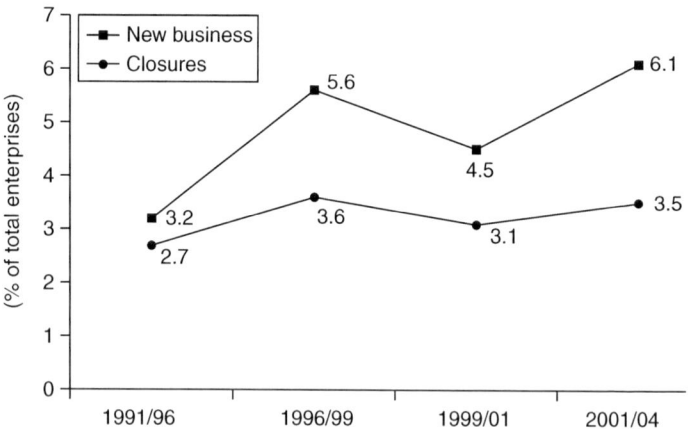

Figure 12.1 Trends in new business launches and closures by number of enterprises
Source: METI.

Based on the SME basic low, the METI has set up the 'small and medium enterprise policy making council'. This council leads SME policy, policymaking systems, and definitions of SMEs. It investigates a wide variety of matters concerning SMEs in general, including finances, banking, and labour. It submits reports and documents, expresses opinions, present explanation in response to request by Ministers. The government bases its policies towards SMEs on these reports. Council members are made up of people such as officials from the METI, representatives of SME support institutions and business groups, people with academic experience in SMEs, and lawyers.

12.2 Actors

12.2.1 R&Ds

The basic plan of S&T for 2001/2005 had a budget of 24 trillion yen over five years. The current basic plan of S&T (2006/2010) has a budget of 25 trillion yen. Four major priority areas (life science, ICT, environment, nanotech/materials) are defined in the basic plan of S&T and the goal is to promote innovation for sustainable growth.

The distribution of public funding in R&D is mainly done by the Ministry of Education, Culture, Sport, and S&T (65% of the total budget) for basic research and by the METI (16% of the total budget) for applied research, through S&T to innovation in the enterprises (see Table 12.2 and Figure 12.2).

The METI has defined a *strategic technology roadmap* for R&D which displays improvement and progress of technologies generated from R&D, and enhancement of desired functions with clear deadlines. The roadmap also describes the technological challenges and the desired

Table 12.2 Distribution of public funding in R&D in Japan (in 2006)

Ministry of Education, Culture, Sport, S&T	65%
Ministry of Economy, Trade and Industry	16%
Japan Defence Agency	5%
Ministry of Health, Labour and Welfare	4%
Ministry of Agriculture, Forestry and Fisheries	3%
Ministry of Land, Infrastructure and Transportation	2%
Others	5%
Total	100%

Source: Takayuhi Sumita, Director, METI.

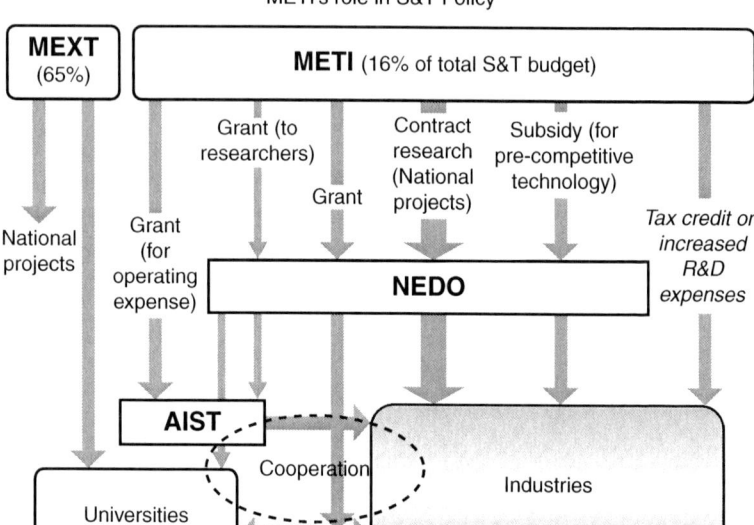

Figure 12.2 Distribution of public funding in R&D in Japan
Source: Takayuki Sumita.

functions of the technologies in order to satisfy market and social needs, the objective being to prioritize critical technologies.

One of the priorities of METI's policy in the field of R&D is the *establishment of regional consortium clusters*. These are defined as networks of regional industries, universities, and research institutes that can create dynamic innovations under cooperative and competitive relationships. Some 17 regional industrial clusters are being promoted by METI's regional offices, and 290 local universities and 9,800 private companies are involved in the 17 clusters.

In June 2006 the government also launched a new policy initiative for the strengthening of global competitiveness and productivity improvement. One of the core concepts is the 'Innovation Super High-Way'. The government encourages making the linkage between science, technology, and business stronger and thicker, with two-way flows of knowledge and human resources to concentrate on fusion of various knowledge through alliances and cooperation between all the people concerned. The objective is that Japan will be a global innovation centre, the place of experimentation of innovation, and to create accumulation of highly advanced knowledge on manufacturing in every sector.

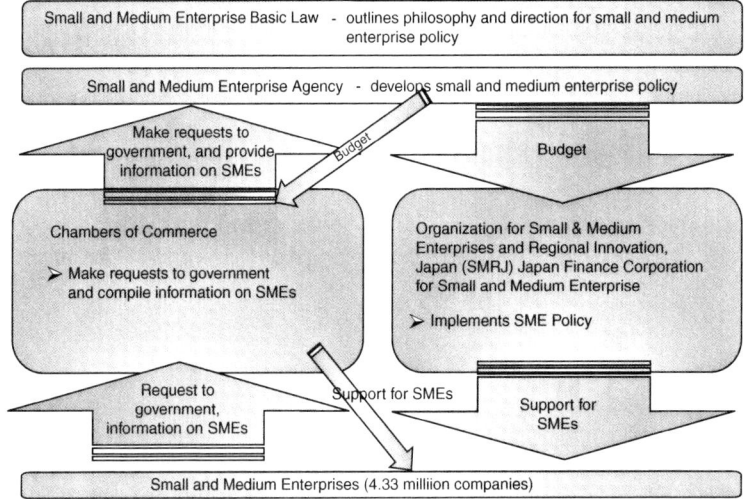

Figure 12.3 Framework for SME policy
Source: 'Japanese Policy on Small and Medium Enterprises', Small and Medium Enterprise Agency, METI, March 2007.

For certain economists, the aim of the new industrial policy in Japan is to promote specific sectors, to bridge the gap between research and product development and hasten the commercialization of seed technology and to promote specific sectors. For Weiss (2005), 'in particular, echoing earlier large-scale projects, METI is now sponsoring numerous R&D consortia at the core of its strategy to regain word leadership in the critical sector of semiconductors'.

12.2.2 SMEs

The framework for SME policy outlines the philosophy and the direction of public support to develop SMEs. The Chambers of Commerce compile and provide information on SMEs to government and to the 'small and medium enterprise agency'. This agency implements SME policy and has a budget of 162 billion yen for 2007 (see Figure 12.3).

12.3 Instruments

12.3.1 R&Ds

The Japanese government has promoted R&D through direct subsidies, special deductions for R&D costs, and low-interest loans from public financial institutions (Harayama, 2001). As we noted in the previous section, a large number of government institutions provide direct or indirect public support to R&D in Japan. Assessing a clear pattern of support by instrument is difficult.

For Noland (2007: 7), 'in quantitative terms, the direct subsidies are the most important component of government support, about twice a large as the tax provisions in most years. Implicit subsidies through the provision of low-interest loans have been relatively unimportant; government support for research organization is approximately as large as direct subsidies'.

One of the Ministry of Education's roles in S&T Policy is to provide *grants* to researchers; grants for operating expenses, *subsidies* for precompetitive technology to support the efforts of industries in the field of R&D. One of approach used by METI is *tax credit* on increased R&D expenses. The objective is to provide tax incentives for private sector R&D to strengthen incentives to increase R&D.

12.3.2 SMEs

Uesugi Iichiro (Deputy Director of the small and medium enterprise agency) underlined that success or failure to obtain financing smoothly is of primarily importance for SMEs, since that has a direct impact on survival or exit. Large enterprises have access to diverse forms of financing including the issuance of shares or bonds. The Japanese government aims to alleviate many of the problems incurred by information asymmetry in SME financing, particularly in the periods of low economic growth and after the bursting of the Japanese bubble.

Government SME financing organizations supplement private sector bank financing in traditional financial markets. The funding received from government financing organizations amounts to 9.3% of the total of SME financing (2006) (see Table 12.3). The two main types of government SME financing are:

- government financing for business creation and management reform of existing SMEs;
- Safety net financing in times of credit uncertainty such as chains of bankruptcy or in times of natural disasters such as earthquakes.

For example, *public finance corporations* may provide to SMEs low interest loans without guarantors, with a financing limit of 10 million Yen, at annual interest rate of 2.2%. This public funding represents 56,000 cases per year with a total lending of around 200 billion yen.

Table 12.3 SME financing in Japan (September 2006)

	In trillions Yen	In (%)
Private financial institution	232.0	90.7
SME finance corporation	6.8	2.7
Public finance corporation	7.6	3.0
Commercial or industrial association bank	9.3	3.6
Total	255.7	100.0

Source: METI.

Table 12.4 SME favourable tax system

	Corporate tax central government (%)	Corporate tax Regional tax
Large enterprises	30	7.2% + size-based corporate tax
SMEs	22	5% depending on annual income deep to 9.6%

Source: METI.

Such low-interest financing without guarantors concern small enterprises with limited assets or with hypothetical value, and unskilled or unstable management.

Another system is the *credit guarantee systems*. Credit associations guarantee borrowed amounts to private-sector financial institutions to facilitate supply of financing to SME lacking credits. If the guaranteed SME is unable to make repayments, subrogate repayments are made with the network of 52 credit associations established throughout Japan. The guaranteed amount from the 52 credit associations was approximately 29 trillion yen in 2006. The government provided the grants and monitoring for these 52 credit associations to support the credit guaranteed systems. METI has mentioned that this credit guarantee system association will create 'an anonymous database of data from more than 2.2 million cases of SME finance from the 52 credit association under the guidance of the small and medium agency, with the aim of supporting the risk assessment of the private sector banks'.

SMEs also benefit from a favourable tax system. The corporate taxes from central government or region are lower than for large enterprises (see Table 12.4).

Moreover, tax benefits for SMEs are put in place to provide policy incentives: depreciation or tax deduction for purchasing equipment, when introducing IT systems, to invest in human resources (education and training costs), to invest in research and development. One of the major SME policies in Japan is to *encourage business creation*. In order to be successful the METI has established with the Chambers of Commerce a business start-up academy where start-up may receive support from a senior advisor to formulate a business plan, to acquire capital to set up the business and to study successful examples of business start-ups and procedure. A business creation financing system based on public finance corporations intervene for start-up with unsecured funding or no guarantor with a financing limit of 10 million Yen. Approximately 30,000 cases totalling 92 billion Yen were covered by this system between July 2001 and October 2006.

The government also provides support for *internationalization* to major SMEs. As SMEs cannot acquire easily information on foreign customs' procedures or investment regulations, or find foreign business partners, the government provides SMEs with specialist trade and investment advisors for each foreign country made up of former employees of trading companies or manufacturers with practical foreign experience: there are around 300 advisors for approximately 2,000 cases per year.

12.4 Industry sector and structure

The total R&D expenditures for the manufacturing sector were 17.9 trillion yen in 2005, and this amount has increased for the sixth consecutive year. The ratio of total R&D expenditure in Japan (as a percentage of DGP) exceeds 3% which is extremely high compared with other countries. In volume, Japan's research expenditure amounted to US$118 billion, equivalent to approximately 40% of that of the United States, which amounted to US$312 billion. Researchers in Japan numbered approximately 680,000 full-timers, approximately 50% of the US figure. It is interesting to note that the industrial sector represents 60% of the total, universities approximately 36%, and public organizations only 4%.

In FY 2005, if the research expenditure used for natural science is divided according to the nature of research 'basic research, application and development', the research expenditure used for development amounted to 63% of the aggregate research expenditure, that used for application approximately 23%, and that used for basic research amounted approximately to 14%. Compared with FY 2004, the aggregate research expenditure rose by 5.6%, of which the research expenditure used for development, basic research and application rose by 6.1%, 5.2% and 4.6% respectively.

The research expenditure of manufacturing industries is concentrated in large Japanese firms (defined as more than 10 billion yen capitalization). They represented 76.2% of the total research expenditure of manufacturing industries in 2006, compared with 50–60% in the 1980s for the same sample of large enterprises.

The total research expenditure amounted to 13 trillion yen in FY 2005. Of the total research expenditure of the business sector, manufacturing industries represented 86%, the service industry 5.1%, and the information and communication industry 4.1%. In the manufacturing sector (11.2 trillion yen in FY 2005) the electrical machinery industry represents 30.9%, the automotive industry 16.3%, the mechanical sector 8.2%.

From the point of view of the ratio of research expenditure to sale, the situation is different. The pharmaceutical industry has the highest ratio of research expenditure of sales by industry in the manufacturing sector. The precision machinery industry is second (7.7%) and the information and communication machinery and appliance industry third, at 6.7%. Compared with the US firms, the ratio of R&D expenditure to sales was at almost the same high level in the automotive, pharmaceutical, and steel industries. However, in the electrical machinery, chemical and information processing industries, R&D investment measured as the ratio of R&D expenditure to sales was lower than in the United States.

Assessing the sectoral pattern of public support policy in Japan is however very difficult. Direct subsidies and R&D tax deductions are generally reported only at aggregate level. If we look at the project defined by the Council for Science and Technology, the sectors receiving the most funding in 2004 were: basic science (260 billion Yen), life science (72 billion Yen), information technology (30 billion Yen), environment (21 billion Yen), social infrastructure including disaster mitigation (17 billion Yen) and nanotechnology (5 billion Yen). In 2007, the METI's four priority areas were: life science, IT, environmental science, and nanotechnology. The new industries that will be supported to meet social needs will be: robots, fuel cells, digital content, digital consumer electronics (Sumita, 2007).

One of the measures of the public support policies to the different sectors of the economy is given by the ratio of implicit capital subsidy to investment for different industries. The implicit capital subsidy is measured (Noland, 2007) by direct subsidies and indirect subsidies, such loans at rates below the prevailing market interest rate or the preferred accelerated depreciation allowed under the tax system. The implicit capital subsidy to investment ratio was generally low, less than 5% in Japan, but it is interesting to note that sectors such as mining petroleum and coal products, or iron and steel, were net beneficiaries in the mid-1980s. Noland (2007) proposed also to look at sectoral tax data per sector for the period 1974–90. The conclusion was that 'for the most part, Japanese manufacturing was taxed in order to provide subsidies for other sectors (such as agriculture and mining). Again, it is revealing that textile was the one manufacturing sector that was a significant beneficiary – a stereotypically, large, established and declining sector' (p. 6). Of course, the Japanese government has also promoted high-technology sectors.

12.5 Public sector and public procurement

State ownership of manufacturing enterprises is very limited in Japan, especially in comparison with a many European countries. The government is not even a minority shareholder of any manufacturing industry. Moreover, there is no monopoly in sectors such as railways, for example. The Japanese government permits private competition even with its own companies. For example, the government-owned Japanese National Railways is competing with private railway companies.

Public procurement in Japan has no specialized authority and is undertaken in a decentralized way by each procurement entity on its own. There is no national procurement agency.

A survey of government procurement is published regularly,[2] but this covers in principle only contracts made by central government entities and public corporations and products and services whose value exceeds the threshold of 17 million yen in 2001. Independent administrative institutions such as national research institutes and national museums are not covered by these surveys.

Looking at the most important entities in Japanese public procurement, Japan post accounted for the largest share of public procurement in 2005 (18.2% of the total), followed by the corporate national university (15.4% of the total) (see Table 12.5).

The total value for government procurement of goods and services for 2005 was 913 billion yen, a decrease of 12.5% from 2000 (see Table 12.6).

In 2005, about 76% of the total value of goods procurement by the Japanese government was contracted through open tendering procedures. In contrast, 66% of the total value of services procurement was contracted through single tendering procedures.

Table 12.5 Entities with large procurement in 2005 (value basis)

1	Japan Post	18.2%
2	National University corporation	15.4%
3	Ministry of Land, Infrastructure and Transport	11.1%
4	Ministry of Finance	8.1%
5	Ministry of Health, Labour and Welfare	4.0%
6	National Police agency	3.3%
7	Ministry of Internal Affairs and Communication	3.0%
8	National Hospital organization	2.3%
9	Ministry of Justice	2.3%
10	Inter-University Research Institute corporation	1.7%

Source: Japan's Government Procurement Policy and Achievements, 2006.

Table 12.6 Total value and number of government procurement contracts in Japan (Yen and number of contracts)

	2000	2005	Change 2005/2000 (%)
Total value	10,431	9,130	−12.5
Total number of contracts	15,348	11,548	−24.8

Source: Products and services covered by government, procurement, survey (http://www.kantei.go.jp.foreign/procurement/2006).

12.5.1 Foreign penetration of public procurement

In 2005, foreign goods and services accounted for about 10.3% of the total procurement value compared to 14.7% in 2000. Products and services from the United States accounted for about 48% of the total foreign products and services public procurement compared with 29% only from the EU on the value basis. The foreign share was particularly high for a limited number of products: Aircraft (83%), mineral products (65%), medical equipment (37%) and medicinal and pharmaceutical products (34%). For the public procurement of services, on the other hand, the foreign share is low, except for telecommunication services (27%).

12.5.2 Procurement contracts by products and services categories

Government procurement by product amounted to about 549 billion yen in 2005. The products with the largest shares was 'office machinery and data processing equipment', which accounted for about one-third of total procurement value, followed by 'telecommunication and sound recording and reproducing apparatus' (8% of the total).

Government procurement by services amounted to about 335 billion yen; 66% of this was spent on 'computer and related services'.

12.5.3 Award procedures and innovation policy

As a general rule, a contract is awarded to the lowest price tender, provided that the price does not exceed the ceiling price evaluated in advance by the procuring entity. There is no reference to innovation in the Japanese documents on public procurement. However, for certain products, public purchase of prototypes is an integral part of the process. This is the case in energy efficient technologies, where aspects of innovation within public procurement can be observed.

Where the lowest-price award method is deemed inadequate, the adoption of the overall greatest value (OGV) evaluation method is encouraged. However, in 2005, this OGV approach was limited and represented less than 5% of total procurement. Some 25% of these contracts were awarded to foreign products and services. In the areas of computer products and services, telecommunications products and services, and medical technology products and services, when large procurement is conducted it is obligatory to apply the OGV.

Each ministry follows its own procurement process and so its own has standard forms and regulations for contracts.

12.6 Evaluation and efficiency of public support policy

The evaluation of Japanese industrial policy has drastically changed over time. To a large extent, the perception of this evaluation was highly sensitive to the economic performance of Japan.

In the 1980s and the early 1990s there was a perception in the United States that the success of the Japanese economy was widely explained by the public support of successful new industries: funding R&D, inducing banks to lend them long-term investment capital at low interest, making tax concessions in favoured sectors, and restricting imports to assure high profit margins on domestic sales. Papers such as Tyson, L. A. (1992) underlined that Japanese industrial policy was one of the major explanations of the economic growth of the Japanese economy in the 1970s.

In contrast, recent evaluation (Porter at al., 2000) claimed that Japanese industrial policy had failed to pick up high-tech and growing industries and has sustained declining and inefficient sectors. For Porter and Sakakibara, the country's post-war economic prosperity was widely explained by internationally successful sectors where internal competition was invariably fierce. In contrast, the sectors in which competition was restricted prove to be those where Japan was not internationally successful (Porter and Sakakibara, 2004). Moreover two industries, the automotive sector and consumer electronics, perceived as the most successful Japanese industries in world markets, did not benefit from extensive government support, in contrast to some other industries such as chemicals and steel. Noland (2007) underlines that evidence indicates that most Japanese government resources went to large politically influential 'backward' sectors, suggesting that political economy considerations may be central to Japanese industrial policy. He underlines also that the two of Japan's most successful industries (the automotive and consumer electronics industries) have enjoyed no special government support and that for the computer-related industry there was no unusual government support in term of subsidies, loans, or tax advantages. For example, the Japanese government's R&D expenditure in the semiconductor field have been far less than half of the US government's expenditure in the same sector in the 1980s.

Finally, in a recent article (2005), Kiyota and Okazabi state that 'these negative impacts do not necessarily mean that the industrial policy was a failure. These policy tools were mainly applied for purposes other than promoting growing industries, including the adjustment of declining industries and the construction of social infrastructure. As presented in the figures of public support policy (Noland, 2007) the patterns of public interventions in Japan has been largely determined by political considerations, in which large, declining sectors exerted a disproportionate influence.

12.6.1 Evaluation of R&D policy

The comparison of global competitiveness by the International Institute for Management Development in Geneva shows that in the case of Japan, the global competitiveness ranking was relatively low (17th) but that the technology related ranking was quite high: number 2 compared to number 1 for the United States. The ranking of the technology-related index was based on indices such as the aggregate R&D expenditure, the number of researchers, the number of research papers released, the number of cases of foreign patents acquired, interest in science and intellectual property protection.

A recent study by the Economist Intelligence Unit also ranks Japan, Switzerland, the United States, and Sweden as the top four innovators among the 82 economies observed from 2002 to 2006. The study defines innovation as 'the application of knowledge in a novel way, primarily for economic benefit'. The number of patents a country generates per million people was considered as the most appropriate measure of innovation. 'Because Japan's population is only 42% of that of the US, its ratio of patents per million populations is 3.5 times higher than the United States – and indeed the highest such ratio at all.' EIU (2007, 12) Reasons given for this performance are the Japanese economy's large proportion of high-technology activities that are more innovation-intensive than traditional industries. More generally, Japan's resource-poor economy has taken an 'innovative or die' approach, and there is a symbiotic relationship between many large companies and innovative associated SMEs. Another factor explaining this performance of Japan as top country for innovation is its proportionately greater investment in R&D than the other major countries, including the United States. The EIU study states that, despite efforts to boost its innovation performance, the EU is unlikely to close the 'innovation gap' with Japan and the United States in the next five years.

12.6.2 Evaluation of SME policy

The RIETI (Research Institute of Economy, Trade and Industry from the METI) has conducted a large study on SME financing in Japan. The RIETI study shows that (1) credit guarantee systems play positive roles in obtaining loans; (2) companies providing guarantees are subject to more frequent monitoring and are more likely to build long-term relationships with banks; (3) high-risk high-tech SMEs that are prone to moral hazard provide more guarantees. The conclusion is that in Japan the credit guarantee system is complementary to, and not substitute for, classic monitoring by banks and relationship lending.

More precisely, the study has measured the effects of the special credit guaranteed system by companies before and after the induction of the programme. The authors found that this public programme improved not only the financing environment of SMEs but also the performance of the SMEs (profit margins, tangible sets to total assets). However the positive effect of the programme is not observable for companies with a very low equity ratio (a good indicator of high credit risk).

Another article (Honjo and Harada, 2006) investigated the effects of public policy and financial structure on the growth of SMEs. Using a panel data set on SMEs in the manufacturing industry, the authors examined whether or not SME public policy and financial structure effect firm growth. They found that public policy and cash flow have a positive impact on the growth of SMEs.

12.7 Conclusion

In the 1970s and 1980s, active public support policies were invoked with respect to Japan, even if data on public support policies showed that established and declining sectors were also large beneficiaries of sectoral policies. Moreover, at the beginning of the 1990s, Japanese public support, measured as a share of manufacturing GDP, was below the OECD average rate. Finally, SMEs and R&D represented around 67% of total public support expenditure at that time (1993) and are still today clear priorities for the Japanese government.

In the 1990s, after the crash of the Tokyo stock market, the Japanese economy entered a decade of economic stagnation. Japan faced significant challenges in encouraging innovation and competition. The new public policy offered approaches such as deregulation, the strengthening of competition policy, enhancing innovation and supporting entrepreneurship. The change of public support philosophy was also reflected by the change of the basic structure of the MITI and the change of the name to METI.

Japan is perceived as a top country for innovation and the technology-related ranking of the global competitiveness of Japan is relatively high. As it is approaching the global technological frontier, clearly Japan continues to pursue selective intervention policies to promote high-tech sectors. The council for science and technology policy chaired by the Prime Minister establishes the basic policy planning, the resources and the review of national S&T projects. The Ministry of Education (65% distribution of public funding in R&D for basic research mainly to universities and national projects) and the METI (16% distribution of public funding in R&D for applied research and innovation mainly to enterprises) are the key actors in Japanese S&T policy. METI continues to emphasize a sector-specific approach in S&T, and its priority areas, approved by the council for S&T, are of four cutting-edge industries with competence and three new industries to meet emerging social needs.

Throughout the period of economic stagnation, SMEs were the big sufferers and the closures of SMEs was systematically higher than the percentage of new business launches. Particularly in depressed industries such as construction and retail sectors, many indebted and poorly performing SME exited from the market. The objective of the new SME policy was the development of diverse and vigorous SMEs. Government SME financing organizations supplement private banks and the fund received from government organizations amounts to 10% of total SME financing. Public finance also corporations provided low interest loans without guarantors to SME, and credit association supported by the government has put in place a credit guarantee systems to facilitate supply of financing to SMEs lacking credits.

Direct subsidies are the most important components of the Japanese public support policies to S&T, being about twice as large as tax provisions. Low interest loans have been relatively important and direct public support for research organization is approximately as large as direct subsidies.

Public procurement in Japan has no specialized authority and is undertaken in a decentralized way by each procurement agency. Foreign goods and services accounted only for about 10% of total procurement value in 2005, compared with about 15% in 2000, and the foreign share is only high in the aircraft, medical equipment, and pharmaceutical industries. As general rule, a contract is awarded to the tendered on the basis of the lowest price and there is no reference to innovation in the Japanese document on public procurement. Where the lowest price award method is inadequate, the adoption of the overall-greatest value evaluation is encouraged but represents less than 5% of total procurement.

The evaluation of the effectiveness of Japanese sectoral industrial policy has changed over time and to a large extent was highly sensitive to the country's economic performance. In the United States in the 1980s it was believed that the success of the Japanese economy was widely explained by public support policies to specific sectors, but recent evaluation claimed that Japanese industrial policy has failed to pick up high-tech and growing industries and has sustained declined sectors. However, if sectoral policies have failed, horizontal policies to support R&D and SME were clearly welfare-enhancing. The investigation of the effect of public policy towards SME on the part of the METI found that the public programme improved the financing and the performance of SMEs. Finally Japan is considered to be one of the top innovators with greater investment in R&D than the other major countries reviewed.

Conclusions

After half a century of controversy about the costs and benefits of implementing industrial policy, economists' attitude toward public support to business is now taking an intermediate position between the past two extreme views, that is, state planning and intervention versus completely free market mechanisms as the main driving force of economic development. A large majority of economists considers that public action could combine with private initiative to foster restructuring, diversification, and technological dynamism. It appears, therefore, that an up-to-date analysis of the debate and evidence on the costs and benefits of pursuing industrial policy is timely. The present book tries to fulfil this mission drawing on recent developments in the theoretical and empirical literature and on the experience of five industrialized countries (Germany, the United Kingdom, France, the United States, and Japan). It offers a structured and up-to-date analysis relating theoretical arguments, implementation approaches, and effectiveness of industrial policy.

Theory presents the choices of public support to business as the results of the trade-off between 'market failures' and 'government failures', that is, in which cases the market (government) can do better than the government (market) in achieving a given objective. Market failures are related to imperfect information (which may, for instance, impact on a firm's innovation), externalities (which may induce sub-optimal decisions if not taken into account), and market power (which may incite a government to support specific domestic industries in order to give them advantage on international markets). Government failures are also related to imperfect information (government officials are not necessarily better informed than private agents), conflict with other policies (e.g. competition and trade policies), and self-interest seeking (desire to win elections, corruption, lobbying, and capture).

Empirical evidence strongly supports the existence of a positive relation between public support and private R&D expenditures. In contrast, there is hardly any solid evidence that such support can induce a significant increase in productivity, especially in the long run. There are even cases where support crowds out private investment in physical capital. Research on the relationship between public support and firm locations suggest that the ability of the different schemes to influence the location of firms is weak. Meanwhile, market incentives (market size, infrastructure, natural resources, presence of other firms, etc.) for agglomeration appear to be stronger than government-side incentives. There are only a few empirical investigations of government failures in relation to public support. They confirm the risk that weak institutional environment coupled with strong vested interests may entail significant efficiency losses and wasteful public spending.

The comparison of the amounts of public support across countries, even focusing on two instruments (subsidies and public procurement), is not easy due to differences in data definitions and availability. To secure as much comparability as possible, the definition, based on National Accounts data, used by the Commission services has been adopted in this study. The analysis shows that public procurement as a share of GDP is broadly similar across the five countries (especially since 2001). However, looking at public procurement, according to the functions as defined in the National Accounts reveals interesting differences across the five countries. The first difference between the three European countries on the one hand and the United States and Japan on the other is in the importance of the function of 'social protection'.[1] While in France and Germany 'social protection' takes up more than 60% of the total amount of public procurement (UK, 14%), the corresponding share in the United States and Japan does not exceed 4% and 3% respectively. Procurements in percentage of GDP pertaining to 'economic affairs' are in contrast much higher in the United States and Japan than in the European countries: 1.1% in France, 1.84% in Germany, 1.54% in the United Kingdom, 2.30% in the United States and 3.18% in Japan. This suggests that, compared with the United States and Japan, European countries use public procurement as an instrument of public support for industry to a much smaller extent. A similar picture emerges regarding subsidies.

The comparison of the public support framework across countries shows that the main objectives are quite often the same: science and technology, development of small firms, regional policy, and energy efficiency. However, the countries allocate very different amounts of

Conclusions 205

support to each objective. For example, regional policy is more important in countries with considerable regional disparities, and SME policy is more important in large countries.

The countries also apply different rules, procedures and instruments to attain their objectives. There are at least two models of public support policies. The first model is found to be primarily 'soft' in nature, consisting of advisory support, encouragement of partnerships, and the dissemination of best practices. The policy management is generally decentralized and the public support programmes are provided by agencies, wholly or partly funded by central government. This Anglo-Saxon approach to industrial policy is characterized by a low level of subsidy.

The second model is found to be more interventionist. Industrial policy is characterized here by large amounts of subsidies to companies and in some case the state is a shareholder of many enterprises. When mergers and acquisitions take place, in particular by foreign enterprises, the role of the state may be very significant. Generally, the government has a clear responsibility of deciding strategic industrial priorities, and competitiveness remains a very sensitive issue in public debate. This is the case in the three other countries.

A by-product of our analysis is that the impact of public support policies remains seriously under-researched, although most extensive subsidy programmes affect domestic resource allocation and income distribution. At the international level, such programmes may also cause distortions in international resource allocation by affecting competitiveness. Moreover, faced with the multiplicity of objectives of public support policies and with their interrelationships, it is increasingly difficult to judge to what extent a public support programme is a success or not. In many countries covered here there is an insufficient number of reports (or none at all) devoted to evaluating the real economic effectiveness of support public policies. More research on the economic impact of public support policies is crucially needed.

Another point concerns the widespread idea among economists that public procurements play an important role in the success of the United States regarding advanced technology. Recently, the United Kingdom also decided to better target its procurement policy toward fostering R&D. However, evidence remains mainly anecdotal, and systematic quantitative analyses are very scarce. The role of public procurements deserves ambitious investigation if one wants to obtain a clear view on their positive effect on growth.

Notes

1 Public Support to Business: An Overview

1. We include R&D in the externalities category under the heading of knowledge externalities.
2. As stated in the Introduction, economists often include rescue to sector or firms in difficulties and equity purposes among public support objectives. For clarity and efficacy, this study does not cover these aspects.
3. Chapter 4 presents a more detailed discussion of this subject.

2 Cases for Public Support: Market Failures

1. An example of investment guarantee can be found in South Korea practice, where the regime of President Park gave implicit investment guarantees to leading Chaebols engaged in new areas of investment. However, this type of public support is open to moral hazard and abuse (Rodrik, 2004).
2. An optimal tariff is one that improves a country's terms of trade to the detriment of its trading partners.

3 Argument Against Public Support: Government Failures

1. In other documents the Commission cites other goals such as consumer welfare (e.g. Merger Regulation) or total welfare (e.g. state aid to R&D).

4 Instruments of Support: Subsidies and Public Procurement

1. The appellate body has ruled that the existence of a benefit is to be quantified by comparison with the market place. The Appellate Body Report in Canada Aircraft (WT/DS70/AB/R2, 2 August 1999) noted that the existence of a benefit is a core element of the definition of a subsidy 'only' in cases where the financial contribution provides the recipient with an advantage over and above what it could have obtained on the market will the government's financial contribution be considered to have conferred a benefit and will a subsidy thus be deemed to exist. 'If the public or publicly directed financial contribution is provided under the same conditions as a private market player would have provided, then there would be no reason to impose any discipline, simply because the financial contribution was provided by the government.'
2. OECD National accounts of OECD countries, vol. 1, p. 369, 2005 and United Nations 1993, system of national Accounts, chapter VII, D3.
3. The Classification of the Functions of Government (OECD Secretariat: 30 April 1997) provides a definition for each function. For instance,

economic affaires concern services and goods provided to the administration of applied research and experimental development, operation of government agencies engaged in applied research, support for applied research and commercial and labour affairs undertaken by non-government bodies such as research institutes and universities. It also includes the administration of labour affairs and services (e.g. the formulation and implementation of general labour policies and regulations concerning labour conditions) and the administration of general economic and commercial affairs and services (e.g. the formulation and monitoring of economic and commercial policies and regulation).
4. Neven (2004) proposed to define the relevant market in state aid as the set of products which would be seriously affected by a subsidy to a particular firm. This definition has not the same objective as market definition for antitrust. Once the market definition is achieved, it will be necessary to identify how the state aid affects the behaviour of the recipient and to identify how the strategy of the recipient affects the competitors in the relevant market.
5. The Dispute Settlement Body consists of all WTO Members and has the authority to establish 'panels' of experts to consider the case and to accept or reject the panels' findings. The panels are like tribunals but the panellists are chosen in consultation with the countries in dispute. They consist of three to five experts who prepare a report on the evidence which concludes who is right and who is wrong. The panel may decide that the subsidy measure does break the WTO rules. The panel's findings can be appealed to the Appellate Body, whose report is final.
6. In the United States, the federal government has no state aid control at the federal level for controlling or coordinating the aids by the individual states. The Constitution grants Congress the power to regulate commerce 'among the several states'. Under a legal theory known as the negative commerce clause, the Supreme Court can strike down state taxes and regulations that have the effect of taxes when it finds them to be protectionist, favouring businesses within a state and thus discouraging national commerce. However, there is no recent evidence that subsidies have ever led to interstate litigation. In 2006, the Supreme Court took up a case (DaimlerChrysler v. Cuno, No. 04-1704, and Wilkins v. Cuno, No. 04-1724) about the legality of tens of billions of dollars in tax breaks that states and local governments award businesses each year to build new factories and offices. But the case was filed by a group of Ohio residents, not other states whose interests might have been harmed. Russia, another state with a federal structure, has recently adopted a state aid control legislation, which applies only to state aid granted by the regions, and not to the federal level spending.
7. Such concerns may arise, for instance, under the situation of considerable uncertainly about the probable costs of meeting by buyer's requirements when they are difficult to specify in a simple way. The bidders are likely to differ in their estimates. If bidders were to bid in line with their cost estimates, the bidder with the lowest cost estimate would win the tender, but this bidder would probably have underestimated the cost of delivering the required goods or services. Therefore, rational bidders are expected to bid with a sufficient safety margin to avoid an outcome in which winning a tender may lead to losses. As for the safety margin, it might be expected to

be larger, the greater the uncertainty about the true cost, and the larger the number of bidders, so that the price paid by the buyer can increase as a result of allowing more participants to submit bids.
8. For a numerical approach, see Bajari (2001).
9. Incumbency advantage means that a public contractor, due to the fact of having a procurement contact once or even several times, develops a better understanding of the public sector's requirements and needs or has made investments that provide advantages over other firms.

5 Effectiveness of Public Support

1. Although, this may be an indirect policy factor stimulating private R&D expenditure.
2. In particular, some macroeconomic growth models include R&D as an endogenous factor of growth. In particular, Segerstrom (2000), shows that subsidies towards R&D can promote or reduce long-run economic growth, subsidies change allocation of resources between horizontal and vertical innovations. While in a short run innovation is expected to increase efficiency or bring about other positive results, in the long run, however, it might result in increased complexity. Thus, a permanent R&D subsidy can have a negative impact on economic growth. However, there is no robust theoretical result and the main outcome is quite ambiguous.
3. The reasons of firms' difficulties (e.g. market decline and poor management) are based on the rescue and restructuring state aid decisions of the European Commission. The latter generally provide some information about the reasons why the company, which is the beneficiary of the aid, ran into business difficulties.
4. The British New Deal for Young People is a policy that prevents young people from entering long-term unemployment.
5. They present a model in which politicians fund projects that are wasteful as a way to signal their diligence, and voters rationally reward them for this.
6. The sample includes 32 countries: Hong Kong, India, Japan, Korea, Malaysia, Singapore, Thailand, Austria, Belgium, Denmark, Finland, France, Germany, Greece, Ireland, Italy, Netherlands, Norway, Portugal, Spain, Sweden, Switzerland, Turkey, United Kingdom, Canada, Mexico, United States, Brazil, Australia, New Zealand, Indonesia, and Hungary.
7. The authors measure concentration in a way that may appear counterintuitive in regard of the traditional concentration ratio widely used by industrial economists.
8. Japan's benchmark countries are Italy, Finland, Austria, Australia, France, and the Federal Republic of Germany. For Korea, the countries of comparison are Uruguay, Portugal, Malaysia, Mexico, and Panama.

6 Subsidies and State Aid

1. The International Monetary Fund's Government Finance Statistics is also a possible source on government subsidies but the definition used by the IMF is narrow.

2. See also the methodological remarks at http://ec.europa.eu/comm/
   competition/state_aid/studies_reports/conceptual_remarks.html
3. As mentioned in the autumn 2006 report, the manufacturing sector in the scoreboard includes the traditional manufacturing sector but also aid for general economic development, aid for horizontal objectives, SMEs environment, energy saving, employment and training. Therefore, aid to manufacturing may be overestimated.

7 Public Procurement

1. According to Evenett and Hoekman (2005) one source of this uncertainty comes from the fact that data on total government expenditure levels, in particular on central government outlays, include certain payments (such as compensation for government employees) that are not usually the subject of state contracts with private sector firms of other suppliers. Moreover, the data do not take account of 'in-house' activities (i.e. when public authorities provide services themselves). There have been few attempts to correct for these factors. The latest comprehensive study is OECD 2002 *The Size of Government Procurement Markets* (Paris) which employs the System of National Accounts (SNA) to compute the magnitude of procurement of goods and services by state bodies in 106 developing countries in 1998.
2. See the Annexes 1 to 5 of the Appendix I of the Agreement of Government Procurement.
3. Although the EU members are signatories of the GPA, they did not report to the WTO figures on public procurements.
4. *Intermediate consumption* consists of the value of the goods and services consumed as inputs by a process of production, excluding fixed assets whose consumption is recorded as consumption of fixed capital. The goods and services may be either transformed or used up by the production process.
5. *Social transfers in kind* consist of individual goods and services provided as transfers in kind to individual households by government units and Non-Profit Institutions Serving Households (NPISHs), whether purchased on the market or produced as non-market output by government units or NPISHs. They may be financed out of taxation, other government income or social security contributions, or out of donations and property income in the case of NPISHs.
6. Troinfetti (2000) uses the same data source.
7. It concerns services and goods provided to the population in case of sickness, disability, old age and death. See *Classification of the Functions of Government*, OECD Secretariat: 30 April 1997.
8. The figures refer to defence procurements not to the defence budget in general.
9. This concerns services and goods for the functioning of police and fire protection, law courts, prisons, etc.
10. This concerns services and goods provided to the administration of applied research and experimental development, operation of government agencies engaged in applied research, support for applied research and commercial and labour affairs undertaken by non-government bodies such as research institutes and universities. It also includes the administration of

labour affairs and services (e.g. the formulation and implementation of general labour policies and regulations concerning labour conditions) and the administration of general economic and commercial affairs and services (e.g. the formulation and monitoring of economic and commercial policies and regulation). See *Classification of the Functions of Government,*, OECD Secretariat: 30 April 1997.

8 Public Support in Germany

* Christian Lechner is the main contributor to this chapter. He is Professor at the Toulouse Business School.

1. OECD (1998) 'Spotlight on public support to industry'.
2. The term Mittelstand refers to medium-sized companies rather than to small firms and traditionally includes companies with up to 500 employees compared to the limit of 250 employees used by the EU. Governments in Germany have often refused to define the Mittelstand by size criteria, preferring to define it as a particular spirit, or by the unity of ownership and management. Support programmes in Germany targeted to 'SMEs' vary widely in their understanding of SMEs. Some follow the EU definitions for sales and employees, others the German Mittelstand definition of 500 employees (also adopted by the Federal Ministry of Economy) and others again a maximum sales volume of €500 million.

9 Public Support in France

1. Aid to companies in financial distress is, in contrast, considered by the authors of the report as a form of social policy, even though the government presents it as an element of industrial policy. Such aid has concerned, for example, the shipbuilding, textile, and steel industries.
2. The Beffa report began with a worrying report on the competitiveness of French industry, recording an overall decline of the weight of France in industrial added value, from 7.5% of total industrial added value in the OECD countries at the beginning of the 1980s to 6% at the end of the 1990s; a low degree of specialization in high-tech industries. High-tech industries (OECD definition) contributed 14% of industrial added value in France in 2000, versus just fewer than 20% in Japan and 28% in the United States; a low degree of industrial specialization in international trade; and a low degree of innovation.
3. For businesses that are claiming this credit for the first time and for those which have not claimed it in the last five years, the rate is 50%.
4. A patent is considered triadic if it is filed at the European, Japanese and the US Patent Office. In general, only invention with a very high potential for worldwide exploitation is patented as a triadic patent.

10 Public Support in the United Kingdom

1. At present the Department for Business, Enterprise and Regulatory Reform encompasses functions from the former Department of Trade and Industry with the Better Regulation Executive (BRE), previously part of the Cabinet Office.

2. Stephen Byers is a former Secretary of State for Trade and Industry (December 1998–June 2001).
3. RSA is only available for up to 15% of 'eligible' project costs, which primarily include buildings, plant and machinery, and land, the rest of the cost of the project must be met by the firm itself. There is also a cost-per-job ceiling that mitigates against large capital-intensive projects.
4. In reality, RSA grants have been particularly useful as an incentive for foreign direct investment (FDI). Value of grants to foreign firms is estimated to be in receipt of over 40% of RSA.
5. It seems that this aspect of the Enterprise Fund is being investigated by the European Commission for compatibility with its state aid rules.

11 Public Support in the United States

1. See also http://www.census.gov/govs/www/class06.html
2. In September 2004, the Supreme Court announced that it had agreed to review a federal appeals court ruling that certain Ohio tax credits granted to business as an incentive to expand operations in the state violated the Commerce Clause of the US Constitution. The federal appeals court reached its conclusion on the grounds that the economic effect of the Ohio tax credit is to encourage further investment in-state at the expense of development in other states and that the result is to hinder free trade among the states. The Supreme Court has ruled in favour of the State of Ohio, for a surprising reason. Since the case was, first, brought by Ohio residents rather than by other states (whose interests might have been harmed), it argued that the plaintiffs did not have a sufficient interest (standing): *New York Times*, 1 March 2006.
3. The 'B-index' measures the relative attractiveness of R&D tax treatment in a given jurisdiction. The more favourable the tax treatment of R&D, the lower is the index.
4. Except for one case: DaimlerChrysler v. Cuno, No. 04-1704, and Wilkins v. Cuno, No. 04-1724. In 2006, the Supreme Court took up the case about the legality of tax breaks that states and local governments award businesses each year to build new factories and offices. But the case was filed by a group of Ohio residents, not other states whose interests might have been harmed.
5. Information on all government assistance schemes is available from the Catalog of Federal Assistance, a database of all federal programs available to business and other entities: http://www.cfda.gov
6. Large, Fortune-500 companies participating as a single firm must pay at least 60% of total project costs while small- and medium-sized companies working on single firm ATP projects must pay a minimum of all indirect costs associated with the project.
7. Department of Agriculture, Department of Commerce, Department of Defence, Department of Education, Department of Energy, Department of Health and Human Services, Department of Homeland Security, Department of Transportation, Environmental Protection Agency, National Aeronautics and Space, Administration, National Science Foundation.
8. Department of Defence, Department of Energy, Department of Health and Human Services, National Aeronautics and Space Administration and National Science Foundation.

12 Public Support in Japan

1. SMEs are defined in Japan as enterprises with less than 300 employees: in 2005 they represented 71% of total employment and 99.7% of the total number of enterprises.
2. The surveys are published in the annual report 'Japan's Government Procurement Policy and Achievements'.

Conclusions

1. This concerns services and goods provided to the population in case of sickness, disability, old age, and death. See Classification of the Functions of Government, OECD Secretariat: 30 April 1997.

Bibliography

Ades, A. and Di Tella, R. (1997), 'National champions and corruption: Some unpleasant interventionist arithmetic', *The Economic Journal*, vol. 107, no. 443, pp. 1023–42.

Aghion, P., Bloom, N., Blundell, R., Griffith, R. and Howitt, P. (2005), 'Competition and innovation: An inverted U relationship', *Quarterly Journal of Economics*, May, vol. 120, no. 2, pp. 701–28.

Aghion, P. and Cohen, E. (2004), 'Education and growth', Council of Economic Analysis, Paris.

Aghion, P. and Howitt, P. (2005), 'Appropriate growth policy: A unifying framework', The 2005 Schumpeter lecture, Amsterdam, 25 August 2005.

Aghion, P., Harris, C., Howitt, P. and Vickers, J. (2001), 'Competition, imitation and growth with step-by-step innovation', *Review of Economic Studies*, vol. 68, pp. 467–92.

Aiginger, K. (2007), 'Industrial Policy: Past, Diversity, Future; Introduction to the Special Issue on the Future of Industrial Policy', *Journal of Industry Competition and Trade*, vol. 7, pp. 143–6.

Amsden, A. H. (1989), *Asia's Next Giant: South Korea and Late Industrialization*, New York and Oxford: Oxford University Press.

Arrow, K. (1962), 'Economic welfare and the allocation of resources for innovation', in Nelson, R. R. (ed.) NBER, *The Rate and Directions of Inventive Activity, Economic and Social Factors*, Princeton, NJ: Princeton University Press.

Asia Pacific Economic Cooperation Economic Committee (1999), 'Assessing APEC trade liberalization and facilitation – 1999 Update', The APEC Secretariat, Singapore.

Audretsch, D. B. (2003), 'Standing on the shoulders of midgets: The US Small Business Innovation Research Program (SBIR)', *Small Business Economics*, vol. 20, pp. 129–35.

Aydin, U. (2007), 'Promoting industries in the global economy: Subsidies in OECD countries, 1989 to 1995', *Journal of European Public Policy*, vol. 14, no. 1, pp. 115–31.

Baldwin, R., Forslid R., Martin P., Ottaviano G., and Robert-Nicoud, F. (2003), *Economic Geography and Public Policy*, Princeton, NJ: Princeton University Press.

Bajari, P. (2001), 'Comparing competition and collusion: a numerical approach', *Economic Theory*, vol. 18, pp. 187–205.

Bajari, P. and Summers, G. (2002), 'Detecting collusion in procurement auctions', Stanford University, Department of Economics, Working Paper 01014.

Bardhan, P. (1971), 'On the optimum subsidy to a learning industry: An aspect of the theory of infant industry protection', *International Economic Review*, vol. 12, pp. 54–70.

Bayrische Staatsregierung (2007), www.bayern.de/politik/staatsregierung, accessed on September 2007.

Bibliography

Beasp, R., Weinstein, D. E. (1996), 'Growth, economies of scale, and targeting in Japan (1955–90)', *Review of Economics and statistics*, vol. 78, pp. 286–95.

Beath, J. (2002), 'UK industrial policy: Old tunes on new instruments?', *Oxford Review of Economic Policy*, vol. 18, pp. 221–39.

Becker, G. S. (1985), 'Public policies, pressure groups, and dead weight costs', *Journal of Public Economics*, vol. 28, pp. 329–47.

Becker, B. and Pain, N. (2003), 'What determines industrial R&D expenditure in the UK?', National Institute of Economic and Social Research.

Beffa, J. L. (2005), Pour une nouvelle politique industrielle, Rapport au Président de la République, La Documentation Française.

Bergström, F. (1998), 'Capital subsidies and the performance of firms', SSE/EFI Working Paper Series in Economics and Finance, No. 285.

Besley, T. and Seabright, P. (1998), 'The effects and policy implementation of state aids to industry: An economic analysis', *Economic Policy*, vol. 13, pp. 15–53.

Bianchi, P. and Labory, S. (2006), 'Empirical evidence on industrial policy using state aid data', *International Review of Applied Economics*, vol. 20, no. 6, pp. 603–21.

Black, D. and Hoyt, W. (1989), 'Bidding for firms', *American Economic Review*, vol. 79, pp. 1249–56.

Bloom, N., Griffith, R. and Van Reenen, J. (2002), 'Do R&D tax credits work? Evidence from a Panel of countries 1979–97', *Journal of Public Economics*, vol. 85, pp. 1–31.

Bond, E. and Samuelson, L. (1986), 'Tax holidays as signals', *American Economic Review*, vol. 76, pp. 820–6.

Bosma, N. and Harding, R. (2006), GEM – Global Entrepreneurship Monitor 2006, Boston, MA: Babson College.

Boss, A. and Rosenschon, A. (2006), *Der Kieler Subventionsbericht. Kieler Diskussionsbeiträge 423*. Kiel: Institut für Weltwirtschaft.

Boylaud, O., Nicoletti, G., and Scarpetta, S. (2000), 'Summary indicators of product market regulation with an extension to employment protection legislation', OECD Economics Department Working Papers No. 226.

Brander, J. A. and Spencer, B. J. (1983), 'International R&D rivalry and industrial strategy', *Review of Economic Studies*, vol. 50, pp. 707–22.

Brander, J. A. and Spencer, B. J. (1985), 'Export subsidies and international market share rivalry', *Journal of International Economics*, vol. 18, pp. 83–100.

Brander, J. A. (1986), 'Rationals for strategic trade policy and industrial policy' in Krugman (ed.), *Strategic Trade Policy and the New International Economics*, Cambridge: MIT Press, pp. 23–46.

Brosig, J., Guth, W., and Weiland, T. (2006), 'Collusion mechanisms in procurement auctions: An experimental investigation', Faculty of Economics and Management, University of Magdeburg, Max Planck Institute of Economics.

BSF (2007), Bayrisches Staatsministerium der Finanzen: Bayern's Finanzen – Ausgezeichnet! München.

Buelens, C., Garnier, G., Meiklejohn, R. and Johnson, M. (2007), 'The economic analysis of state aid: Some open questions', *European Economy Economic Papers*, N. 286, September.

Buigues, P.-A. (2001), 'State aid and market failures: The quantification issue', in Ehlerman, C. and Everson, M. (eds), *European Competition Law 'Selected issues in the field of State Aids'*, Oxford, UK: Hart Publishing.

Buigues, P-A., Jacquemin, A. and Sapir, A. (1995), 'European Policies on competition, trade and industry: Conflicts and complementarities', Surrey: Edward Edgar.
Bund der Steuerzahler (2007), Subventionen. Report 4 April 2007, www.steuerzahler.de
BVK (2006), *Bundesverband Deutscher Kapitalbeteiligungsgesellschaften: BVK – Statistik 2006*, Berlin.
Byers, S. (2000), 'A discussion on an active industrial policy: Lessons from Long bridge', Institute for Public Policy Research, London, September.
Cabral, L. M. B., Cozzi, G., Denicolò, V., Spagnolo, G. and Zanza, M. (2006), 'Procuring innovation', CEPR Discussion Paper No. 5774.
Calzolari, G. and Spagnolo, G. (2006), 'Reputational commitments and collusion in procurement', Stockholm School of Economics; Department of Economics, University of Bologna.
Caves, R. E. (1987), 'Industrial policy and trade policy: The connections', in Kierzkowsk, H. (ed.), *Protection and competition in international trade. Essay in honor of W. M. Corden*, Oxford: Basil Blackwell.
Clifford, Mark L. (1994), *Troubled Tiger: Businessman, Bureaucrats, and Generals in South Korea*, Armonk, NY: M. E. Sharp.
Coggburn, J. D. (2003), 'Exploring differences in the American States' procurement practices', *Journal of Public Procurement*, vol. 3, no. 1, pp. 3–28.
Cohen, E. (2006), 'Theoretical foundations of industrial policy', *EIB Papers*, vol. 11, no. 2, pp. 84–107.
Cohen, E. and Lorenzi, J. H. (2000), *Politiques industrielles pour l'Europe, la Documentation Française*, Paris.
Collie, D. R. (2000), 'State Aid in the European Union; the prohibition of subsidies in an integrated market', *International Journal of Industrial Organization*, vol. 18, no. 6, pp. 867–84.
Compte O., Lambert-Mogiliansky, A. and Verdier, T. (2005), 'Corruption and Competition in Procurement', *RAND Journal of Economics*, vol. 36/1, pp. 1–15.
Coriat, B. (2000), 'Entre politique de la concurrence et politique commercial, quelle politique industrielle pour l'Union européenne?', supplément G in La Documentation Française, édition CAE Report no. 26: Politique industrielle, Paris, France.
Cozzi, G. and Impulitti, G. (2004), Technology Policy and Wage Inequality, Rome and New York Universities: Mimeo.
Devereux, M., Griffith, R. and Simpson, H. (2007), 'Firm location decisions, regional grants and agglomeration externalities', *Journal of Public Economics*, vol. 91, pp. 413–35.
Dewatripont, M. and Seabright, P. (2006), 'Wasteful public spending and state aid control', *Journal of the European Economic Association*, vol. 4, no. (2–3), pp. 513–22.
Dierx, A., Pichelmann, K. and Röger, W. (2004), 'Product market reforms and macroeconomic performance in the European Union', in Dierx, A., Ilzkovitz, F. and Sekkat, Kh. (ed.), *European Integration and the Functioning of Product Markets*, Surrey: Edward-Elgar, pp. 171–97.
Dimitris Skuras, D., Tsekouras, K., Dimara, E. and Tzelepis, D. (2006), 'The effects of regional capital subsidies on productivity growth: A case study of the Greek food and beverage manufacturing industry', *Journal of regional Science*, vol. 46, no. 2, pp. 355–81.

Doyle, C. and van Wijnbergen, S. (1996), *American Federalism: Competition Among Governments*, Lexington, KY: D. C. Heath.
Eaton, J. and Grossman, G. M. (1985), 'Optimal trade and industrial policy under oligopoly', *The Quarterly Journal of Economics,* vol. 100, pp. 383–406.
Economic Intelligence Unit (2007), 'Innovation: Transforming the way business Creates' *The Economist Intelligence Unit.*
Ehlermann, C.-D. and Goyette, M. (2006), 'The interface between EU State aid Control and the WTO disciplines on subsidies', *European State Aid Law Quarterly,* vol. 4, pp. 695–718.
European Commission (2005), Public Procurement for Research and Innovation, Directorate-General for Research.
European Innovation Scoreboard (2006), Comparative analysis of innovation performance, European Commission, Brussels. 'Innovations: les nouveaux modes de financement', Cahier Industries, Ministère de l'industrie, April.
Evenett, S. and Hoekmann, B. (2003), 'Transparency in procurement regimes and market access: What can we expect from international trade agreements?', in Arrowsmith, S. and Trybus, M. (eds) *Public Procurement: The Continuing Revolution,* Kluwer Law International: The Hague.
Evenett, S. and Hoekmann, B. (2005), 'Transparency in procurement: Market access, transparency, and multilateral trade rules', *European Journal of Political Economy,* vol. 21, pp. 183–63.
Evenett, S. (2005), *Would Enforcing Competition Law Compromise Industry Policy Objectives?* University of Oxford: Mimeo.
Falch, M. and Henten, A. (2005), 'Industrial policies in an information society context', Paper presented at Euro CPR, Potsdam.
Falk, M. (2004), 'What drives business R&D intensity across OECD countries?' WIFO Working Paper No. 236/2004.
Fingleton, J., Ruane, F. and Ryan, V. (1999), 'Market definition and state aid control', in Meiklejohn, R. (ed.), *State Aid and the Single Market,* European Economy Reports and Studies, no. 3.
Fong, G. R. (2000), 'Breaking new grounds or breaking the rules', *International Security,* vol. 25, no. 2, pp. 152–86.
Freeman, C. (1982), *The Economics of Industrial Innovation,* London: Frances Pinter.
Freeman, C. (1995), 'The national system of innovation in historical perspective', *Cambridge Journal of Economics,* vol. 19, pp. 5–24.
Friederiszick, H. W., Röller, L. H. and Verouden, V. (2008), 'European state aid control: An economic framework', in Paolo Buccirossi (ed.), *Handbook of Antitrust Economics,* Cambridge, MA: MIT Press, pp. 625–70.
Goto, Akira and Wakasugi, Ryuhei (1988), 'Technology Policy', in Ryutaro Koniya, Masahiro Okuno and Kotaro Suzumura (eds), *Industrial Policy of Japan,* San Diego, CA: Academic Press, pp. 183–204.
Greenwald, B. and Stiglitz, J. (2006), 'Helping infant economies grow: Foundations of trade policies for developing countries', *American Economic Review,* vol. 96, p. 2.
Gual, J. (1995a), 'The coherence of EU policies on trade, competition and industry', CEPR Discussion Paper No. 1105.
Gual, J. (1995b), 'The three common policies: An economic analysis', in Buigues P., Jacquemin, A. and Sapir, A. (eds), *European Policies on Competition,*

Trade and Industry: Conflict and Complementarities, Surrey: Edward Elgar, pp. 3–48.

Gual, J. (2000), 'Reducing state aid in the European Union', in Neven, D. and Roller, L.-H. (eds), *The Political Economy of Industrial Policy in Europe and the Member State*, New York: Stigma, pp. 11–23.

Gual, J. (2001), 'Aggregate targets for state aid reduction in the European Union' in Ehlermann, C. and Everson, M. (eds), European competition law annual 1999, Oxford: Hart, pp. 77–90.

Gual, J. and Jódar, S. (2006), 'Vertical industrial policy in the EU: An empirical analysis of the effectiveness of state aid', *EIB Papers*, vol. 11, no 2, pp. 80–105.

Guellec, D. and Van Pottelsberghe, B. (2003), 'The impact of public R&D expenditure on business R&D', *Economics of Innovation and New Technology*, vol. 12, no. 3, pp. 225–43.

Hall, B. H., Link, A. N. and Scott, J. T. (2003), 'Universities as research partners', *Review of Economics and Statistics*, vol. 85, pp. 485–91.

Hall, B. and Van Reenan, J. (2000), 'How effective are fiscal incentives for R&D? A review of the evidence', *Research Policy*, vol. 29, pp. 449–69.

Harayama, Yoko (2001), 'Japanese technology policy: History and new perspectives' RIETI, Discussion Paper Series 01-E-001 Tokyo.

Harland C., Gibbs, J. and Sutton, R. (2000), 'Supply strategy for the public sector: Framing the issues', *Conference 2000 Proceedings,* pp. 342–51.

Harris, R. and Robinson, C. (2004), 'Industrial policy in Great Britain and its effects on total factor productivity in manufacturing plants, 1990–98', *Scottish Journal of Political Economy*, vol. 51, no. 4, pp. 528–43.

Hart, J. (2001), 'Can industrial policy be good policy?', paper presented to the conference on *The Political Economy of Policy Reform*, Louisiana: Tulane University.

Haskel, J., Pereira, S. and Slaughter, M. (2002), 'Does inward foreign direct investment boost the productivity of domestic firms?' NBER Working Paper No. 8724.

Hausmann, R. and Rodrik, D. (2003), 'Economic development as self-discovery', *Journal of Development Economics*, vol. 72, pp. 603–33.

Hausmann, R. and Rodrik, D. (2006), 'Industrial policy as predicament', prepared for the seminar organized by the Center for International Development at Harvard University on 9 September 2006.

Hellman, J. and Schankerman, M. (2000), 'Intervention, corruption and capture: The nexus between enterprises and the state', EBRD Working Paper No. 58.

Hellman, J., Jones, G. and Kaufmann, D. (2000), 'Seize the state, seize the day: State capture, corruption and influence in transition', World Bank Policy Research Working Paper No. 2402, Washington, D. C.

Henten, A. (2005), 'Are industrial policies irrelevant or obsolete?', in Verhoest (ed.), *Contradiction, Confusion and Hubris: A Critical Review of European Information Society Policy*, pp. 47–51.

Holbrook, D. (1995), 'Government support to semiconductor industry: Diverse approach and information flows', *Business and Economic History*, vol. 24, no. 2, Winter, pp. 133–65.

Honjo, Y. and Harada, N. (2006), 'SME policy, financial structure and firm growth: Evidence from Japan', *Small Business Economics*, vol. 27, no. 4–5, December.

Hornbeck, J. F. (2007), 'Trade adjustment assistance for firms: Economic, program, and policy issues', Report to the Congress, Congressional Research Service.
Hozic, A. A. (1999), 'Uncle Sam goes to Siliwood: Of landscapes, Spielberg and hegemony', *Review of International Political Economy*, vol. 6, no. 3, pp. 289–312.
Huck, S. and Konrad, K. (2001), 'Merger profitability and trade policy', Unpublished manuscript.
Hunja, R. (2003), 'Obstacles to public procurement reform in developing countries', in Arrowsmith, S. and Trybus, M. (eds) *Public Procurement: The Continuing Revolution*, The Hague: Kluwer Law International.
Hyytinen, A. and Toivanen, O. (2003), 'Do financial constraints hold back innovation and growth? Evidence on the role of public policy', ETLA Discussion Paper No. 820.
IfM (2007), *Der volkswirtschafliche Bedeutung von Familienunternehmen. IfM-Materialien 172*, Bonn: Insitut für Mittelstandsforschung.
Jansen, H. (2004), Transfers to Germany's eastern Länder: a necessary price or a permanent drag, *European Commission Country Focus,* vol. I, no. 16.
Jaumotte, F. and Pain, N. (2005), 'An overview of public policies to support innovation', OECD Economics Department Working Papers No. 456.
Jones, D. S. (2002), 'Procurement practices in the Singapore Civil Service: Balancing control and delegation', *Journal of Public Procurement*, vol. 2, no. 1, pp. 29–54.
Kamps, C. (2005), 'New estimates of government net capital stocks for 22 OECD Countries 1960–2001', IMF Staff Paper.
Katz, M. L. and Shapiro, C. (1985), 'Network externalities, competition, and compatibility', *The American Economic Review*, vol. 75, pp. 424–40.
Katz, M. L. (1986), 'An analysis of cooperative research and development', *Rand Journal of Economics*, vol. 17, no. 4, pp. 527–43.
Kaufmann, D. (2005), 'Six questions on the cost of corruption with World Bank Institute Global Governance Director Daniel Kaufmann', Governance and Anti-Corruption website, www.worldbank.org/ wbi/ governance.
Keen, M. and Marchand, M. (1997), 'Fiscal competition and the pattern of public spending', University of Essex: Mimeo.
Ketels, H. M. (2007), 'Industrial policy in the United States', *Journal of Industry Competition and Trade*, vol. 7, pp. 147–67.
Kiyota, K., Okazabi, T. (2005), 'Foreign technology acquisition policy and firm performance in Japan, 1957–70 Micro-aspects of industrial policy', *International Journal of Industrial organization*, vol. 23, pp. 563–86.
Kokko, A. and Gustavsson, P. (2004), 'Regional integration, FDI, and regional development', *EIB Papers*, Vol. 9, no. 1, pp. 110–35.
Krugman, P. (1991a), *Geography and Trade*, Cambridge: MIT Press.
Krugman, P. (1993), 'The current case for industrial policy', in Salvatore, D. (ed.), *Protectionism and World Welfare*, Cambridge: Cambridge University Press, pp. 160–79.
Krugman, P. and Obstfeld, M. (1994), *International Economics*, third edition, New York: Harper Collins.
Lach, S. (2002), 'Do R&D subsidies stimulate or displace private R&D? Evidence from Israel', *Journal of Industrial Economics*, vol. L, pp. 369–90.

Laffont, Jean-Jacques (1996), Industrial policy and politics, *International Journal of Industrial Organization*, vol. 14, pp. 1–27.
Laffont, J-J. and Tirole, J. (1991) 'Auction Design and Favoritism', *International Journal of Industrial Organization*, vol. 9, pp. 9–42.
Lall, S. (2004), 'Reinventing industrial strategy: The role of government policy in building industrial competitiveness', Report to the Intergovernmental Group on Monetary Affairs and Development (G-24).
Lambert, A. and Sonin, K. (2005), 'Corruption and collusion in procurement tenders', Center for Economic and Financial research (CEFIR), Working Paper 2005–25.
Lambert, A. and Kosenoky, G. (2006), 'Public markets tailored for the cartel: Favoritism in procurement auctions', PSE, Paris-Jourdan Sciences Economiques: mimeo.
Layard, R. (2001), Welfare-to-Work and the New Deal, Centre for Economic Performance, London: London School of Economics and Political Science.
Leahy, D. and Neary, J. (2001), 'Robust rules for industrial policy in open economies', CERP Discussion Paper No. 2731. or *The Journal of International Trade and Economic Development*, vol. 10, pp. 393–409.
Lerner, J. (1999), 'The government as venture capitalist: The long-run impact of the SBIR program', *Journal of Business*, vol. 72, no. 3, 285–318.
Levy, J. D., Miura, M., Park, G. (2003), 'Existing etatisme? New directions in state policy in France and Japan', Working Paper, Berkeley: University of California, November.
Lichtenberg, F. (1995), 'Economics of defense R&D', in K. Hartley and T. Sandler (eds), *Handbook of Defense Economics*, Vol I, Amsterdam, The Netherlands: Elsevier Science.
London Economics (2004), Ex-post evaluation of the impact of rescue and restructuring aid on the international competitiveness of the sector(s) affected by such aid, Final Report to The European Commission – Enterprise Directorate-General.
Lorenz, E. H. (1992), 'Trust, community and cooperation: Toward a theory of industrial districts', in Storper, M. and Sctoo, A. J. (eds), *Pathway to Industrialization and Regional Development*, London: Routledge.
Lucas, R. (1988), 'On the mechanism of economic development', *Journal of Monetary Economics*, vol. 22, pp. 3–42.
Markusen, A. (1995), 'Interaction between regional and industrial policies: Evidence from four countries', Proceedings of the World Bank Annual Conference on Development Economics, The World Bank.
Martin, L. L. (2002), 'Performance based contracting for human services: Lessons for public procurement?' *Journal of Public Procurement*, vol. 2, no. 1, pp. 55–71.
Martin, S. and Valbonesi, P. (2006), 'State aid to business', in Bianchi, P. and Labory, S. (eds), *International Handbook of Industrial Policy*, Surrey: Edward-Elgar, Forthcoming.
Mauro, P. (1998), 'Corruption and the Composition of Government Expenditure', *Journal of Public Economics*, vol. 69, no. 2, pp. 263–79, August.
Mayer, T. (2004), 'Where do foreign firms locate in France and why?' *EIB Papers*, vol. 9, no. 2, pp. 38–61.

McCrudden, Ch. (2004), "Using public procurement to achieve social outcomes", *Natural Resources Forum*, vol. 28, pp. 257–67.
Meiklejohn, R. (1999), 'The economies of state aid', *European Economy*, vol. 3, pp. 25–31.
Messerlin, P. (1999), 'External aspects of State aids' in European economy', in Meiklejohn, R. (ed.), *State Aid and the Single Market*, no. 3.
METI (2007), 'Japanese policy on small and medium enterprises', Small and Medium Enterprise Agency, March.
METI (2007), 'Trends of R&D activities regarding Japan's Industrial Technologies', Industrial Science and Technology Policy and Environment Bureau, April.
Midelfart, H. and Overman, H. (2002), 'Delocation and European integration: Is structural spending justified?' *Economic Policy*, vol. 17, October, pp. 321–59.
Mo, P. H. (2001), 'Corruption and Economic Growth', *Journal of Comparative Economics*, vol. 29, no.1, pp. 66–79, March.
Montani, G. (2005), 'The role of the European Budget in European Economic Policy', *The Federalist*, vol. XLVII, no. 3, pp. 136–68.
Mühlenkamp, H. (2003). Zur Förderung der mittelständischen Wirtschaft durch Privatisierungsmassnahmen und öffentliche Aufträge, in Bouncken, R. (ed.), *Management von kleinen und mittleren Unternehmen und Gründungsunternehmen*, Wiesbaden, pp. 237–63.
Nail, J. and Brown, H. (2006), 'Identifying technology flows and spillovers through NAICS coding of ATP project participants', NISTIR 7280 (Economic Study).
National Performance Review (1993), 'From red tape to results: Creating a government that works better and costs less', Darby, US: DIANE.
National Science Foundation (NSF) (2006), *Science and Engineering Indicators 2006*, Arlington, VA: National Science Foundation.
Nelson, R., Baumol, W. and Wolf, E. (1994), *Convergence of Productivity: Cross-National Studies and Historical Evidence*, Oxford: Oxford University Press.
Neven, D. (2004), 'State aid and distorsions of competition', Presentation EAGCP, DG COMP, 16th June.
Neven, D. and Seabright, P. (1995), European industrial policy: The Airbus case', *Economic policy*, vol. 21, pp. 314–44.
Nezu, R. (2007), 'Industrial Policy in Japan', *Industrial Policy in Japan*, vol. 7, pp. 229–43.
Noland, Marcus (2007), 'Industrial policy, innovation policy, and Japanese competitiveness', Working Paper, 07-4, Washington, D.C.: Peterson Institute for International Economics.
Noland, Marcus and Pack, H. (2003), Industrial policy in an era of globalization: Lessons from Asia, Institute of International Economics.
OECD (1998), 'Spotlight on public support to industry'.
OECD (2001), 'Competition policy in subsidies and state aid', DAFFE/CLP(2001)24, 12 November.
OECD (2003a), The sources of economic growth in OECD Countries.
OECD (2003b), Tax incentives for research and development: Trends and issues.
OECD (2006), Evaluating government financing of business R&D: Measuring behavioral additionality, *OECD Documents* DSTI/STP.

OFT (Office of Fair Trading) (2004), 'The effects of public subsidies on Competition', Report prepared for the O.F.T. by frontier Economics, November.
OFT (Office of Fair Trading) (2007), 'Guidance on how to assess the competition effects of subsidies', O.F.T. 829, January.
OXERA (2006), 'Feasibility study for econometric assessment of the impact of tax credits on R&D expenditure', http://www.oxera.com/main.aspx?id=5362
Pack, H. (2000), 'Industrial policy: Growth elixir or poison?' *The World Bank Research Observer*, vol. 15, no. 1, pp. 47–67.
Parisi, M. L. and Sembellini, A. (2003), 'Is private R&D spending sensitive to its price? Empirical evidence on panel data for Italy', *Empirica*, vol. 30, pp. 357–77.
Park, C. H. (1970), *Our Nation's Path: Ideology of Social Reconstruction*, Seoul, Korea: Hollym.
Park, C. H. (1971), *To Build a Nation*, Washington, D.C.: Acropolis.
Pegnato, J. A. (2003), 'Assessing federal procurement reform: Has the procurement pendulum stopped swinging?' *Journal of Public Procurement*, vol. 3, no. 2, pp. 145–75.
Pelzman, S. (1976), 'Toward a more general theory of regulation', *Journal of Law and Economics*, vol. 19, pp. 211–40.
Porter, M. and Sakakibara, M. (2004), 'Competition in Japan', *Journal of Economic Perspectives*, vol. 18, no. 1, pp. 27–50, Winter.
Porter, M. E. (1999), 'Clusters and competition' on competitions, Harvard Business School Press.
Porter, M. E., Takeuchi, H. and Sakakibara, M. (2000), *Can Japan Compete?* Basingstoke: Macmillan.
Pritchard, D. and MacPherson, A. (2005), 'Manufacturing technology to Japan: Surrendering the US aircraft industry for foreign financial support', Canada-United States Trade Center Occasional Paper no. 30, Department of Geography, State University of New York.
Report prepared for the Office of Fair Trading (OFT) (2004), 'Assessing the impact of public sector procurement on competition', www.oft.gov.uk
Rey, P. (2001), 'On the form of state aid', in Ehlermann, C. and Everson, M. (eds), *European Competition Law. Selected issues in the field of State Aids*, Oxford, UK: Hart Publishing, pp. 141–48.
Rodriguez-Clare, A. (2004), 'Clusters and comparative advantage: Implications for industrial policy', Inter-American Development Bank.
Rodrik, D. (1995), 'Trade and industrial policy reform', in Srinivasan, T.N., Chenery, H. and Behrman, J. R. (eds), *Handbook of Development Economics*, vol. III, Amsterdam, The Netherlands: Elsevier, pp. 2925–82.
Rodrik, D. (1996), 'Coordination failures and government policy: A model with applications to East Asia and Eastern Europe', *Journal of International Economics*, vol. 40, no. (1–2), pp. 1–22.
Rodrik, D. (2004), 'Industrial policy for the twenty-first century', JFK School of Government, Harvard University: Mimeo.
Rodrik, D. (2006), 'Industrial development: Stylized facts and policies', JFK School of Government, Harvard University: Mimeo.
Röller, L. R., Friederiszick, H. W. and Neven, D. J. (2003), 'Evaluation of the effectiveness of state aid as a policy instrument', Report to DG ECFIN, European Commission.

Romer, P. (1990), 'Endogenous technological change', *Journal of Political Economy*, vol. 98, no. 5, pp. 71–102.

Rose-Ackerman, R. (1997) 'The political economy of corruption', in Elliott, K. A. (ed.), *Corruption and the Global Economy*, Washington DC, Institute for International Economics, pp. 31–60.

Rosovsky, H. (1985), 'Trade, Japan, and the year 2000', *New York Times*, September.

Ruttan, V. (2005), 'Military procurement and technology development', Working Paper, Department of Applied Economics College of Agricultural, Food, and Environmental Sciences University of Minnesota.

Sachverständigenrat (2000), Sachverständigenrat zur Begutachtung der gesamtwirtschaftlichen Entwicklung: Chancen für einen höheren Wachstumspfad. Jahresgutachten 2000/2001, Wiesbaden: Statistische Bundesamt.

Sachverständigenrat (2003), Sachverständigenrat zur Begutachtung der gesamtwirtschaftlichen Entwicklung: 20 Punkte für Wirtschaft und Wachstum. Jahresgutachten 2002/2003, Wiesbaden: Statistische Bundesamt.

Sachverständigenrat (2006), Sachverständigenrat zur Begutachtung der gesamtwirtschaftlichen Entwicklung: Widerstreitende Interessen – Ungenutzte Chancen. Jahresgutachten 2006/2007, Wiesbaden: Statistische Bundesamt.

Sakakibara, M. and Branstetter, L. (2003), 'Measuring the impact of US research consortia', *Managerial and Decision Economics*, vol. 24, no. 2–3, pp. 51–69, March-May.

Sakakibara, M. and Porter, M. (2001), 'Competing at home to win abroad: Evidence from Japanese industry', *The Review of Economics and Statistics*, vol. 83, no. 3, pp. 310–22.

Sapir, A., Aghion, P., Bertola, G., Hellwig, M., Pisani-Ferry, J., Rosati, D., Viñals, J. and Wallace, H. (2003), An agenda for a growing Europe: Making the EU system deliver, Report to the President of the European Commission.

Schapper P., Veiga Malta, J. N. and Gilbert, D. L. (2006), 'An analytical framework for the management and reform of Public Procurement', *Journal of Public Procurement*, vol. 6, no. 1/2, pp. 1–26.

Shipp, S., Wang, A., Campbell, S., Wisniewski, L., Levin, K. and O'Brien, J. (2006), 'Measuring behavior additionality in ATP joint venture projects: Findings from the advanced technology program', Evaluating government financing of business R&D: Measuring behavioral Additionality, OECD.

Schwartz, G. and Clements, B. (1999), 'Government subsidies', *Journal of Economic Surveys*, vol. 13, no. 2, pp. 119–47.

Scott, M. F. (1989), *A New View of Economic Growth*, Oxford: Clarendon Press.

Segerstrom, P. S. (2000), 'The long-run growth effects of R&D subsidies', *Journal of Economic Growth*, vol. 5, pp. 277–305.

Simon, H. (1996), *Hidden Champions*, Cambridge, MA: Harvard Business School Press.

Simon, H. (2007), *Hidden Champions des 21. Jahruderts*, Stuttgart: Campus Verlag.

Smith, M. (1985), *Military Enterprise and Technological Change*, Cambridge: MIT.

Spencer, B. and Jones, R. (1991), 'Vertical foreclosure and international trade policy', *Review of Economic Studies*, vol. 58, pp. 153–70.

Statistisches Jahrbuch (2006), Statistisches Bundesamt: Wiesbaden.

Steenblik, R. P. (2003), 'Subsidy measurement and classification: Developing a common framework' in 'Environmentally Harmful subsidies. Policy challenges, OECD, Paris, pp. 101–41.
Subventionsbericht der Bundesregierung (2006), Bericht der Bundesregierung über die Entwicklung der Finanzhilfen und der Steuervergünstigungen für die Jahre 2003 bis 2006 (20. Subventionsbericht), Köln: Bundesanzeiger Verlagsgesellschaft.
Sykes, A. O. (2003), 'The economics of W.T.O. rules on subsidies and countervailing measures', *John M. Olin Law and Economics*, Working Paper No. 186, The Law School, University of Chicago.
Takayuki Sumita (2007), 'Technology policy in Japan – The role of government and academia', METI, February.
Tanzi, V., and Davoodi, H. (1997), 'Corruption, Public Investment, and Growth', International Monetary Fund Working Paper: WP/97/139, October.
Thai, K. V. (2001), 'Public procurement re-examined', *Journal of Public Procurement*, vol. 1, no. 1, pp. 9–50.
Thai, K. V. and Grimm, R. (2000), 'Government procurement: Past and current developments', *Journal of Public Budgeting, Accounting and Financial Management*, vol. 12, no. 2, pp. 231–47.
Tietje, C. (2004), 'Current developments under the W.T.O. agreement on subsidies and countervailing measures as an example for the functional unity of domestic and international trade law', Mars: Martin-Luther-Universiteit.
Tilton, M. (1996), *Restrained Trade: Cartels in Japan's Basic Materials Industries*, Ithaca, NY: Cornell University Press.
Toivanen, O. (2006), 'Innovation and research policies: Two case studies of R&D subsidies', *EIB Papers*, vol. 11, no. 2, pp. 54–79.
Thomas, C. J. (2001), 'Collusion and optimal reserve prices in repeated procurement auctions', Federal Trade Commission, Washington D.C., Working Paper No. 242.
Tomiuram, E. (2003), 'Changing economic geography and vertical linkage in Japan', Research Institute for Economics and Business Administration, Kobe University.
Trionfetti, F. (2000), 'Discriminatory public procurement and international trade', *World Economy*, vol. 23, pp. 57–76.
Tyson, L. A. (1992), *Who's Bashing Whom? Trade Conflict in High-Technology Industries*, Washington D. C.: Institute for International Economics.
Uesugi Lichiro (2006), *SME Financing: What We Have Found*, Tokyo: METI.
Valila, T. (2006), 'No policy is an island – on the interaction between industrial and other policies', *EIB Papers*, vol. 11, no. 2, pp. 8–33.
Vernohr, B. and Meyer, K. (2007), The German miracle keeps running: How Germany's hidden champions stay ahead in the global economy, Working Paper, Berlin School of Economics, March.
W.T.O. Trade Report (2006), 'Subsidies, trade and the W.T.O', pp. 45–226, July.
Wade, R. (2003), *Governing the Market: Economic Theory and the Role of Government in East Asian Industrialization*, Princeton, NJ: Princeton University Press.
Warda, J. (2001), 'Measuring the value of R&D tax treatment in OECD countries', OECD STI Review, No. 27, OECD.

Weiss, L. (2005), 'Global governance, national strategies: How industrial states make room to move under the W.T.O', *Review of International Political Economy,* vol. 12, no. 5, December, pp. 723–49.

Williamson, O. (1975), *Markets and Hierarchies: Analysis and Antitrust Implications,* New York: Free Press.

Wren, C. (2001), 'The industrial policy of competitiveness: A review of recent developments in the UK', *Regional Studies,* vol. 35, no. 9, pp. 847–60.

Wren, C. (2005), 'Regional grants: Are they worth it?' *Fiscal Studies,* vol. 26, no. 2, pp. 245–75.

Young, A. (1991), 'Learning by doing and the dynamic effects of International trade', *The Quarterly Journal of Economics,* vol. 106, pp. 369–405.

Zysman, J., Tyson, L. A. and Dosi, G. (1990), 'Technology, trade policy and Schumpeterian efficiencies' in de la Mothe, J. d. L and Ducharme, L. M. (eds), *Science, Technology and Free Trade,* New York: Columbia University Press.

Index

accountability, government 26
actionable subsidies 38
administrative corruption 78
Advanced Technology Program
  (ATP) 174, 175–6, 180–1
Agence de l'Innovation Industrielle
  (AII) 146, 150, 151
Agence Nationale de la Recherche
  (ANR) 146, 152
agglomeration 15, 21, 24
Agreement on Government
  Procurement (GPA) 43, 101
Agreement on Subsidies and
  Countervailing Measures (SCM
  Agreement) 29–30, 38
aid mechanisms, in France
  156–7, 159
American Competitiveness Initiative
  (ACI) 172
Annual Respondents Database
  (ARD) 70
antitrust law 170–1
Asia-Pacific Economic Cooperation
  (APEC) 45
assessment issues, on public
  support 55–7
asymmetric information 56
Austria 89
automotive sector 199
Azerbaijan 78

banking sector
  in Germany 125
  in Japan 186
barriers to entry/exit, subsidies
  and 36
Bavaria 129
bribes 74
British public support 160–9
  actors 161–2
  instruments 162–7
  objectives of 160–1
  outcomes 167–8

for science and technology
  163–4
for small business 166–7
Bund 121–3
Business Environment and
  Enterprise Performance Survey
  (BEEPS) 77–8
business support agencies 21
Buy American Act 178
buyer power, of public sector 47–8

capital subsidies 195–6
capture 26–7, 77–9
cartels 24
case studies 56
cash subsidies 7
Central Contracting Registration
  (CCR) 178
cluster development 134
coal industry 128, 139
Coase, Ronald 11
Colbertist model 141
Cold War 171
collusion 24, 50–1, 74
Commision des Marchés Public de l'Etat
  (CMPE) 152–5
competition
  impact of subsidies on 34–8
  imperfect 16–19, 23–4
  oligopolistic 17, 19
  perfect 24
  public procurement and 46–54
competition policy 22–4, 160–1
competitive clusters, in France 147–8,
  150–2
Congress 172
constant returns to scale 24
consumer electronics 199
cooperation 15–16
corruption xix, 27, 74–7, 78
countervailing duty (CVD) 39–40
credit guarantee systems 193
credit subsidies 7

crowding in 56
crowding out 56

defence objectives, of subsidies 96
defence spending 105, 172, 181–2
demand, stability of 51
Department for Business, Enterprise & Regulatory Reform (DBERR) 161–2, 169
Department for Innovation, Universities and Skills (DUIS) 161–2, 169
Department of Trade and Industry (DTI) 160, 161
Deregulation Subcommittee 185–6
developed countries (DCs), international trade and 4
direct network effects 13

East Asian industrial policy 12
Eastern Germany 116–17, 136, 138
econometric analysis 56–7
  of political economy 75–81
  of R&D 58–60
  of state aid 66
  of subsidies 37–8
Economic Development Administration (EDA) 175
economic efficiency 131–2
economic growth
  in Germany 123
  industrial policy and 80–1
  in post-war Japan xix, 79, 198
economies of scale 17
education 105
efficiency objectives 37, 96–7, 99–100
elections 25–6
empirical evidence
  on arguments against public support 73–81
  on arguments for public support 57–73
energy 93, 117, 137, 184
enterprise, spirit of 133–5
entry barriers, subsidies and 36
environmental protection 93, 111, 132
equity objectives, of subsidies 96–7
equity subsidies 7, 87

European Communities (EC)
  Treaty 31–2, 40–1
European Innovation Scoreboard 155
European Structural Funds 72
European Union (EU)
  approach to subsidies 40–3
  competition policy 24
  definition of subsidies in 31–3
  public procurement in 44–5
  public support policies in 94–8
  state aid in 91–4
  vertical industry policies in 66–7
exchange rates, overvalued 7–8
Exist programme 133
export promotion 17, 184
export subsidies 38
externalities 5, 11–16, 18–19
  knowledge 12–13, 18, 21
  negative 11
  network 13–14, 57–8
  positive 11
  spatial 14–16, 18–19, 21, 24

favouritism 27
Federal Acquisition Regulation (FAR) 178
federalism 121–2, 138
firm location 68–73
fiscal instruments 21
Fonds de compétitivité des entreprises (FCE) 147
foreign direct investment (FDI) 68–9
foreign goods 197
France 69
  aid mechanisms in 159, 156057
  public procurement in 104, 105, 106, 111, 152–5
  public sector structure 152–5
  public support in 140–59
  R&D in 155–6, 158
  regional policy in 143
  subsidies in 98
free trade 4
French public support 140–59
  actors 145–50
  changes in 157–8
  decline in 141
  evaluation and efficiency of 155–7
  funding system for 156–7, 159

French public support – *continued*
 grand projects 140–1
 industry sector and structure 150–2
 instruments 149–50
 national champions 140
 objectives of 142–4
 overview of 144
 sectoral distribution of 144

game theory 16
geographic concentration 14–16
German Council of Economic Experts 136
German public support 115–39
 actors 121–5
 evaluation and efficiency of 132–7
 industry sector and structure 127–8
 instruments 125–7
 objectives of 116–21
 overview of 118–21
 regional nature of 137–8
 sectoral distribution of 138–9
Germany 41, 95–6
 banking sector in 125
 development of Eastern 116–17, 136, 138
 federalism in 121–2, 138
 industrial policy in 115–39
 municipalities in 123–5
 private equity in 134–5
 public procurement in 104, 105, 107, 111, 128–32
 public sector structure 128–32
 reunification 41, 95, 115, 137
 subsidies in 98
 tax system in 136–7
Global Entrepreneurship Monitor (GEM) 135
goods, compatibility of 14
governance quality, state capture and 79
government accountability 26
government failures xviii, 4–5, 20–8, 203
 from imperfect information 20–2
 political economy 25–7
government funding; *see* state aid

government procurement; *see* public procurement
Government Procurement Act (GPA) 177–8
Government Procurement Experts Group 45
government subsidies; *see* subsidies
GPA; *see* Agreement on Government Procurement (GPA)
grants 87, 133, 192
Great Britain; *see* United Kingdom
Greece 63–4, 89
green energy 117, 137
gross domestic product (GDP)
 public procurement as share of 101–5
 subsidies as share of 88, 94–5, 98, 99

health care, public procurement for 8, 21, 43, 54, 103, 111
high-tech industries 142–3
horizontal support 5–6, 30, 33, 87, 202

imperfect competition 16–19, 23–4
imperfect information 5, 10–11, 18, 20–2
import tariffs 22, 25
indirect network effects 13–14
industrial innovation 142–3
industrial policy 3
 British 160–9
 conflicts with other policies 22–5
 corruption and 76–7
 East Asian 12
 in France 140–59
 in Germany 115–39
 indirect costs of 23
 interventionist approach to 205
 in Japan 184–203
 Latin American 12
 macroeconomic TFP growth and 80–1
 political economy and 25–7
 soft approach to 205
 U.S. 170–83
 views on xvii–xx
 see also public support to business

industry concentration 14–16
industry sector and structure
  in France 150–2
  in Germany 127–8
  in Japan 194–6
industry-university partnerships 181
infant industries
  learning process for 3–4
  subsidies to 3–4
information issues 10–11, 18, 20–2, 56
innovation
  country rankings for 199–200
  encouragement of 21, 58–60, 133
  in France 155, 158
  funding of 142–3
  German public support for 125
  industrial 142–3
  in U.S. 174, 175–7
instruments
  of British public support 162–7
  of French public support 149–50
  of German public support 125–7
  indentifying 20–1
  of Japanese public support 191–4
  optimality of 21–2
  public procurement 43–54
  subsidies 29–43
  of U.S. public support 173–9
interest groups 26–7
intermediate consumption 209n4
International Monetary Fund (IMF) 6, 208n1
international trade
  dynamic effects of 4
  public procurement and 43–6
  see also trade
Ireland 89

Japan 79, 81
  deregulation in 185–6
  post-war economic boom in xix, 79, 198
  public procurement in 104, 105, 110, 111, 196–8, 202
  public sector structure 196–8
  public support policies in 94–8
  R&D in 184–5, 189–92, 194–5, 199–200
  small business support in 187–9, 191, 192–4, 200
Japanese public support 184–203
  actors 189–91
  evaluation and efficiency of 198–200
  industry sector and structure 194–6
  instruments of 191–4
  objectives of 187–9
job creation 71–2

knowledge economy 144
knowledge externalities 12–13, 18, 21
Korea; see South Korea

labour training 13
Länder; see Germany
Latin American industrial policy 12
'learning by doing' effect 3–4, 17
less developed countries (LDCs), international trade and 4
LINK scheme 164
Lisbon Summit 140
lobbying 26–7
local content subsidies 38

Manufacturing Extension Partnership (MEP) 174
manufacturing industry 3, 15, 33, 59, 184, 195, 196, 209n3
Manufacturing Extension Partnership (MEP) 175
market concentration, subsidies and 34, 36
market failures xviii, 4–5, 10–19, 203
  degree of 37
  externalities 11–16, 18–19
  imperfect competition 16–18, 19
  imperfect information 10–11, 18
  instruments for addressing 20–2
  measurability of 56
market power 5
merger policy 21
mergers and acquisitions (M&As) 24, 186
military spending xvii–xix, 105, 172, 181–2

Ministry of Economy Trade and
    Industry (METI) 187, 189–90, 201
Moldova 78
monetary instruments 6, 20–1
monopolies 127
municipalities, German 123–5

National Accounts 31, 85–7, 94,
    96, 99–100
National Committee on Aeronautics
    (NACA) 182
negative externalities 11
network externalities 13–14, 57–8
New Deal for Young People 72,
    208n4
new economic geography (NEC) 15
New Länder; see Eastern Germany

OECD countries, public support
    policies in 89–91
Office of Fair Trading 34
Office of Government Commerce
    (OGC) 162, 169
Office of Management and Budget
    (OMA) 178
oligopolistic competition 17, 19
Organisation of Economic
    Cooperation and Development
    (OECD) 7
Oseo 146–7, 150
overall greatest value (OGV)
    evaluation method 198

patents 24, 140, 155, 158, 200, 210n4
perfect competition 24
pharmaceutical industry 195
Pôles de compétitivité 147
policy mix 22–5
political cycles 25–6
political economy 25–7
    corruption 27
    econometric analysis of 75–81
    elections 25–6
    lobbying 26–7
    public procurement and 44–5
Portugal 74
positive externalities 11
prequalification criteria 50
President 172

private equity, in Germany 134–5
procurement; *see* public procurement
procurement subsidies 7
productivity, impact of state aid
    on 62–8
profitability 11
prohibited subsidies 38
public aid; *see* state aid
public finance corporations 192–3
public funding, competitiveness
    of 56
public order objectives 96, 111
public procurement 8–9, 21, 43–54
    aggregate assessment of, using EU
        definition 102–4
    competition and 46–54
    corruption in 74–5
    divergent assessments of 101–2
    empirical evidence on 57–60
    foreign penetration of, in
        Japan 197
    in France 104, 106, 111, 152–5
    by functions 105–11
    in Germany 104, 105, 107, 111,
        128–32
    international trade and 43–6
    in Japan 196–8, 202
    knock-on effects of 53
    long-term effects of 51–3
    objectives of 131–2
    policy objectives 45–6
    politica context of 44–5
    quantitative analysis of 101–12
    as share of GDP 101–5
    short-term effects 49–51
    in U.S. 177–9, 181–2
public research centers 21
public sector 47–8
public sector structure
    in France 152–5
    in Germany 128–32
    in Japan 196–8
public spending, wasteful 26, 74
public support policies
    in EU, U.S., and Japan 94–8
    in OECD countries 89–91
public support to business
    arguments against 20–8
    assessment issues 55–7

public support to business – *continued*
   cases for 10–19
   country comparisons on 204–5
   defined 3
   economists' attitudes toward 203
   effectiveness of 55–82
   empirical evidence on arguments against 73–81
   empirical evidence on arguments for 57–73
   in France 140–59
   in Germany 115–39
   instruments of 6–9, 29–54
   in Japan 184–203
   motivations for 3–5
   objectives of 116–21, 142–4, 160–1, 171–2, 187–9
   overview 3–9
   theories on 203–4
   types of 5–6
   in United Kingdom 160–9
   in United States 170–83
   see also industrial policy
pull effect 52
pull factors 8
push factors 8

quantitative analysis
   of public procurement 101–12
   of subsidies 85–100

regional development, state aid for 93–4
Regional Development Agencies (RDAs) 161, 162, 165
regional policy 68–70
   in France 143
   in Germany 137–8
   in Japan 185
   in United Kingdom 164–6, 169
Regional Selective Assistance (RSA) 62, 70, 71, 165–6
regional support 68–9
regulation subsidies 7
research and development (R&D) 12
   decisions about, and subsidies 36–7
   evaluation of Japanese policy toward 199–200
   in France 155–6, 158

grants 133
impact of public procurement on 58–60
in Japan 184–5, 189–92, 194–5
public support for 117
state aid for 60–2, 94
tax credits for 150
in United Kingdom 162
in U.S. 173–7, 179
Russia 78

science
   British public support for 163–4
   Japanese public support for 195
   U.S. public support for 171, 173–5
SCM Agreement; *see* Agreement on Subsidies and Countervailing Measures (SCM Agreement)
Scotland 63
sectoral distribution 92–4, 150–2
Selective Assistance Management Information System (SAMIS) 63
Service for General Economic Interest (SGEI) 89
Small and Medium Enterprises (SMEs) 9, 22, 38
   financing for 192–3
   French public support for 143, 152, 155, 159
   German public support for 125, 132–5, 139
   Japanese public support for 187–9, 191–4, 200–2
   public support for 117–18, 121
   state aid for 94
   tax benefits for 194
   U.S. public support for 179–80
Small Business Act 178
Small Business Innovation Research (SBIR) 174, 176–7, 179–80
Small Business Technology Transfer (SBTT) 174, 177
Small Firm Merit Awards for Research and Technology (SMART) programmes 62–3
small firms 166–7
SMART/SPUR programmes 164, 169
social protection 105

Index 231

social transfer 103–4, 209n5
soft loans 87
South Korea xix, 17, 74–5, 79–81
spatial externalities 14–16, 18–19, 21, 24
special interest groups 26–7
stability of demand 51
standards 14
start-up companies
 in Germany 135
 public support for 117–18
state aid 32–3, 40–3
 disparities between Member States 91–2
 empirical evidence on 60–73
 in France 156–7
 influence on firm location 68–73
 objectives ofr 93–4
 quantitative analysis of 91–4
 sectoral distribution of 92–4
 see also subsidies
State Aid Scoreboard 86, 91
state capture 26–7, 77–9
state monopolies 127
strategic trade 21
strategic trade theory (STT) 16–18
Structural Adjustment Programs (SAPs) xvii
structural instruments 20–1
structural policies 6
subsidies 6–8, 21–2, 29–43
 actionable 38
 capital 195–6
 cash 7
 classification of 96
 countervailing measures 39–40
 credit 7
 data sources for 85–6, 87, 99
 definition issues 28–35, 85, 98
 dispute settlement 40
 econometric analysis of 75–6
 economic analysis of 37–8
 equity 7, 87
 EU approach to 40–3
 export 38
 impact of, on competition 34–8
 local content 38
 measures of 85–9, 99
 objectives of 96–7
 procurement 7
 prohibited 38
 rules for 38–43
 as share of GDP 88, 94–5, 98, 99
 tax 7, 87
 in U.S. 179
 WTO disciplines 38–43
Subsidies and Countervailing Measures (SCM) 85–6
Sweden 65, 68, 89
System of National Accounts (SNA) 85–7, 94, 96

tariff monopolies 127
tariffs 4, 22, 25
tax benefits, for SMEs 194
tax credits, for research 150
tax reliefs 21, 126–8
tax subsidies 7, 87
tax system, German 136–7
TCS scheme 164
technical progress
 productivity 62–8
 R&D 58–62
technological change 15–17
technology policy 160–1, 163–4, 171, 173–5, 187, 189–91, 195
Total Factor Productivity (TFP) 62–4, 66–8, 80, 167–8
trade
 public procurement and 43–6
 strategic 16–18, 21
Trade Adjustment Assistance (TAA) program 175
trade policy 17, 22–3, 25
trade protections 4
training 13
transition economies 78
transparency, in public procurement 50
triadic patents 155, 210n4

Ukraine 78
United Kingdom 70–1, 89
 institutional structure of 171–2
 public procurement in 104, 105, 108, 111

232   Index

United Kingdom – *continued*
  public support in 160–9
  regional policy in 164–6, 169
  subsidies in 98
United States
  industry-university partnerships in 181
  military spending in 181–3
  public procurement in 104, 105, 109, 111, 177–9, 181–2
  public sector structure in 207n6
  public support policies in 94–8
  trade policy of 17
U.S. public support 170–83
  actors 172–3
  instruments of 173–9
  objectives of 171–2

outcomes 179–82
structured subsidized programmes 175–7

vertical industry policies 66–7
vertical support 5–6
video cassette recorders (VCRs) 57–8

wasteful spending 26, 74
welfare maximization 24
World Competitiveness Report (WCR) 76
World Report on Subsidies 6
World Trade Organisation (WTO) 6
  definition of subsidies in 29–30
  SCM notifications 85–6
  subsidy rules 38–40, 41–3